FROM THE BLACK SEA:

THROUGH

PERSIA AND INDIA

FROM THE BLACK SEA:

THROUGH

PERSIA AND INDIA

EDWIN LORD WEEKS

GYAN

Published by

Gyan Publishing House
5, Ansari Road
Daryaganj, New Delhi-110002
Phone: 011-47034999, 9811692060
E-mail: books@gyanbooks.com

Distribution Network
gyanbooks.com
India, USA, Canada, UK, Australia

ISBN: 978-93-6433-112-8 (PB)

First Published, 1896

2nd Impression 2024

Printed at: Gyan Press, Delhi.

FROM THE BLACK SEA: THROUGH PERSIA AND INDIA
Author: EDWIN LORD WEEKS

FROM THE BLACK SEA

THROUGH

PERSIA AND INDIA

BY

EDWIN LORD WEEKS

ILLUSTRATED BY THE AUTHOR

NEW YORK

HARPER & BROTHERS PUBLISHERS

1896

PREFACE

THESE preliminary lines of explanation are only to show why this journey was undertaken at such an unfortunate moment, and that there was some underlying method in its apparent madness. When the route was first mapped out, it was our intention to follow the line of the Trans-Caspian Railway to Samarcand, and thence to Herat, and through Afghanistan to India. But the political situation and the civil war in Afghanistan rendering such a trip hazardous, we decided to take the trans-Persian direction, and to enter Persia near Meshed.

As Mr. Theodore Child's well-known work on Russia had made him favorably known in official circles, the Russian government had kindly offered us every facility in passing through its territory. With the permission from the War Department to visit Central Asia came an urgent telegram from the American legation at St. Petersburg, advising us not to go on account of the cholera, which, after devastating Meshed, had left Persia and invaded the Russian provinces. We were then leaving for Constantinople by the *Camboge*, and finding that she would not proceed to Batoum, by reason of quarantine, we were again forced to change our route. This time we elected to follow the old caravan road from Trebizond, on the Black Sea, to Tabreez, through the mountains of Kurdistan, that country of indefinite boundaries.

In short, there was no other route left open to us; we must either turn back, or, setting our faces forward, head straight for the Persian frontier, five hundred miles away, and we decided to go on.

EDWIN LORD WEEKS.

CONTENTS

CONTENTS

ILLUSTRATIONS

FROM THE BLACK SEA
THROUGH PERSIA AND INDIA

BY CARAVAN FROM TREBIZOND TO TABREEZ

Trebizond, July 22, 1892.—A blue bay, calm and peaceful, lies before us as we look out from under the awnings of the *Camboge*, and the city, a compact mass of white and yellow masonry, rises in terraces along the shore. An amphitheatre of barren hills encircles the bay. We are rowed to the custom-house; and Artemis, the Armenian dragoman, whom we had engaged at Constantinople, has been instructed to save us trouble at any expense. An ancient Turk, who has been detailed to burrow into our bags and boxes, mercifully ignores the fire-arms and cartridges, but pounces at once on Murray's hand-books for Bengal and the Punjaub, and Adams's Cable Codex, which he scrutinizes severely. The printed page in an unknown language is considered by the Ottoman official to be fraught with peril to the peace of all true believers. These suspicious volumes are detained for the examination of the censor, but were kindly returned to us on the following day, duly indorsed on their fly-leaves, to the effect that nothing detrimental to the religion of Mohammed had been found.

At last we are allowed to pass through the ponderous inner gate, and joyfully follow the porters carrying our baggage, who are struggling up the roughly paved street towards the little hotel. This hotel is kept by Greeks: and the vine-shaded stoop, reached by a steep flight of steps on each side, is not uninviting.

Trebizond is a city of some thirty thousand inhabitants. Persia begins here, practically if not politically, and the road from Trebizond, through Erzeroum, to Tabreez, or Tauris, the largest city in Persia, is undoubtedly the oldest caravan route in the world. All the merchandise from the north of Persia to western Europe and England passes over it, and the return traffic is equally important. The time of transit is rather uncertain. We were told in Tabreez that it often took three months from Persia to the Black Sea by camel caravans, which usually travel by night, and rest during the day. When they reach a grassy nook, or fertile hollow high among the hills, the beasts are unloaded and turned out to pasture, while the drivers light their camp-fires and brazen samovars under roughly extemporized shelters of rugs and hempen mats, erected among the square bales of merchandise packed at Tabreez or Teheran.

The main bazaar of Trebizond, which is interesting on account of the variety of its products from the East and the far West, has one long artery partly roofed over, and some narrower parallel veins of commerce straggling up and down the hill; it is particularly rich in the embroidered bags and saddlery and the roughly picturesque mule trappings of Asia Minor and Kurdistan. Here, too, are weapons of every description, from the silver-hilted pistols and swords left by the Kurdish cavaliers, to the latest Martini and Winchester rifles. The genuine Smith & Wesson revolver is not rare, but more frequently still is the clever imitation made in Russian workshops.

In the centre of the town is a small park-like enclosure, much frequented by resident Persians as a tea-garden, and nothing stronger than effervescent lemonade is sold there. Near by are several great caravansaries with court-yards, where the "arabas" and other quaint vehicles from the

CAMEL CARAVAN BY MOONLIGHT

interior are put up. A winding road bordered by pleasant gardens and cemeteries with venerable black cypresses leads to the hills high above the bay. Down this road come the Kurdish horsemen and the long camel trains led by flat-faced and ruddy Tartar drivers, their sunburnt cheeks shaded by shaggy peaked caps of camel's-hair or sheepskin. The leading camel, always a majestic brute, carries his head proudly aloft, decorated with a ponderous mass of colored tassels and jingling bells.

A favorite resort in the late afternoon is a little Persian tea-garden by the road-side, looking down on the harbor and the distant town. The view is like a vignette, framed by trellises with vine leaves and the drooping fronds of the weeping-willow. Pink rhododendrons and white-flowering shrubs are set in moss-covered pots and boxes. A rude projecting balcony, higher up, over the shrubbery, is frequented by Turks, whose turbaned heads cut like black silhouettes against the pale orange of the evening sky. Only tea is served here, and the waiters are two Persian boys, who bring it in small glass cups, together with burning coals in metal trays, for the kalyans and cigarettes of the loungers at the little round tables. A row of distant and slender cypresses of inky blackness is pencilled against the sky.

July 23d.—The strange little table d'hôte at the hotel is filled at the dinner hour by a company of Levantines and Greeks. All wear the fez. My neighbor, a burly sunburnt man, is relating in French a recent adventure among the mountains beyond Erzeroum. He was sleeping at night in a hut, when five armed Kurds entered through the window, bound him hand and foot, and carried off his money, clothing, and other belongings. Although this narrative is addressed to a young Greek at the end of the table, it is not lost on the two strangers who

IN THE TEA-GARDEN

had planned this campaign at the Café Américain, and matured it definitely in the uproar of the Casino. It is needless to say that the Kurds were not taken into account. They look blankly at each other, and think of the rouleaux of napoleons, of sovereigns, and the precious packages of five-pound notes and roubles which they hope to carry safely through Kurdistan and over the Persian border. The victim of this midnight aggression proves to be an English subject in the employ of the Ottoman tobacco monopoly, which fact may have had something to do with his misfortune. When he finds that we have the same mother-tongue, he offers us much frank and sound advice, urging us particularly not to sleep in tents beyond Erzeroum. As he usually passed the night in village huts or in road-side "khans," he had invented an insect-proof sleeping-tent, constructed of white muslin, shaped like a long cube, at least three yards in length and two in height. When in use, this tent is suspended from the ceiling or walls by a cord at each corner, so that the bottom lies upon the floor. The entrance is a round hole at one end, with a long sleeve-like funnel, through which he who would sleep in peace wriggles in, letting the sleeve drop behind him. It is an admirable invention, and we order a pair of them.

With the advice and assistance of the consular dragoman we lay in a stock of liquors and canned provisions for emergencies. Two means of conveyance are open to us from Trebizond to Erzeroum—either a train of pack-horses and mules, or an araba, which will carry all our baggage, and in which our dragoman and cook can sleep. We decide upon the latter, but we should have lost less time had we taken pack-horses.

An araba, it should be explained, is a great lumbering tented wagon, much lighter than it appears to be, and not unlike an American "prairie schooner." The best arabas are built in Russia. The cart has four wheels, but no springs; the sides slope inward from above, and the tail projects backward beyond the hooped tent which covers the forward part. The four horses are harnessed abreast to a single long pole. This vehicle seems at first sight to be rudely and clumsily constructed, but upon examination it will be found that the toughest wood and the best iron and steel only are employed. This cart will stand any amount of rough usage, and the threatening perils through which ours passed unscathed are almost beyond belief. It is not easy to give the faintest notion of the roads, if roads they can be called, over which our arabas labored with ever-increasing vicissitudes, and as we approached the soaring passes near the boundary of

Persia they rolled and thundered over the rocks, straining and pitching like ships in foul weather. Let the reader imagine a heavy army wagon, laden with baggage and men, dragged by four horses over the higher passes of the Alps—not over macadamized roads, such as the Simplon, but over mule tracks like the Grimsel Pass, and sometimes as high as the Dent-du-Midi—and then over sections of road partly destroyed by landslides and heavy rains, and down the slippery banks of rivers or the beds of mountain torrents. Imagine these passes of six, seven, or nine thousand feet in height to occur not once or twice only, but day after day and week after week, through the wilderness of mountains south of Ararat and along the borders of Kurdistan. We once rode a hundred yards in the araba down the bed of a river, and the sensation was like that of being tossed in a blanket. It is hardly necessary to say, then, that our luggage suffered far more from the endless grating and grinding of each package against its neighbor than if it had been packed on horses. We had brought our saddles from Paris, and secured fairly good horses for ourselves. The staff consists of Artemis, the dragoman; Diamante, the cook, a native of Trebizond; the driver of the araba, a crusty and superstitious old Persian; and a younger man, part owner of the horses, with one or two supernumeraries.

As soon as our various chests, packages, and the tents are placed in the wagon the rear is filled up and fenced in with the musty old pack-saddles of the horses, to be used on their return journey. After all our later experiences of pack-saddles I can remember none that were as malodorous as this first instalment, and we could not but pity the dapper dragoman who was compelled by perverse fate to leave the flesh-pots of Pera and eat, drink, and sleep in this tainted atmosphere.

Everything is ready at last, passports are covered with numerous visas in Turkish and Persian, and our stock of provisions stowed in the cart. The driver cracks his whip, and the procession winds slowly up the hill in the noonday heat. There had been heavy rains a few days before, and the roads were reported to be in bad condition. Two hours from Trebizond we reach a stretch of deep mire. The men go on in front to reconnoitre, and conclude to drive ahead; the horses sink deeper as they advance, the mud reaches their girths, and the wagon wheels are buried to the hubs. Blows and kicks avail nothing, and the poor animals soon cease to struggle. Then the baggage is taken out and carried to a place of safety, and some laborers are found who dig out a passage with their shovels. A mule train coming in the opposite direction is even in a worse plight; one heavily laden donkey is only kept from sinking out of sight by his broad pack-saddle; an old worn-out horse, after hopelessly floundering close to the bank where the mud is deepest, resigns himself to his fate, tormented on one hand by showers of blows and kicks, and on the other by clouds of flies which settle on his face, the only visible portion. But all are rescued after heroic efforts, and a few hours further on this scene is partly repeated, but we extricate ourselves with less difficulty.

Djèvizlik, July 24th.—A small neat village, with a long main street lined by houses with widely projecting eaves, a café or two, and a small khan or rest-house. All day we follow the road, now dry and dusty, along the side of a deep valley, far above the stream, which we cross by a bridge at daybreak. We look down on highly cultivated slopes, sunny vineyards, and up to the forest-clad heights on either side. The clustered white houses of the villages, and the tin-roofed bell-towers of Armenian churches and convents, sparkling in the sunlight, recall in a measure the Val d'Aosta, and the Val Savaranche.

Taschkeupreu, July 25th.—Here we halt for the night, quite in the heart of this Turkish Switzerland. Mounting a rickety wooden staircase from the road, we unpack our belongings in the small but clean guest-room of the khan. From a raised platform built against the railing of the veranda we watch the arrival of the other four arabas and the unloading of their freight of homeward-bound Persians as they draw up in the street below. These travellers settle themselves on the green turf, along the whitewashed wall of a low house adjoining the khan, and spread out all their paraphernalia of rugs and blankets, samovars, and copper pots. Wreaths of mist which have been accumulating in the valley below now settle among the pine-clad slopes above us, and a gray twilight envelops all. Fires flash out along the street; there is a sound of sizzling and frying, with the attendant odors. The horses are picturesquely grouped in circles around the hempen trays attached to the poles of the wagons, in which their barley is supplied. After the culinary functions are over, the drivers and some of the pilgrims organize a sort of country dance. All stand in a row, one or two of them sing a monotonous chant, agitating their handkerchiefs, while the rest beat time with their feet. Several of the spectators seated along the stone wall which borders the road are roughly but good-naturedly dragged up and made to take part in the performance.

July 26th.—Our road still ascends through magnificent forests with towering beeches, poplars, and evergreens. Streams of water cross the road, and there is a dense and tangled growth in the deep ravines below. Sometimes we are blockaded by trains of little ox-carts carrying timber. The wooden trucks of these carts when in motion keep up a monotonous shrieking and groaning which can be heard a mile away. Squads of Turkish infantry occasionally pass, on their way to the interior. At a turn of the road the forest ceases, and we come at once upon a country of ochre-tinted, glaring hills, sparsely dotted with stunted evergreen shrubs. We halt at mid-day on a high, bare ridge. A fresh breeze blows straight in our faces from the line of snow-streaked ridges a day's journey beyond us. Henceforward these snow-spotted heights are always in sight, but never by any chance do we reach them. The landscape is severe and monotonous, but there is variety within its monotony. We descend steep hill-sides shaded by scattered pines. The sun burns fiercely; at times a boisterous wind envelops us in clouds of dust; this is almost a relief, as it helps us to resist the ever-increasing drowsiness. There are places where the yellow cliffs behind us reflect an overpowering glare, and we ride through a stratum of heated air like the breath of a furnace. Yet the pocket-thermometer held on the saddle seldom shows more than 105° Fahr., save in these exceptional spots. The nights at this elevation are almost invariably fresh and cool.

Erqui, July 27th.—To-day an accident nearly led to the utter wrecking of the araba and its contents, and one of the horses is so badly injured that we shall have to replace him at the next town. We enter a series of deep and narrow ravines, with walls of no great height, but rocky and savage in character. The road, narrow and rudely built, passes in one place under an overhanging cliff on the left, and some fifteen feet below, on the other side, lies the channel of a torrent. There is not room for the four horses to past abreast, and scarcely room for the

ACCIDENT JUST BEFORE BAIBOURT

breadth of the araba, but the men urge their beasts on, with shouts and blows. The outermost horse falls over the ledge, and hangs suspended by the bit and one or two straps which have not parted, vainly struggling to find a foothold on the sliding soil. The road caves in and crumbles away under the feet of the second horse, and he, too, is dragged down. Then the men in the cart throw their weight on the inner side, which restores its balance, and cutting loose the fallen horse, manage to rescue the second. The poor brute which fell first is badly cut and bruised.

Baibourt, July 28th.—We enter this city in a whirlwind of yellow dust. A steep and tawny ridge of rock rises above it, bearing like a crest the irregular broken walls and flanking towers of an ancient citadel, presumably of Byzantine origin. Following in the wake of the Persian arabas, we reach the lofty entrance of a great caravansary. The carts are driven under the arch into a dark and foul-smelling stable. A steep and narrow stairway takes us to an upper guest-room of the khan. Here we find high clay platforms on three sides, divided by low railings into sleeping compartments, carpeted with straw matting, suggestively dingy; a clay fireplace occupies one end, but our cooking is done outside in the passage. Half-way down the dark and unswept stairs a door opens into the common guest-room and café combined. Our fellow-travellers have grouped themselves picturesquely on the wide platforms. The drivers and muleteers are mending their multicolored rags, and the great brass samovars are steaming over the fireplaces. The picture has the rich and bituminous tone of a Teniers, but the high, peaked fur caps are more suggestive of Russia or Siberia than of Holland. As Baibourt is a garrison town, a Turkish gendarme soon makes his appearance, and hangs about while our baggage is being unpacked. When we go out to see the town he is our guide, and in one of the covered bazaars, roofed with sticks, tattered patches of awning, cobwebs, and filthy straw mats, we come to a café with a ram-shackle wooden gallery, which we reach by means of a tottering stairway. From this elevated station we look down on the market-place and the moving crowd through a haze of dust and flying straw, which partially veils the view of the yellow ridges

INTERIOR OF CAFÉ AT BAIBOURT

above. Two more police officers of higher rank saunter in and partake of our coffee and cigarettes. They ask many questions of our dragoman, and looking at our hand-cameras, insinuate, but with perfect courtesy, that these forbidden weapons are not to be used here. This official warning comes too late, however, for the gallery and the two officers themselves already figure among our souvenirs of Baibourt. Here let me add that we never had reason to complain of rudeness on the part of these functionaries, but they gave us a deal of trouble, nevertheless. I was not prepossessed by our quarters for the night at the khan, and ordered my sleeping-tent to be hung up on the trembling wooden balcony which jutted over the stable door. Half the town assembled in the street below to look up at my preparations for retirement. My camp-bed was first taken inside and unfolded, and as the candle within made a huge transparency of the tent, the elaborate gymnastics shadowed upon the walls must have been vastly entertaining, judging from the deep murmurs and grunts of satisfaction. The night was far from peaceful, however. The noise and uproar of the bazaar continued till a late hour; two fleas had found an entrance somewhere, and Keating's powder had no terrors for them. The effluvium of the stable below rose through the cracks in the floor; an injured puppy lamented plaintively all through the night, and there were catcalls, and occasionally the ear-piercing howls of a pack of street dogs hunting down an intruder to the death. Rising above all, the long-drawn groans and shrill shrieks of distant ox-carts. When my candle was extinguished I could see that my neighbor, a shop-keeper opposite, was also a sufferer from insomnia; he had lit his lamp, and crooned to himself with the wailing cadences of his race. When the morning light appeared we felt that many more such nights would be sorely trying, and we inwardly resolved to keep to the tent and the open country in future, come what might. The debatable border-land of Kurdistan is still some days distant.

Ilidja, July 31st.—A straight and dusty road over a plain leads to this village, which is famous for its warm sulphur springs, with bathing establishments, frequented by the upper ten of Erzeroum. These springs ooze from the ground and spread out into marshy pools in the centre of the village. Erzeroum is visible high up on the flank of a range of mountains, a white speck near the patches of snow.

Erzeroum, August 1st.—The gateway of this fortified stronghold is protected by a moat and drawbridge, and earth-works apparently of modern construction. There are sentries on the ramparts above. The first impression of the town is not seductive. Low stone huts, with their supply of winter fuel—cakes of dried dung—stacked in black pyramids about the doors, uneven paths where the dust lies deep, or rises in clouds to mingle with the pungent smoke of the morning fires. Far above, on our right as we enter, rises a desolate range of moutains, and the rare patches of snow descend nearly to the level of the town. On the left, to the eastward, rises a hill with a battery on its summit, which commands the approaches on all sides. As we draw near to the heart of the city we pass the place of slaughter, environed by gory mire, where the carcasses of slain animals are suspended on poles and scaffoldings. There are many well-stocked European shops with supplies of all kinds, and the bazaars where old saddlery, weapons, and rugs are sold are uncommonly rich in bric-à-brac, which is not for us, however, with our long route to the Persian Gulf stretching before us. We are taken to a high four-storied building, with a billiard-room and café under Persian management at the top. The place is not repulsive outwardly, but it proves to be a noisome den within, and there is no other shelter available at present. We had a brief interview with the chief of the custom-house, who allowed us, under protest, to have our luggage unloaded at the hotel. He seems to have repented his leniency, however, and soon sends a subordinate after us, who insists upon prying into our boxes, but with a little diplomacy he is persuaded to refrain.

Upon arriving at any town, the first step is always to have our passports examined, and as the consul is absent, his dragoman undertakes to make the necessary arrangements. He at once finds something wrong in our dragoman's passport, which gives him permission to go as far as Van only, but not to cross the frontier into Persia. Now Van is not on our route, but far to the southward. This passport was made out at Constantinople under consular supervision, and the Consul-General had been most carefully informed as to our projected route. It seems that all Armenians are regarded with suspicion just now on account of a plot against the Turkish authority, recently discovered, in which many of their leading men were implicated. On the next morning the consular dragoman, in order to explain the state of affairs, visited the Vali, or military governor, who, being an orthodox Turk of the old school, was rather a difficult man to deal with. In the afternoon we were told that matters were going on well, and that the Vali had promised his signature.

August 2d.—In the course of our rambles about the town this morning we visited the palace of the governor, a large yellow-washed barrack without interest, and called upon the chief of police, a tall soldierly man, who received us with frank cordiality, and was lavishly hospitable to the extent of cigarettes and coffee.

Erzeroum was once a Persian capital, and there are still some remains of that epoch: a mosque with two slender minarets on either side of a narrow pointed arch; the entire structure, although ruinous, is rich with carved stone-work and brilliant tiles; and near it stands a basilica-like building rather Byzantine in character, as well as the remains of an old fortress and citadel. There is a large Persian quarter, where the people sit on little

CAMEL'S HEAD AND TRAPPINGS

stools along the shady side of the street, with their glass cups of tea and bubbling kalyans.

This is the first day of the great annual festival of Hassan and Houssein, which is honored throughout all Mussulman Asia. A procession with banners, and flagellants smiting their bared breasts, passes the hotel. In the afternoon the consular dragoman appears with an air of hopeless dejection, and says that the Vali, at the last moment, had refused to indorse our dragoman's passport, and that our new friend the chief of police, who had discussed our projects with us in his lame but sympathetic French, had advised him not to sign that document. The prospects of getting away from Erzeroum now began to look desperate. It would be next to impossible to find another interpreter, or indeed any sort of a substitute. Our unhappy dragoman, who had been much depressed since his arrival, now showed unmistakable signs of bodily fear, and begged us tearfully not to desert him. Even should he succeed in crossing the frontier with us, he dared not return alone without his passport, and would be liable to arrest by any Turkish subaltern, with a prospect of imprisonment and the chain-gang. But one alternative seemed open to us, one last chance. We concluded to demand an interview of the Vali, through the authority of the consulate in the person of its dragoman, and should he grant us an audience, to make the most of our slight official position, and insist on our dragoman's passport in order that we might arrive at Teheran, where we were expected by the legation at a certain date. Our official go-between shook his head dubiously over this proposition, but promised to do his best, with the air of one who is about to stake his all on a forlorn hope. During the interval of suspense we visit the Persian consul, to have our papers put in order for

Persia, and to draw up a contract with the chavadars,* whom we expect to engage for the journey to Tabreez. A young Greek merchant, to whom we bring letters of introduction, receives us in a handsomely decorated tent behind his house. At the breakfast which follows the French consul is present, and a few other Europeans drop in. Nothing can exceed their kindly and sympathetic interest in our projects, but it is evident that they regard our plan of reaching Persia by this route as an almost hopeless wild-goose chase. A company of Persians who came with us from Trebizond in an araba intend going on to Tabreez with the same vehicle when we are ready to start. But our new friends are quite sure that the road will shrink to a mere goat-path beyond Erzeroum, and advise us to buy pack-horses or mules. Then some one suggests Kurds and brigands, and in the vivid reminiscences which follow we and our plans are almost forgotten. We both felt rather despondent when we took leave of our kind entertainers, but were more than ever anxious to get away from Erzeroum. It was impossible to work here, as the Vali had sent a message forbidding us to sketch or photograph on this side of the border. I could not leave the house for a moment without being followed by spies, but their occupation was no sinecure, as they were obliged to keep me in sight, which entailed endless marching and countermarching for no apparent object. The hotel where we had encamped was filthy beyond description, but the upper floor, monopolized by the Persian billiard-room and tea-counters, seemed clean by comparison. I had amused myself by making a sketch of the interior, and contemplated another from the

* The man who has charge of the horses, and is usually part owner of them, is called the "chavadar."

balcony, which overlooked the low roofs of the town and the hill beyond with its battery. A friendly Persian who sat smoking in the doorway warned me that we were being watched from below.

August 3d.—His Excellency has condescended to receive us. We are conducted to a long room where he is seated, cross-legged, upon a divan at the opposite end. He wears a short gray beard, and is costumed in white drill, patent-leather boots, and a fez. On his right are several officers occupying a row of chairs against the wall. The trial of this important case takes up at least an hour. Our advocate, the dragoman of the consulate, seems to have the gift of persuasive eloquence, judging from the impassioned fervor of his opening speech, interrupted at intervals by the sharp cross-questioning of the Vali. At last we are told that our dragoman, Artemis, must present a request for a new passport in the form of a petition, which he (the Vali) would sign. As a condition, we must promise to make no sketches, photographs, or notes on this side of the boundary, and the zapti, or mounted gendarme, who is deputed to accompany us to the next *étape*, has orders to keep an eye on our movements, and to delegate his authority to the officer who relieves him. All these pompous restrictions amount to nothing, and once out of sight of the town we end by doing exactly as we please.

August 4th.—It was with no little sense of relief that we rode out from the gates of Erzeroum into the open country, but with a haunting fear that the Vali might suddenly repent of his generosity.

A few hours' ride takes us to the foot of a bold promontory of rock, capped by the ruins of another Byzantine fortress. The town, or rather large village, is built along the side. Our tent is pitched near the base, and on the

WATERING HORSES ON THE EUPHRATES—NOONDAY

edge of an emerald-green meadow, with many springs and pools of water. The Persian araba empties its contents near us. Our friends begin their devotions early the next morning, as it is the most important day of the Moharrem. Before sunrise they spread their prayer-carpets and scarlet coverlets on the dewy turf. The meadow is dotted with kneeling and standing groups. Their sombre kaftans and tall black caps of Astrakhan are sharply relieved against the distant ridges now lighted up with the first flush of sunrise. Other groups are busy over the samovars and camp-fires, from which the smoke ascends in spirals, and the animals are led to water or grouped around the tented arabas. The Persians want to take a day's rest in honor of their holiday, but with the Erzeroum experience fresh in our minds, we are anxious to push on, and, after a few hours' delay as a concession to our friends, we begin the day's march, and the other araba follows reluctantly in our wake.

Deli-Baba, August 10th.—The officer on duty who comes to the tent to inspect our papers is accompanied by a species of Cossack whom we had seen prowling about. He is clad in a long-skirted gray frock crossed by cartridge-belts, and a tall gray lamb's-wool cap, which, with his blond beard, gives him a decidedly Russian appearance. But he proves to be in the Turkish service. We are within a few hours of the Georgian frontier, and these fellows wear anything indiscriminately by way of uniform.

August 11th.—We are early in our saddles, as we have been advised to make all haste over the Taya Pass, and not to spend the night in the village half-way, near the summit. Five men were killed there a fortnight ago, our guard tells us, the same gray-skirted Georgian who came to the tent last night, and he has been promised an extra fee to spur on the drivers of the arabas. One soon learns to take these "tales of the border" with a liberal allowance of salt and a certain amount of fatalistic resignation, yet there is substantial if not reassuring evidence that they have some foundation of truth. The road ascends abruptly into a labyrinth of deep and sombre ravines, crossing again and again the same torrent, overshadowed by echoing walls of black rock. At noon we gallop into a high and treeless valley, and halt in a Kurdish village consisting of a few cave-dwellings built like dens in a rocky hill-side, each with its black pyramid of winter fuel at the entrance. As there is neither shade nor shelter we seat ourselves along a stone wall in the full glare of the sun. In spite of the elevation the heat is intense. The Kurds who surround us are handsome stalwart fellows, with their girdles well furnished with silver-mounted pistols and swords, and they show a friendly and professional interest in our heavy battery of Winchesters and Smith & Wesson small-arms. One scowling beetle-browed giant might figure as a stage captain of the "Forty Thieves." Beyond this village the ascent of the Taya Pass begins, which is approximately eight or nine thousand feet above the Black Sea. The higher slopes above us lose much of their grandeur as we approach them, and partake of the character of elevated Swiss pasture-lands, pierced here and there by sharp ridges of rock, but there are no patches of snow near us, and only a few are visible on the more distant summits. A thunder-storm which had been slowly gathering breaks over us as the wagons begin the ascent, and the dust which lay deep on the road becomes a gluey paste. The four horses of our araba struggle frantically under lash and kicks, but are unable to move the cart; one horse is entirely useless. The Persian araba, which has the better team, mounts slowly but surely upward. Ishmael, the driver, seeing our difficulty, halts a few hundred yards above us, and unhitching his best horse, leads him down and attaches him to our wagon, which is then dragged up to the level of his own. This manœuvre is repeated until we reach the summit of the pass, just before twilight. But the events of the day are not yet over. Although the rain has ceased, the road is in a worse condition than ever, and the descent, of unparalleled steepness, ends in a gulley. Twilight is deepening, and our halting-place is far below us. At the bottom of the first hill the road has been washed away, and the ravine which cuts it in two has banks six feet in height. Down the first bank the horses plunge and slide, while the men hang on to the back of the araba, which is almost perpendicular. The foremost araba capsized, but it has been righted again and the baggage replaced. The extra horse is again attached to our cart, while all hands take hold of the wheels. Frenzied by the wild yells and the cracking of whips, the five horses leap and struggle up the opposite bank. Here the outer edge of the road has been undermined by the torrent and washed away. All the men in the Persian araba get out, and with armfuls of stones and bowlders fall to and piece out the road. Miracles of apparently reckless driving were performed, while we waited breathlessly, expecting the final catastrophe, which seemed inevitable. The prospect of being wrecked with all our baggage and valuables in the wildest part of the Kurdish hills was imminent enough to disturb the resigned fatalism of a Mussulman. There are moments when one may reiterate "Kismet" and "Imshallah," bnt these talismanic words no longer produce the desired tranquillity of mind. The dramatic interest of the situation quite equalled that of a cyclone at sea. As we descend we enjoy a brief interval of peace.

ENTERING TAYA PASS

We have leisure to look at the landscape, which seems far richer and more luxuriant than any we have seen since leaving the valleys near Trebizond. In the hollows of the hills there are marshy pools surrounded by tall reeds, thickets of tangled vines, and great clusters of flowering shrubs varied and brilliant in color. The difficulties of the road diminish, until at last we reach the stony channel of a mountain stream, which is as a macadamized road compared with the route above. Down this natural highway we drive to our destination, and in the gathering darkness come suddenly into a Kurdish village. A horse-fair is being held in the market-place, which is crowded with mountaineers. Our camping-ground is on the edge of a brawling stream beyond the village, in a sinister hollow surrounded by desolate bowlder-strewn heights. As Child suggested, it seemed a fitting background for robbery and assassination. Artemis, shaking with chills and fever, begs to be allowed to sleep in the chief's house in the village behind, so that he may be under cover. We are thus left without guide or interpreter, but our energetic cook, Tatoŝ,* with whom we could only communicate by signs and a sort of Volapük composed of fragments of Turkish, English, and French, is a host in himself, and soon settles us comfortably in our tent. He engages the chief of the village to watch at our tent door, and the Persian caravan encamps near by. Our minds are filled with the exciting events of the day, but, lulled by the monotonous noise of the water, we are just dropping off to sleep when a long low whistle like a curlew's call acts like a cold douche on our overstrained nerves. We listen intently. The call is answered after a short interval

* Tatos had been engaged at Erzeroum to replace his incapable predecessor.

by a similar whistle from the rocky ridge which hems us in, and this is echoed again from another crag still farther off. There is no cause for apprehension, however, as it proves to be only the signal of the chief to the watchers posted on the surrounding hills. But all through the night in our waking moments we are vaguely conscious of his warning whistle at regular intervals, followed by gradually attenuated responses. In this strange and forbidding landscape, heard above the noise of the torrent, it produced a singularly weird and uncanny impression.

Kizildize, August 12th — Mount Ararat.—Since day-

IRRIGATION CANAL AND ARMENIAN GIRL

break we have been slowly mounting by long zigzags a pass which seems to rival in height the Taya Pass, which we left behind us but yesterday. Our map gives it 2350 metres only. Tatos had

MOUNT ARARAT

taken my horse, while I climbed by the short-cuts, leaving the caravan toiling slowly on far below. From the highest point another gorge opens below and beyond us, and all at once the mighty mass of Ararat rises straight from the plain, a dazzling snow-capped cone, uplifted by long purple slopes, flecked with the shadows of high-sailing summer clouds. By noon we are down in the long valley which follows the southwestern slope of the great peak. Here we look for a good halting-place with water, but can find no trace of a spring. The governor of some little province, with his servant, had joined us on the road. Both are armed, and the governor wears one of the high-peaked white hoods in vogue among travelling Ottoman officers as a protection against the glare. We were persuaded to invest in these appendages while at Erzeroum, and Artemis had ordered a hoop to be inserted in the front of each hood. His appearance was delightfully grotesque, with his short and dumpy figure surmounted by this huge and flapping edifice of white linen, not unlike a New England Shaker bonnet.

We leave the caravan behind, and, accompanied by the zapti and the governor, who is finely mounted on a pacing Arab, ride on in quest of water. The governor holds a hasty conference with the zapti, who dashes suddenly up a hill-side and peers about from the summit. Wheeling quickly, he tears downhill, and as he flies past, my horse bolts and follows him. Wild yells and calls are heard from the direction in which we last saw the caravan. The zapti slips a cartridge into his Martini, and we all gallop on in the direction of the cries, stimulated by the excitement of our horses and the exhilaration of the moment. The mystery is cleared up when we find the wagons hidden in a fold of the volcanic hills. The guard had seen a party of five armed horsemen observing us from a hill-top, and the governor considered the neighborhood unsafe. Both were anxious to press on to the last frontier station, where we were to pass the night. Meanwhile our men had found a spring, and were watering the horses. The yells which had so alarmed the guard were intended only to call us back. There is no shelter, and although the noonday sunshine is slightly veiled by haze, the heat is intense. We lie down in a hollow like a rifle-pit, and eat a hasty but voracious lunch. We are soon mounted again, and follow in a compact squad behind the wagons through a strange and ever-changing landscape, past tawny ledges of rock and clumps of low thorn-trees, crossing fords where broad sheets of white pebbles frame in the narrow water channels, reflecting the indigo-blue of the zenith. The long, grand slopes of Ararat, leading up to its dazzling cone of snow, are always on our left, and the lesser summit, bare of snow, now comes into view. Here we have a little difference with the governor, who would like to strike across to Bayazid, and take our zapti with him. Before sundown we reach the station, a fortified camp with a large custom-house. Here we find a *cordon sanitaire*, and caravans from Persia or from the Russian dominions are subjected to a quarantine of five days. Great camel trains dot the plain on the right with their encampments. The custom-house enclosure is like a large caravansary, filled with a motley crowd of Kurds, Circassians, and Persians. Here our luggage is again overhauled, and the officials want to have it all unloaded, but they show themselves amenable to reason, and examine it in the araba. This function being over, we drive on to our camping-ground, a narrow sloping plain between two yellow and rocky hills. Here a new cause of annoyance interferes with our repose, and postpones the hour of "Nirvana." We had already advanced more money for the araba and horses than we had engaged to do by the contract, as the men swore that they had spent their last piastre in buying fodder for the animals. At this frontier station they were obliged to pay an export, or rather drawback, duty for the wagon and horses of several Turkish liras, or pounds, to the custom-house. This money would be refunded when they presented the receipt on the return trip. There was but one course open to us—to pay down the money to the officers and get the drivers' stamped receipt. Our passports were again vised, for the last time in the Sultan's dominions. Our camp is well guarded to-night. The Kurdish chief of the district, bearing on his black Astrakhan cap a gilded badge with the lion and the sun of the

Persian Shah, assures us that "he is responsible for our safety." He is a tall, white-bearded, and soldierly old man, with the bearing of a prophet or a Schamyl, and we sleep with a feeling of perfect security.

Ovadjik, August 14th.—To-day we are well over the border. In spite of the warnings of our European friends, we have slept peacefully during the greater part of our journey in our tent, unmolested by brigands. Although most of the Europeans whom we had met thus far seemed to stand in awe of the Kurds, we left their country with the impression that they were not bad fellows.

KURDISH SHEPHERD

There are but a few days more of the mountains, and then we shall begin to miss that element of uncertainty which added a little flavor to the monotony of the dusty road, and made us appreciate more keenly the value of life. Another source of joy for the moment is the fact that we no longer run the risk of being detained by Turkish officials. We are now approaching Khoi, the first Persian town of any size; but the road has not begun to improve, as we expected. Here it is a mere track, easy enough to follow where it lies along a breezy ridge of high pasture-land, but dangerous again when it plunges down into the depths of deep gullies beset with all manner of obstacles. A young Kurdish shepherd joins us on the road, and plays bucolic airs on a reed pipe. The prospect of gaining a half-kran* by posing as a model induces him to follow us to our halting-place at noon. Here our men conclude to purchase another horse, and the few half-maimed and spavined animals which the village can show are brought forth. After much heated discussion they select a horse, for which they pay about eight dollars (in our currency). Knowing that it is useless to apply to us for more money, they borrow the amount of Ishmael, the driver of the Persian cart. In the afternoon we begin another interminable descent, where the ample mule-track, which was quite sufficient for the arabas, shrinks to an uncertain goat-path. Amid towers of dust, and with much rattling and shaking, we descend to the first Persian village. Here the poplars begin; there are melon patches, and actual houses of mud, with windows and wooden lattices. The sky is overcast, and the wind, which shakes the tent walls, is raw and chilly, although it is the middle of August.

August 15th.—Still another pass, with long winding defiles. The Persian "trooper" who replaces our Turkish escort is a lamentable, dejected creature, clad in rags, and mounted on a donkey. He rides sadly behind my companion, who, with his great height and bulk, girt about with arms, and his bronzed face, has the air of a brigand. Our protector, as he rides between the protected, looks like a malefactor in custody. At noon we are caught in a thunder-storm—a deluge in which, notwithstanding water-proofs, we are well drenched.

As we descend the pass the hot sun comes out, the clouds roll back, and disclose far below us a long and

* Kran, the Persian coin representing the nominal value of a franc. It is worth much less in reality, owing to the amount of alloy.

PERSIAN GUARD

fertile valley. A blue lake gleams in the middle of the valley, and we have a premonition that we shall have to cross it. The road is heavy with mud, and our progress desperately slow. At last we come to a stand-still on the heights above a swollen river. After some unsuccessful attempts to reach the other side, we wait a little until the water has begun to subside, and then venture into the stream, which just reaches the bottom of the wagon. The worst is still before us, and at the beginning of twilight we reach the flooded meadow we saw from the pass. It is traversed by ditches and streams, necessitating many detours in order to reach the village beyond. Here the ground is like a wet sponge; there is no dry spot whereon to pitch a tent, and we must perforce, wet and sodden as we are, pass the night in a mud hut. Artemis, chattering with fever, conducts us to the house which he considers the best in the village. The araba draws up in a sea of mud, opposite a square hole in a mud wall, within which there is a fragrant lake of yellow mire. On the left a door leads into a stable, and in front, across the yard, is the room which we are to occupy. It is being swept, while our baggage is carried in, piece by piece. In order to reach the door we follow along a slippery bank, sloping on the right into the miry pond, and bordered on the other side by a row of deep pits. The room is low and dark, but with a fairly clean floor, which is strangely hot, for here the family bread is baked, and the hot air rises from the furnace below, through a round hole in the floor. A door opens on one side into the family living-room and bedroom combined, which is dark and grewsome, but well populated. On the left, a narrow opening leads into the sleeping quarters of the four-legged occupants of this Noah's ark. A buffalo pokes his long head into our room, and leaves but little space for us to circulate among our baggage. While we are still unpacking, the cattle come home from afield, and file through our bedroom, a long and weary, but orderly procession, into the buffalo's apartment. There are sheep and goats, kids, a dejected horse, a cow and two calves, an ungainly buffalo calf and its mother. As Artemis is now in the throes of a chill, it strikes us both that the dry, hot air of this room would be more suitable for him than the stable effluvia, so he is dosed with quinine and bundled into bed over the oven. The ridge of greasy mud, with an abyss on each side, along which we pick our uncertain way to the stable, recalls, in its dramatic possibilities, the passage of an ice cornice on the "Dent Blanche." In the stable there is certainly more space and air. A high platform of clay, with a fireplace, occupies one corner, and here the energetic Tatos installs his kitchen; our camp-beds, and the dinner-table, covered with a clean white napkin, are placed as far as possible from the horses' heels; a very creditable dinner is then served, beginning with an omelet which would not disgrace the Café Américain. Regardless of the squealing and kicking of our fighting stallions, we sleep well, and so does Artemis, thanks to our self-sacrifice in giving him the oven. In the morning we are still damp and somewhat stiff from yesterday's wetting, but none the worse for it. As we pack our bags by candlelight, a subdued piping and clucking comes from a hole in the wall behind my valise; this is the hen-coop, and, excited by the artificial daylight of the candle, the inmates issue forth, picking their way daintily over our belongings, as they would have done over our heads had we slept there. Our hostess, with a pile of freshly baked flat loaves of bread, which proves to be the best we have yet had, now comes in, bearing her youngest on one shoulder. The baby's face is covered with suspicious looking pimples, but we can do nothing by way of medical aid—the case is too far advanced—and we can only regret that vaccination is not compulsory in Persia.

August 16th, near Khoi.—We had been fondly hoping that our chariot would meet with no further trouble, but after slowly mounting a long series of terraces, another great mountain gateway opens below us; as we descend we look down on a richly cultivated plain, hemmed in by still grander mountain ridges, and in the centre of the plain are the gardens of Khoi. Down steep and rocky slopes the carts are driven to the river-bed below. Here one of our friends from the other araba, a Persian gentleman of fine presence, who had been in a manner recognized as the chief of their company, takes leave of us, for his garden, filled with a dense growth of poplar and apricot trees, skirts the bed of the stream. Now the other araba, some distance ahead of us, breaks down, and the valiant Ishmael is in sore distress. One of his wheels, so often patched and tied up with strings, has given out at last. But our driver, who has been often assisted by Ishmael, promises to send back one of our wheels on a donkey when we reach the village. The other araba will then follow with our wheel to the camping-ground, and in the morning all hands will fall to and patch up the old one again. Once over this, the last of the passes before Tabreez, we have a fresh series of impediments to progress, and we learn that the passage of a Persian village is as rich in thrilling and dramatic episodes as the ascent of a pass, and quite as much to be dreaded. As it rarely happens that any wheeled vehicle invades this region, we seldom find a village with a navigable road traversing it. The road is usually wide enough at the entrance, so that it is easy to get in, but, alas, how often we despair of getting out! The mud-holes and quagmires which diversify the road on the outskirts are always passable at this season, but once inside the village, the road forks and ramifies into a series of narrow lanes between mud-walled gardens. Down the centre of the widest lanes there is often a deep and narrow stream or ditch bordered by poplars or willows, and with steep clay banks. The space between the ditch and the crumbling walls of dried mud frequently narrows to a mere bridle-path. Then comes the *mauvais quart d'heure*, the moment of suspense and peril. The wheels on one side are high up on the bank, on the other stuck fast in the mire of the ditch. The men hang on to the upper side of the cart, while the driver showers curses and blows upon the horses, which are kicking and struggling, some on the bank and some below, while all the village turns out to be "in at the death." Veiled women with babies and dirty-faced children, turbaned moullahs, and old men of fierce and uncompromising aspect, with shaggy eyebrows and gray beards dyed flaming orange and scarlet with henna. More than once it seemed as if the end had come, but somehow, by hook or crook, we always pulled through, to drive on with bated breath until we reached the next obstacle. This often took the form of a narrow bridge with a hole in the middle, sometimes half concealed and made into a pitfall by sticks and straw laid over it. This is the Persian fashion of repairing roads.

August 17th.—As we have met no travellers or caravans coming from Tabreez, we know nothing of what has been going on in Persia. There are already rumors of cholera in some of the villages which we have passed through. Can it be that after leaving Meshed, where it began, and spreading northward through the Russian provinces to Batoum, it has again returned to Persia?

My horse shies as we pass a road-side fountain; two men are washing a naked corpse, which has a strangely bluish tint about the temples.

Khoi.—A large walled city, with moat and drawbridge, sloping walls and battlements of rose-tinted mud. We ride down a shady but dusty avenue crowded with citizens who are looking on at an Armenian religious procession, with priests and banners. We halt for lunch at a caravansary, just outside the city gate, and, climbing up to the broad wooden balcony just over the entrance, we find several of our Persian fellow-travellers, who are already installed. After a long resistance we have at length capitulated to the Persian watermelon, and begin to believe that there is no harm in him. In a country where the brackish water is impossible to drink, the filtered and sweetened juice in the heart of a melon seems to be nature's own substitute; but our dragoman, who had become sadly intemperate in the matter of melons and sliced cucumbers, now began to show the disastrous results of his indulgence. His face, which was round and ruddy at the outset, had become elongated and haggard, and his flabby cheeks hung in wrinkled folds. In vain we physicked him and dosed him with cholera mixture and quinine; we invariably caught him the next day after an indisposition surreptitiously devouring forbidden fruit. While we are eating on the balcony, during the space of

A CHOLERA INCIDENT NEAR KHOI

an hour or two, thirteen bodies are deposited in the cemetery across the way. Plainly there must be something wrong about the sanitary condition of this place. For a short distance beyond Khoi we follow a well-made carriage road shaded by great trees, which ends suddenly at the bank of a river, and we then strike across the hills again.

Tasouidj, August 18th.—All day we ride across a desert plain between ranges of dark volcanic hills. The sun burns fiercely, and a hot wind blows straight in our faces, bringing with it strange and nauseous whiffs of sulphur and heated iron. A far-off horizon of wind-swept water, of the deepest hue of ultramarine, now appears to the southward. As we ride on and on, hour after hour, crossing at times narrow and sunken ravines which descend from the hills on our left, necessitating long circuits in order to find convenient crossing-places, we approach the great salt lake of Urumiyah. Far-off ranges of mountains appear and grow nearer in the amber and rose-tinted afternoon sky; beyond the blue of the water, rocky islets and abrupt cliffs, with ragged serrated outlines, rise above the opposite shores. Range beyond range and islands of fantastic shape seem to melt and quiver in the haze of light, and beyond them the dark blue of the ruffled water is drawn sharply against the western sky. For two days we follow at a distance, and at an elevation far above its level, the winding contours of this inland sea, marvellous in the delicate and ethereal beauty of its coloring, strangely impressive in its sun-steeped desolation. At noonday, in the heat haze, its color seems to fade and die softly away into neutral, intangible tones of opal and pearl, to blaze again into life in a brief glory of rose and scarlet and violet at sunset.

As we left Diza-i-Khalil, the village where we had

passed the night, I turned to enjoy a last glimpse of the lake, and it was my good-fortune to gaze upon the most wonderfully impressive morning sky that I have ever beheld. The dark and featureless plain in the foreground lay under a cloud shadow. It was perfectly calm, and the distant line of water, environed by hills, reflected the mellow and amber tones of the western sky. Long delicate lines and bars of clouds edged with light were pencilled with but slight relief across the clear sky. There was no patch or spot of positive color, but suggestions of turquoise-blue and pale emerald-green and of warm rose seemed to merge one into the other, all enveloped in a golden haze. There were hints of scarlet on the hills beyond the water, where the sun shone through cloud rifts of violet and palest purple in the shadows, but the charm was in the tone, the "enveloppe," to use an atelier phrase.

August 20th, near Mâyun.—To-day we are to reach Tabreez, which lies somewhere between the dark olive-tinted line of its surrounding gardens, barely visible at times from some high point of the plateau. The last night of the journey, twenty-nine days from Trebizond, is passed near a small caravansary. There had been much loss of time on the road, and at twilight there was still no sign of the caravansary, although both drivers protested that it was but twenty minutes farther on. One of our men, a filthy and untruthful old reprobate, who had intrigued at every village to raise the prices of provisions which we purchased, and whose brain was forever weaving plots to extract from us the balance of the contract-money before arriving at Tabreez, had been taken ill on the road. It was impossible to ascertain the nature of his malady. Some of the men believed it to be cholera, others the result of excessive indulgence in opium. Meanwhile there

EARLY MORNING—SHORE OF LAKE URUMIYAH

he lay, an unsightly writhing heap of rags on our baggage under the canvas of the cart. There was no other place to stow him, and his compatriots had refused to take him in at any of the villages along the road, so that we could only hope most devoutly that his disease was not contagious. As he seemed to be at the point of death, and darkness was rapidly coming on, we gave the order to halt by the road-side. The Persian araba kept on, deserting us for the first time, and in the morning we could see that they were right: the caravansary was just in sight. An irrigation channel of running water passed the tent. Its banks were steep and muddy, and the water, decidedly brackish in flavor, was neither clear nor inviting, but no other water was to be had; so we filtered enough to fill the samovar. Even filtered and boiled it was still nauseous, and we quenched our thirst with the cool juice of the melon. We had reason to repent of our intemperance before morning, and were feeling strangely ill at ease when we mounted our horses at sunrise. Tabreez was but two hours farther on. We forded a river crossed by a bridge which was unsafe for the araba, and were soon among the outlying villages and gardens. From this point the custom-house is an hour farther on, and when we halt in front of it the officials come out and insist that the araba shall be driven into the court-yard. This we are inclined to oppose, but Artemis, as usual, fails to show the necessary decision, and while we are still discussing the matter the driver whips up his horses and drives through the gate. Once inside, we are informed that it is Friday, that the headmen have gone to the mosque, and that we cannot have our baggage until the following day. We then decide to find the consul and appeal to his authority. The European quarter is a long way off, and when we reach it we find only mud walls, dusty hollows strewn with ruins, and streets full of holes and pitfalls. A few well-built gateways open here and there into gardens half hidden by brick walls, above which tower pale green poplars. This quarter seems even more lifeless and melancholy than the rest of the town. The consular residence is closed; so too are the houses of other Europeans to whom we have letters. We begin to regret our tent, and the prospect of finding shelter is not promising. The mid-day sun is getting hotter, and the dry wind raises clouds of dust.

With a feeling of relief we meet a European standing at the gate of his house; he is clad all in white, helmet and duck suit. He proves to be a young Austrian, and in a few words of French he explains the mystery of the situation. The cholera is raging; there have been many thousand deaths; and although it is rumored that the worst is over, and that the numbers have begun to diminish, it is still impossible to obtain any reliable figures. The large European colony, with the exception of a few individuals, has left the city, and has taken refuge in the villages on the slopes of the Sahend Mountains. The great bazaars, the most extensive and populous in all Persia, are almost empty, and the few European shops are closed. This, then, was the reason of the empty streets and the hurried funeral processions which we had encountered on the road. Although we had made this long detour to avoid the infected Russian provinces, we have ridden straight into a cholera trap. The life in the open country has been joyous enough, but in every town we have had some unpleasant experience, and this bids fair to cap the climax.

FROM TABREEZ TO ISPAHAN

I.

THE vertical rays of a noonday sun beat down mercilessly in this deserted by-way of Tabreez, and we were driven to take refuge in the narrow patch of shadow under the projecting eaves of a house. While we stood there our newly-found friend explained the situation, which we endeavored to grasp, wondering a little at our own lack of emotion. We were neither of us surprised to find cholera the reigning power, but felt that we might better have gone luxuriously to Samarcand in a saloon carriage than to have ridden through five hundred miles of mountains to see a plague-smitten city. "A pretty state of affairs!" said my companion, as we all strolled along the shady side in search of shelter of some kind, for Tabreez cannot boast of a hotel, in the European sense of the word. After knocking at several doors and finding no one but the door-keeper, always with the same negative answer, our new friend invited us into his own house. Stepping down through a low door in the outer mud-wall, and crossing a brick-paved court-yard, we reached the sitting-room. There is a square tank in the middle of the court, plants in pots are grouped about it, and ranged along the walls is a row of great jars, the usual accessaries of a Persian house now, as in the days of Ali Baba; tall trees cast thin and flickering shadows, for the leaves are crisped and burned by the dry August winds. A pile

PERSIAN MOTHER AND CHILD

of boxes and trunks is visible from the window, stacked in a corner of the yard; they are marked with an English name, and their owner was one of the latest victims of the cholera. Meanwhile there is good wine on the table, and a prospect of something solid as well. Our host, by inviting us into his house, is acting the part of an uncommonly good Samaritan, for in these troublous times he cannot foresee what may happen to the stranger within his gates. While we are sitting at ease around the table he takes our dragoman to task for his stupidity in letting the baggage be driven into the custom-house, as the Persian officials, it is well understood, have no right whatever to meddle with personal property. He at once despatches his own servant to recover it, and to find us a house, where we can unpack. While sitting at the table I had begun to feel strangely uncomfortable and disinclined to take part in the conversation, which had become more general, as a German friend of our entertainer, and one or two Persians, had joined us. An overpowering feeling of drowsiness had taken possession of me, as well as a return of this morning's symptoms. Child produces his bottle of "cholera mixture," but, far from bettering my condition, the effect is immediately disastrous. It is evident from the expression of watchful intensity in our host's eyes what is in his mind. He takes from his pocket two papers containing some white powder, which he administers at intervals, and then shows me into a dark closet, where I can lie down and be at rest; sleep, however, is out of the question, for there is no escape from the swarms of flies, and after a brief period of tranquillity and comparative darkness, I return to the room, and take possession of the divan. Listening dreamily to the hum of voices in French, German, and the strange Persian tongue, I become conscious of returning peace of mind and body, of a blessed sense of perfect comfort, and when the cool of the evening comes I am sufficiently recovered to look forward to dinner with almost the usual interest. I recall these personal reminiscences, which under ordinary circumstances would have no importance, with the presumption that it may interest some one to know how an abortive attack of cholera feels at the very beginning. While we are dining in the court-yard, the servant returns with the welcome news that the minions of the custom-house have yielded up their prey, and that all our baggage has been taken to the house which he has found for us. Escorted by our German friends, and lighted by a huge transparent lantern, which is always carried in front of the belated wayfarer in a Persian city, we set out for our new quarters, a few doors off. At the entrance of the narrow lane leading to the house we are obliged to step over a deep pit, or "khanat," to use a Persian term, and, reaching the low door, we descend a few mossy steps, and cross a small court-yard, strewn with large and juicy mulberries, which have fallen from a great tree covering like a roof the whole enclosure. Our bedroom occupies the greater part of the lower floor, and the walls are panelled off into arched recesses, most useful for storing small articles.

August 21st.—My companion seems quite ill; he complains that all his symptoms of yesterday have returned, accompanied by cramps in the legs. Artemis, also, is in great misery, and wears a most dejected expression, but he has already consumed nearly all the slender stock of remedies at hand, and but one solitary mustard-plaster remains. In ready response to our appeal, we are at once visited by the lady left in charge of the medical department of the American mission, accompanied by one of the leading members of that society. They decide that my friend has cholera, and that Artemis has a milder form of the same malady. Both patients must be removed at once to more airy and accessible quarters, and they generously place the mission school-house, now empty and next door to the dispensary, at our disposal. With their assistance we are quickly installed in the new quarters, which are far more spacious and airy than the little house where we passed the night. Two great rooms connected by folding doors occupy the upper floor; in one of them a comfortable bed has been made ready for the patient, and in the other, where the battered desks and benches of the Armenian school-children have been huddled together at one end, we bestow the dragoman and the dusty, weather-beaten camp baggage. Many doors and windows open on to the flat clay roofs, or terraces, whence the eye commands a wide and desolate panorama of mountains—the far-stretching level of flat roofs, low clay domes in long ranks marking the course of the bazaars, and the encircling heights are all of the same pale reddish hue, cut by the vertical lines of slender green poplars, and the hills of the Sahend group on the south are patched with snow. Straight from these high ridges a cool and bracing wind blew across the house-tops, tempering the heat of the long summer days, and rising at times to a gale in the clear moonlit nights. A line of gaunt and barren desert cliffs hemmed us in on the east, and at sunset their slopes burned with vivid orange and vermilion hues. This was our home for nearly four weeks, while my companion, for the first few days hanging between life and death, gradually recovered his strength. Artemis was soon on his feet again, and he resigned himself with the air of a martyr to his new duties as hospital assistant; he was soon able to occupy himself with the concoction of various savory dishes, as Tatos had no time to cook for him, and very little time for sleep. While the epidemic had been declining in Tabreez, it had broken out in Teheran, and many were the victims. A number of Europeans had fallen, members of the telegraph corps, and of the staff of the "Imperial Bank of Persia." The employés of this latter institution had organized a volunteer corps of hospital assistants which had been of very great service. There were rumors, moreover, of an outbreak at Ispahan and Shiraz. It was then, during the convalescence of my companion, that we discussed two alternative routes which seemed to offer a shorter land journey to India. The route *via* Shuster and the Karun River first suggested itself, but was abandoned when we found that the steamers which touched at the port were not to be depended upon.

The caravan road to Bagdad, and thence by steamer to India down the Tigris, was next considered; it was too late in the season to think of going to Mossoul and down the Tigris by raft, the usual way, and the direct caravan road had its drawbacks. One gentleman connected with the mission, who had just returned from that journey, said that the Turkish officials had confiscated not only his sermons, but his blank paper; and another, who had undertaken a business enterprise, had fallen among Bedaweens, and they had stripped him of all he possessed. Moreover, the plague was then holding high carnival at Bagdad, and the cholera was marching steadily in that direction. Should one escape these evils, there remained the well-known scourge of that city, the "Aleppo button," to be taken into consideration—the little abscess which appears somewhere on the countenance, and leaves a purple lump shaped like a date stone. We concluded then to carry out our original plan, and to keep on *via* Teheran and Ispahan to Bushire. Our enforced detention at Tabreez was rendered more endurable by knowing that we could not go to Teheran until the epidemic was over. Tabreez itself offered but little artistic interest, although the bazaars, as they filled up once more with returning life, were as interesting as any we afterwards encountered. Like all other Persian bazaars, they are long vaulted corridors solidly built of brickwork or masonry, lined with shops on both sides, and with domes at regular intervals. At the top of each lofty dome is a small round opening through which the sunlight streams in, enlivening the long and sombre perspective with vertical shafts of dusty light. One felt as if walking through a gallery of living Rembrandts and Riberas, and where a slender beam of light flecked with motes touched upon a group in front of a shop, or gilded a pile of oranges in a fruit stall, it was as if an electric lamp had blazed out in the purple gloom. A high pointed archway opens here and there into the great court of a caravansary, and the broad track of light streams across the bazaar, edging the hurrying figures with a golden halo. This type of caravansary is not, however, like those where travellers put up on the road, but rather a vast storehouse, a court, surrounded by two tiers of pointed arches or alcoves, the lower one occupied by shops and shaded by awnings. There is always a wide tank in the middle, surrounded by poplar and plane trees. The ground is littered with packages of merchandise enveloped in gunny-bags. Long trains of tall camels chained together blockade the entrance to these enclosures, and one is obliged to steer his way among their legs or dart under the chains in order to enter; and one must be always on the alert to avoid the caravans of laden mules or pack-horses with jingling bells, and droves of donkeys carrying building material, as well as the cava-

INTERIOR OF BAZAAR AT TABREEZ

liers who are mounted on superb horses decked with saddle-cloths of velvet embroidered with gold. Some of these saddle covers were of finest Persian carpeting, or of cloth embroidered with applied designs.

There are no fine mosques or remarkable monuments in Tabreez save the magnificent ruin called the "Blue Mosque," which is covered with exquisite faience, blue in its prevailing tone, relieved by dull black and yellow, and the lofty fragment of a brick citadel called the "Ark." During the convalescence of my companion I found time to explore a portion of the bazaars and the surrounding streets, but never did I succeed in finding a way through the labyrinth of dusty lanes and gardens to the open desert beyond. The streets have but few attractions for the pedestrian who walks for exercise, although the bazaars, as they gradually filled up and resumed their normal aspect, were a never-failing source of interest. But the air in these vaulted and gloomy aisles is close and heavy in midsummer, besides being scented with oppressive and unfamiliar odors, and it is not easy to avoid contact with the swift and silent funeral processions. Naturally one felt drawn towards the open country which lay beyond the city, but the usual limit of these pilgrimages towards the source of the invigorating desert wind was the desolate and sandy cemetery surrounding the city, for here, as in all Oriental countries, the dead seem to occupy far more space than the living.

Owing to the constant care and devotion of our friends, we were soon able to set out again, and while we were preparing for the next move the European colony began to flock back from the hills. Had it not been for their kindly aid we should have been obliged to wrestle with many more difficulties. Artemis was sent back to Constantinople, as a Persian who spoke fairly good French

LOADING THE PACK-HORSES—SUNRISE

had been found to take his place. A new tent was purchased, more roomy than the other, and the bazaars were ransacked for supplies. Although we had been advised to buy all our animals, we finally shirked the responsibility by chartering the lot from a chavadar. When the last load had been adjusted, and we had taken leave of the friends to whom we felt so deeply indebted, following the caravan bells through the dusky gloom of the bazaars, and ploughing over the long sandy avenue beyond, it was with a certain sense of relief that we climbed the desert slopes which flanked the Sahend Mountains, and breathed once more the keen, pure air which blew across the open wastes.

II.

Saidabad, September 15th.—Our camp to-night is on green turf, near the pebbly shore of a brook fringed by willows. My first exploit is to get lamed by a kick, while trying to head off my fugitive steed, who is trotting off bridleless, to have a roll on the grass with his saddle still on. The very first performance of our caravan horses, when we come to the end of the day's march, is to lie down and roll luxuriously, with their loads on, if possible, and to raise a cyclone of dust. The caravan, as well as the commissariat department, is on quite a new footing, and much better organized than before. Tatos, the cook, is still with us, and Abdullah, the new Persian servant, seems capable and trustworthy. We have ten horses in all—two for our personal use, and eight for the baggage and men. As the Persians know how to travel in their own country, we have adopted their fashion of carrying valises and small trunks, and have invested in two pairs of long carpet sacks, in which these articles are packed. Each sack is called a "ma-fresch," and two of them are a load for a horse, one being placed on each side of the saddle, with the weight carefully adjusted. These receptacles are usually made of velvety Persian carpeting, six feet in length by eighteen inches in depth and width, shaped like long narrow boxes, with stout leather handles at each end, and a multitude of straps and buckles. In these sacks all the small packages and valises are placed, water-proof bags with bedding, our iron camp-bedsteads, stools, tables, and carpets, are laid on the top, and after being tightly strapped up, they are lifted into place by the combined efforts of all the men, and corded on to the bulky pack-saddles of the horses. Provisions, wine, and cooking utensils are carried in two quaint chests, made in a Tabreez bazaar, covered with stamped red leather, and provided with short legs, which prevent the cords from slipping off. Another chest, made in Paris, which we meant to leave at Trebizond, is still with us. The horse which the head chavadar rides is more lightly loaded than the others, and picturesquely festooned with bags of fodder and earthen water-jars. Each of these weather-beaten old horses, with head-stall of fringed leather, straps and bridle ornamented with shells and blue beads, and his worn pack-saddle, shredded and patched with many colors, like a beggar's mantle, is a wonderfully interesting study of color. Around their necks, among the many-hued tassels, or from their sides, are hung bells, and bells within bells. Our march through Persia was attended by their monotonous but not discordant music. For at night, while we slept in the tent, the horses, tethered in a long row to a cord outside, munched steadily at the chopped straw in their nose-bags, and in our waking moments we were conscious of the same chimes which we had heard through the day. Each chavadar, clothed in patched and faded blue, or en-

HADJI THE CHAVADAR AND HIS ARAB STEED

veloped in heavy felt overcoat, to keep off the chill of early morning, his face burned and tanned to a rich mahogany tint, is a type of the most primitive, robust order.

This caravan life has a subtle charm of its own when one is in perfect health and things go smoothly, and even when they do not, the minor discomforts of a nomad existence do not weigh heavily on nerves blunted by the open air and a certain amount of healthy fatigue. When one journeys by vestibule train or Wagner sleeping-car, the short space of time between two cities is like an interim, an *entr'acte*, during which one's daily routine is suspended, to be resumed again only when he leaves the train at his destination. But here, where the distances are so vast, the real existence is on the road, and the brief stay in each city, full of feverish, agitated movement and unrest, becomes the interim, and the traveller looks forward to the calm and pure air of the desert plateau beyond and the comfort of his tent. The routine of daily life is a little trying at first, but easily learned; each twenty-four hours is divided into four parts—the period of hurry and activity in the early morning, a longer one of comparative tranquillity on the march, the brief hour of bustle on arriving at our destination, and then, "nirvana," the dreamless sleep of the night. At half-past three or at four A.M. it is time to get up and dress by candlelight, to call for the "samovar" and hot tea, to see that the men in the kitchen tent are astir, and that the chavadars are feeding their horses. Then the small articles are packed, Abdullah brings in breakfast, and while we are eating the chavadars come in to take out the baggage, the first red light from the rising sun shines through the transparent walls, and then the tent itself is pulled down, and we are shivering in the frosty and bracing morning air. Sometimes breakfast is finished on one of the camp-chests while the table is being packed away. When the last load has been secured, and the ground, now strewn with egg-shells and loose straw, has been searched for lost articles, we mount our horses or walk on ahead. Then comes the long day of comparative rest; and when the brief morning chill has passed away, made drowsy by the growing heat of the sun, we nod and sway in our saddles, lulled by the monotony of the slow march and the ceaseless tinkling of the bells. Over deserts of white salt, like new-fallen snow or frozen sleet, where the horizon swims and quivers in the mirage, and over plains floored with black volcanic deposit, we ride on and on, over passes, across rivers and marshy plains, until it is time to hurry on ahead of the caravan and despatch a hasty lunch on some shelterless hill-side, or deep in a gully if the wind blows, and, best of all, where there is a brook in which to cool a bottle of wine. This caravan, unlike the former one, never halts at noon, but keeps on at the same unvarying pace until its allotted task is done. At last the lengthening shadows and the sight of the distant mud-walls of the village where we are to halt warn us that it is time to spur on with the chavadar to select our camping-ground before the baggage animals come up. It was usually our fate to encamp on a ploughed field, and it was no small piece of work to clear the ground of stones and briers; often in a high wind it required the combined strength of all of us to hold the flapping canvas while the pegs were being driven in, and we were fortunate indeed if there were no wet sketches lying about when the dust drove in clouds under the tent. When the cords are well

OUR TENT AT NIGHT

secured the baggage is brought in, carpets are spread out, beds are unfolded, and the ebonite filters are put in working order, so that tea or the refreshing "peg" may be forthcoming. There is often a leisure hour in which to jot down impressions of color before Abdullah comes in to set the table, and after dinner we sit under the canvas awning which projects above the tent door, and smoke, in the crimson after-glow, grand and solemn, in this land of vast horizons.

Turkomanshai, September 17th.—A ruinous caravansary stands by the road-side, and the tents are put up just beyond it on the brink of a deep fissure, through which a narrow stream flows, and the land rises abruptly on the other side. Deep in the gully there is a spring set about with stones, and the men lead down the tired horses to drink. Here, as elsewhere near a village, we are beset with cats—not that we regard them with antipathy, but there are really too many cats. They seem to spring up from the ground, and curl themselves snugly in our beds. When they have been expelled they make a semblance of retreating, but return again to take refuge among our bags and carpets. At the dinner hour they prowl about the door of the tent in anticipation of bones, and pass like illuminated silhouettes across the track of the lantern light.

Mianeh, September 18th.—This is the home of the redoubtable insect of which the bite is believed to be fatal both to men and horses. We were therefore not unwilling to favor the popular superstition by encamping at some distance from the town. We ford a narrow but deep and rushing brook, and put up the tents in a ploughed field. A lurid sunset portends rain, and against this sombre background our camp-followers with their horses and the group of curious villagers tell with unusual force of color. The men have been winnowing grain, and the ground is littered with straw and yellow dust. They all feel a chill in the rising wind, which shakes the tent walls, and have built fires. While the preparations for dinner are going on the chavadars are curry-combing the horses with the curious implement peculiar to this country, which makes a loud humming sound, like a watchman's rattle.

Serchem, September 19th.—We are still jogging on to the tune of the caravan bells over the endless desert plateaux, following the line of the Indo-European telegraph poles. We came suddenly upon them after leaving Khoi and long before reaching Tabreez. Now they stretch away before and behind us, an endless perspective of trim iron masts, each with the name of the famous London firm stamped upon it. By merely touching one of these poles one feels at once *en rapport* with London or Paris, New York, and Bombay. Walking on a mile or more in advance of the caravan, over a billowy plain, which seems vaster than the ocean itself, for the reason that we are always at such an elevation that it is like being on the roof of the world, whence one can look forth over endless space, we are approaching a still higher table-land. Far beyond the plain, tufted with bunches of dry yellow herbage gilded by the setting sun, this great plateau rises above us at a distance impossible to estimate in the clear atmosphere; its surface is broken up into little hillocks, like the waves of a petrified sea, each crest tipped with scarlet from the glowing west, and each long shadow correspondingly violet; and beyond this again rises another and still higher country of purple mountains, and through the gaps of their serrated sky-line other and more distant ranges may be discerned, faint and far away. Looking into the west as the sun sinks, range after range becomes visible, each less purple and more enveloped in golden haze. A wide river valley lay between us and the plateau. In the twilight which follows closely upon the golden after-glow we halted near a village strangely suggestive of the African Sahara.

Zinjan, September 24th.—Having arrived early we intend taking a day of rest, partly on account of the horses. A yellow plain reaches to the city walls: several different roads, like white threads drawn across it, converge at a point of the wall which is probably the entrance. Beyond this yellow line of walls rise a few yellow domes, some dark, spire-like trees, and three bulbous domes of vivid turquoise blue, which glitter in the sunshine against the pink and violet hills. We encamp on the gravel plain well away from the town, but with a view downward into the river valley over the wealth of green foliage confined by low garden walls. Tatos sets out at once for the bazaar, that he may buy the wherewithal with which to feast, for we are to cross another desert, and that which we have just traversed provided but little to satisfy our Gargantuan appetites, which ill accord with the ascetic character of the country. Accompanied by Abdullah, I stroll down to explore the town. From this silent and glaring desert it is but a few steps into the crowded gloom of the bazaars, noisy with the strident din of hammers as we pass through the quarter of the metal-workers, and into the street of the saddlers, where the shopkeepers stare silently at us from their cavernous retreats, fringed about with tasselled and embroidered trappings. We come to a hoary old mosque, which still retains a little of its ancient faience. There are chains across the door, as usual, to exclude the infidel, but Abdullah, who avers that the moullahs of Zinjan are less fanatical than most of their confrères, raises the chain for me to enter. Trusting to the wisdom of this enlightened Persian, I slip through the hallowed portal, and stroll about under the venerable poplars, examining the tile-work adorning the cloisters. Our presence seems to occasion not a little consternation, but apparently no open hostility, and, our inspection over, we bow ourselves out of the sacred retreat. It was the first and only mosque which I entered in Persia, and Abdullah afterwards said that the moullahs did not at all appreciate the honor of our visit.

September 25th.—I was suddenly awakened from a last doze at daybreak by the voice of my companion, Mr. Child, who stated with shocking brevity that his steel trunk had been stolen. Unwilling to believe it, we hunted high and low, but upon examining the "ma-fresch," where it had been left just inside the tent-wall, we discovered that both leather and carpet had been cut through from the outside. He himself was aware of the moment when it had been done, perhaps half an hour earlier; he had heard the ripping sound of the knife, but being half asleep had paid no attention to it. The camp was a scene of confusion for an hour or more. One of the horses had been cut loose by robbers, but turned up again a short distance away. We had a faint hope, of short duration, however, that the thief on breaking open the box would not think it worth while to carry off the clothing which it contained. Of what use could a dress-suit and a "Feringhi's" wardrobe be to a Persian tramp? But nothing was found. We concluded then to send on the caravan, but to stop on our way through the town and complain to the Governor, who, it appeared, was also a prince. As we rode up to the palace gate a company of horsemen were dismounting, one of whom was pointed out as the Governor's deputy. Having heard our statement, he led the way into the inner court, and went in search of his Excellence. After a short delay, a group of officials appeared, follow-

PACKING BAGGAGE BEFORE SUNRISE

ing the dignitary at the head, who, after a courteous salutation, sat himself down in a niche of the wall, making room for us by his side. He seemed greatly concerned, and after asking many questions, consulted with his followers, and said that his Highness was now asleep, but would awaken about noon, when he would probably give us an audience. We had been under the delusion that we were talking to the prince himself, and now, greatly disgusted by the delay, my companion vowed that he had far rather lose his clothes than so much valuable time, and briefly saluting the representatives of power, we mounted and hurried off to catch up with our men.

Sultanieh, September 26th.—Every traveller who has left a record of this journey has spoken of the vast extent of ruins around Sultanieh. M. Jaubert, a Frenchman, who went on a diplomatic mission to Teheran in 1805, and returned by this route, says: "The remains of edifices and fine monuments which cover the plain, together with the testimony of history, combine to prove the vanished splendor of this city, which in the fifteenth century was the depot of a great trade with India." Curzon also speaks of it in similar terms.

As we approached it, late in the afternoon, we passed a summer residence of the Shah, which loomed up like a domed mosque rising above a fortress; and beyond it appeared a still higher and more ancient dome, with fragments of brilliant mosaic still adhering to it. It was twilight before we reached this ruin by a net-work of stony paths, where the horses stumbled among piles of loose bricks and broken walls. It was not easy to pick out a clean piece of ground whereon to pitch the tent, as darkness had come on; there was a cold and benumbing wind, and our baggage animals were still lagging behind. But they appeared at last in the obscurity, and in spite of stiff fingers we unpacked, and were soon comfortably stretched out on our camp-beds, and looking forward to a late dinner. After riding across miles of country comparatively clean, it seemed a strange and annoying fatality that we should always be obliged to encamp near some filthy village in order to procure water, or to get to windward of the cemetery.

In the morning, our surroundings, which we could not see distinctly before, are unusually striking. Close at hand, the great crumbling ruin towers above us. It is the once splendid mausoleum of Shah Khodabendeh, a two-storied octagonal pile, capped by a dome, and with a slender minaret rising from each angle. A great caravan covers the plain, and the men, shapeless bundles enveloped in their clumsy felt mantles, are huddled together over their fires in the misty light of early morning. Our own men, as they bend over the baggage or rise up like silhouettes against the flushed sky, suggest endless combinations for pictures in a rich and mellow scheme of color.

Kazbin, September 28th.—Here we hope to find a vehicle of some sort to take us over the hundred miles of carriage road beginning at Kazbin and ending at Teheran. But alas for our hopes. There is no carriage to be had, not even a droschke, and we must still toil on with the caravan. There are plenty of arabas, but we know from experience how much speed can be gotten out of that vehicle, and at the worst we shall not lose more than two days. The Shah had recently granted a monopoly to the new road company formed in Vienna, and while we were still at Tabreez the *personnel* of the company arrived, bringing their carriages, diligences, and live-stock. After a few days for rest and repairs, they went on to Teheran. In the meantime there is an interim: the old service has been suppressed, and the road is out of repair. The great hotel, charmingly situated in a garden, and looking out into a public square which is a picture in itself, is empty. The broad, shady avenue where this hostlery stands is full of life and movement, and more attractive in aspect than any we have seen yet. As we go along, Tatos buys some cooked "kabobs" at a shop, so that we may have a hot breakfast *al fresco* while the tent is going up. The kabobs of Persia, being made from a sort of spiced minced meat which is moulded into little cakes and grilled, are uncommonly appetizing when at the best, and quite equal to Frankfort sausages.

Safar Khojah, September 29th.—The Shah's highway, considered as an agreeable promenade, or merely as a necessary avenue of approach to a great capital, cannot be considered as a shining success. Straight away in front of us as far as eye can reach, it stretches over a level plain, and up a slight rise, bounded on one side by

THE SHAH'S HIGHWAY

the arrow-straight line of iron telegraph poles. The sky is slightly overcast; a fierce wind blows in our faces, bringing dense clouds of dust, which rise at times to a great height in the distance, often taking the form of water-spouts, or of towering columns of smoke; once enveloped in one of these travelling dust-storms, there is nothing to do but hold our heads down, and with eyes tightly shut ride through it, emerging on the other side white-bearded and powdered like millers. Sometimes we try to avoid these encounters by riding over the rough and broken ground on one side. There are many wrecks by the way of what were once stout ships of the desert, as well as the last remnants of horses, mules, and donkeys, lying where they gave up the struggle for life. The only birds in this drear landscape are the ravens, which hunt in couples, and fly up from the road croaking hoarsely as we approach. There is not even a hard bank of earth or a stone large enough to sit upon when it is time for lunch, and one can only squat ignominiously in the dust.

The rest-houses and caravansaries along the road are better organized than usual, and travel certainly seems to increase as we near the capital. The grand mountain ranges which have skirted our route are no longer in sight, but others are appearing in the distance. Beyond Sukurabad we cross a bridge over a torrent, which would certainly have been impassable for wheeled vehicles, owing to the great holes in the middle; and while mounting the hill beyond it we are overtaken and passed by a squad of cavalry guarding a prisoner. They are variously uniformed, but well mounted, and most of them are soldierly, stalwart fellows. Many wear gray Astrakhan caps, and belong to the regiment uniformed as Cossacks, which is considered the élite of the Shah's army. The wretched captive has his jaw bound up in a blood-stained rag, his hands tied behind him, and he manages with difficulty to balance himself on a donkey. He is a bandit of some sort, and is being taken to Teheran, where he will lose his head, or be strung up by the heels, for Persian justice is summary. Two men not in uniform, but armed with shot-guns, ride close behind. The officers, as they pass, salute us, and begin a conversation through Abdullah. An hour later we overtake the whole party, who have dismounted to eat by a road-side café; the prisoner has been untied, and is fraternizing with the men; the officers signal to us to stop and share their refreshments, but we decline, and hasten on in search of some deep ravine or fissure where we can enjoy a quiet lunch sheltered from the boisterous, dust-laden wind.

October 2d.—As we come to the last few miles before Teheran, the great crescent-like range of the Shimran, powdered with snow, dominates the landscape. Somewhere between us and the great ravines which scar the slopes, in the midst of a long dark line which is beginning to take on the semblance of verdure, lies the city. We have been on the lookout for Demavend, the mighty pyramid of snow twenty thousand feet in height, but the sky is too cloudy in that direction. There is a village in front of us, not an hour from Teheran, and we halt for lunch; a large group of tents surrounding two or three great blue pavilions lies among the gardens on our left. A brook crosses the road with several channels of clear, rippling water, between banks of green turf, and here our carpets are spread, while a bottle of old Kazbin wine, not unlike Marsala, is buried in the brook to cool. Near the café by the road-side are two or three antiquated and cumbersome barouches, which might have been made in the days of the First Empire; another carriage is driven out from a garden gate, with coachman and postilion strangely attired in brown liveries, and with long-skirted frock-coats, recalling the fashions of Louis XV. They seem to have stepped out from a masquerade into this strange Asiatic landscape. They, as well as the tents close by, belong to the Shah, who is on his way to the capital. We soon overtake our pack-horses, toiling on in the now increasing company of other caravans and riders on horse or camel back, all moving towards the long green line of gardens.

III

When approaching one of the world-famous cities of Asia, one has always at least a moment of faint surprise at finding it so dwarfed by its environment of giant mountain barriers, often quite hidden until one is close upon it by some fold of the ground, and so insignificant a speck in the surrounding desolation. The "Kazbin Gate," by which we enter, is a modern structure of fanciful but inartistic design, decorated with enamelled bricks. Abdullah, having been a custom-house officer, and knowing how to deal with his brethren, succeeds admirably in getting us through the gate without having our baggage overhauled. We enter a dusty and glaring new quarter, and turn into a crowded market-place of vast extent, a labyrinth of booths and stalls, shaded by the most ragged, many-colored, and fantastically contrived awnings imaginable. Picking our way through the swarming multitude, clothed for the most part in patched and faded rags, steering the laden horses of our caravan through the jam of donkeys and ragged, weather-beaten camels, among piles of vegetables, hanging meat, rubbish heaps, flies, dust, and débris, we turn into a dark corridor leading to the bazaars of Teheran. How long we were engaged in slowly threading our way through these interminable and dimly lighted aisles it would be difficult to estimate. Progress was necessarily slow by reason of the crush, which seemed to exceed even that of Tabreez, the continual entanglements with camel and mule trains which we met on the way, and the disputes with shopkeepers, as our projecting chests and tent-poles constantly threatened

GRAIN MARKET, TEHERAN

the merchandise hung up in front of their shops. But every step was full of novelty and charm. We lingered for a moment in front of a fascinating cook-shop, where great jars were sunk to the brim in a clay counter, after the fashion of the wine-shops in Pompeii; a few old tiles sparkled like blue and yellow gems, placed irregularly on the wall, in its bituminous depths. Farther on, a veritable European shop displayed second-hand furniture and a brave array of gilded chairs covered with crimson damask. A passage opened into a great roofed warehouse, glittering with huge crystal chandeliers and quantities of cut-glass ware from Vienna. Then we clatter out into the daylight of an open street, and our horses shy at the unwonted apparition of a tramway car, such a horse-car as one meets in the streets of Boston in the summer-time, with transverse seats, freighted with Persians, half hidden by the flapping white curtains. A high archway decorated with plaques of modern faience representing the mythological heroes of Iran and Persian soldiers of to-day, leads to the great oblong square known as the Tup-Meidan, and we pass under it and cross the square, leaving on our right the richly decorated palace of the Imperial Bank of Persia. From this point the different tramway lines start, and there is a veritable cab-stand, with old and battered fiacres. This square may be said to typify the modern architectural art of the country, and without further detail it might be characterized as an astonishing medley of cheap and showy faience, of tinted and stuccoed façades of German descent, and of all that is meretricious, pretentious, and grotesque, recalling, in a measure, an Oriental background at the Opéra Comique, where the Taj-Mahal, Benares, Cairo, and Constantinople are huddled together on one canvas. And yet the whole effect is novel and interesting.

Turning into a long, straight avenue, darkened by over-arching trees, and with European shops on either side, we ride on in quest of a hotel. This is the "Boulevard des Ambassadeurs," so called, half in derision, by the foreign colony. But it is not, however, a misnomer, for here most of the legations are situated, ending with the imposing entrance to the British Embassy, and as usual England

THE BOULEVARD DES AMBASSADEURS, TEHERAN

outshines her continental rivals. This street is an amusing combination of semi-European and Persian life; the little shops have plate-glass windows half filled with a meagre but varied assortment of under-clothing, kerosene-lamps and gas-fixtures, hardware, violins, and sheets of music; there is also a well-furnished barber's shop, with a fine assortment of cosmetics, kept by an Armenian hailing from Stamboul or Pera. There are many high-walled gardens, a hospital, guard-houses for the municipal police, and little Persian cafés or tea shops have placed inviting benches in front of their doors, usually filled by loungers with "kalyans," or water-pipes. The hotel, when found, does not seem as home-like as our own tent, and hearing of another which has just opened, we mount again and follow our guide. The sky has become dark and gloomy, threatening rain, the "boulevard" is heavy with dust and fallen leaves, and the autumnal scent in the air draws us in fancy far from this exotic street and back to the avenues of Versailles or St. Cloud in chill October. At the new Telegraph Hotel we find good cheer and a landlord who takes a personal interest in every detail.

The few days passed in this strange gathering-place of races left a medley of abiding but somewhat confused impressions. As in the changing phases of a dream, the scenes were rapidly shifted, beginning with the joyous evenings in which we were so fortunate as to again enjoy the society of cultured and hospitable Europeans, where the brilliantly lighted drawing-room, but for its broadside of ancient Persian windows, exquisitely latticed and filled in with mosaics of tinted glass, might have looked out on the Parc Monceau. Strange scenes flashed past as we journeyed to remote quarters by the tramway lines through stifling clouds of dust. On one of these excursions my neighbor was an Armenian, whose summer residence was at Bougival, adjoining the premises of Gérôme the painter, and whose son was a student in his atelier at the Beaux-Arts. A familiar face seen at a gateway belonged to a Persian youth who had posed for me in Paris. A busy street through which the tramway passed, lined with nondescript booths and shops, where cobblers stitched at piles of old shoes in the open air amid the nameless litter of a workaday cosmopolitan suburb, looked strangely familiar to us both. My companion thought he had seen its like in South America, while I remembered similar quarters in Bombay or Lahore, where the advancing tide of English civilization leaves a shore-mark of "Cheap Jack" shops.

The last afternoon was passed in driving about in a fiacre, executing last commissions and filling the carriage with bundles. In the windows of one shop a varied line of goods was displayed, from artists' materials and fancy stationery to canned provisions, hosiery, and woollen under-garments; and I had a brief encounter with the voluble little Frenchwoman within, who got the better of me in a bargain for winter flannels. The imposing gilt sign of Madame Chose, Modiste, glittered over a shop across the tramway tracks. In order to fully appreciate the cost of this exotic luxury of Teheran, one should bear in mind that all the European furniture and upholstery, the grand pianos and carriages, the Parisian fashions, and even the ladies which they adorn, are brought into Persia by way of Tiflis and the Caspian Sea to Resht, and transported on beasts of burden over the terrible Kharzan Pass, so often blocked with snow. A fine drizzle had set in as we drove back to the hotel along a dreary and unfinished boulevard, where the chill wind and falling leaves presaged the coming of a winter which we hoped soon to escape in the summer of India.

October 6th.—We have left Teheran far behind, and have resumed once more the familiar home life of the tent.

Having passed the last outlying gardens and graveyards, we enter again the same vast landscape which we left on the other side, and which stretches endlessly before us. The city, with its hurry and bustle, its dark and teeming bazaars, seems already but a brief episode in a long nomadic existence, a dot upon the map. The sketch which I am trying to finish before sundown is little more than a hasty note descriptive of our present surroundings—a long, battlemented clay wall ending with a sloping tower, and the ploughed field in the foreground, are both of the same tone of old-gold from the sunset; the field is traversed by long curving violet shadows cast by the ridges of dry earth, and the background is closed in by the purple wall of the "Shimran," shadowed by a mighty wrack of storm clouds, and freshly powdered with newly fallen snow. Like a ghost, the pale cone of Demavend

PEOPLE WE MEET BY THE WAY

appears and disappears with the flashes of lightning. The road from Teheran is a broad avenue leading to the shrine of Shah Abdul Azim; it is fringed with thickly planted willows and poplars, and at times one might almost fancy one's self in Normandy, save for the well-dressed Persians flocking to the sanctuary, which is but a suburb of the capital, and a pleasure resort as well. The illusion is aided by seeing through the trees the smoke of the train speeding along the only railway in

Persia, which begins at Teheran and ends at the tomb of this favored saint, six miles from the city. Leaving behind the gilded dome of the sanctuary and the muddy streets of the village, we encamped well out in the open country.

October 9th.—A brief statement to the effect that we had just traversed another desert would justly seem but monotonous repetition. But this desert is the very quintessence of all, and though its like may be seen in the Sahara and in Colorado, it never fails to impress every traveller who journeys to Ispahan. It is "a land of deserts and of pits, a land of drought and the shadow of death, a land that no man passed through, and where no man dwells." One forbidding landscape I particularly remember. We came out from some narrow defile and halted for a moment to look down over steep and arid slopes, across a broad and straight river valley, through which ran a slender blue thread of water, to the long fortress-like cliffs which upheld the plateau beyond. Tier above tier, and level-topped, these cliffs rose in successive graded terraces one above another, regularly seamed with vertical fissures like the folds of sculptured drapery, extending far across the horizon, until their converging lines seemed to fade and melt into the sky. And again the landscape utterly changed in character, when from a deep and stony gorge we emerged upon water-worn and crumbling volcanic cliffs, where the then projecting shelves of rock would scarcely bear one's weight, and so high that the eye ranged far over a level plain, black and shining as if floored with coal-dust, to the white glitter of an inland sea. In spite of the brilliant sun the wind was cold and piercing, and Hadji, the stout Tatar chavadar, bent over his saddle as if in pain. When we had at last reached the village, and had chosen a camping-ground on a narrow and stony garden terrace hardly wide enough for the tent, Hadji fell on his face and lay motionless on the ground. He was in a raging fever, and as the cook was also on the sick-list, we had to struggle with the tent ourselves in the roaring wind.

Kushk-i-Bahram, October 11th.—We are still short-handed, and do much of the work ourselves. Hadji is flushed and burning, and has stretched himself out in a niche in the wall of the superb caravansary, where we

THE BATHING-TANK OF THE CARAVANSARY—LATE AFTERNOON

dose him with "Cockle's Pills," quinine, and hot tea. By way of variety, this is a sandy desert which surrounds us, and adjoining the caravansary a circular tank mirrors the deep blue of the sky, and on its stone curb tired travellers and muleteers are bathing in the water or stretched out asleep.

Kum, October 13th.—This last section of the wagon road from Teheran is in better repair, and passes between well-irrigated fields, leading up to the golden dome of Fatima, which rises straight in front, between slender tiled minarets. Kum is one of the most hallowed spots in Persia, and its peculiar sanctity as the mausoleum of many kings has made it a place of pilgrimage, as well as a last resting-place for pious believers who can afford to have their bodies brought here after death. But we met but few of the corpse caravans of malodorous repute, as they mostly journey by night, fortunately for our shying horses.

Kashan, October 14th.—Another ruined city. Many of the bazaars through which we passed on our way to the camping-ground had been long empty and in the last stages of decay. The road on the other side of the town is like a deep channel between high banks of clay, and we were at first puzzled by huge mounds, which proved to be used for storing ice during the summer months. From the level of the upland, where the tents are placed on the very brink of a steep bluff, the distant cone of Demavend is still in sight. Since leaving Teheran the sky has become cloudless again, and the white pyramid, nearly one hundred and sixty miles to the northward, hangs like a cloud in the sky, seemingly detached from the earth, while the high range of the Shimran, which nearly masked it at Teheran, although thirteen thousand feet in height, has dwindled down to a dim gray line.

Kukrud, October 15th.—Filing through a deep valley, of which one side lies under the grateful shadow of almost perpendicular cliffs, and climbing a steep, paved causeway like a Roman road, we find the valley walled across by a huge mass of masonry. This is the great dam, or "Bund," built in the reign of Shah Abbas, who seems to have been as great a builder as Shah Jehan of India. It was intended to irrigate the plain of Kashan by means of sluices. As we turned into this valley we lost sight of Demavend. Once over the wall, and we descend into a second and longer valley, resembling in character the high stony slopes of the Alps below the snow-line. Mounting still higher, the road commands a view of emerald-green meadows and inviting gardens far below. Hadji has already gone on with the servant to choose the ground, and as we follow, leaving the baggage animals behind, the walls of bare and splintered rock, which rise steeply on either side, almost shut out the afternoon sun, while the road plunges downward, and at once enters a green twilight of overarching boughs. This is a new and unexpected phase of Persia. The thickly planted orchards of mulberry and other fruit trees rise in terraces on either hand quite to the base of the rocky walls. Venerable walnut-trees with huge and gnarled trunks stand among the rocks green with moss and spattered with lichens, and mountain brooks ripple over the stones.

Tired of being alone, my horse, who has been listening eagerly for the sound of the bells, lifts up his voice and whinnies loudly. This demonstration evokes a chorus of answering neighs from the other horses far on in the wood, which sets his mind at rest, and he trots on until we find them waiting near the village on a piece of bare ground, under giant walnut-trees. Although the altitude of this village is given as 7250 feet, the cold at night is not so great as we expected, owing to the sheltering trees and the walls of the pass above. The village, a compact mass of square huts built in ascending terraces, rises steeply against the rocky cliffs behind.

IV

Ispahan, October 20th.—Upon the plain which we now entered there was a number of heavily proportioned round towers, each with a smaller turret at the top. These strange landmarks, rising from the dense foliage of parklike gardens, had the effect of mediæval fortress towers, but, unlike the giants of La Mancha, they proved to be not windmills, but only pigeon-roosts. We were an hour or more in traversing the girdle of villages and the first bazaars, but we finally reached the heart of the city, where, passing through an archway under a lofty palace, we came out at the beginning of a long straight avenue or boulevard, shaded by several lines of great trees. Down the centre of this great highway runs a canal, flanked by slabs of stone, expanding into tanks or ponds at regular intervals. On all sides stand ruined palaces and gateways, the remains of former architectural magnificence, pathetic souvenirs of the days when Ispahan was the seat of the most sumptuous court in the world. But it has never recovered from the successive depredations of Jenghis Khan, of Timour, and, later still, the horrors of the Afghan invasion. As late as the seventeenth century it is said to have had over a million inhabitants. As we descend the avenue, through the checkered light and shadow of the towering chenar-trees, we note a richly decorated façade crowned with a lofty pillared hall or "loggia"; the ceiling, which we can see from the street, is still in good preservation, resembling in its exquisite de-

SILVER DOOR OF THE COLLEGE OF ISPAHAN

sign and scintillating color, the silken shawls of Scinde, in which bits of glass sparkle among rosettes of delicate embroidery. Ruined gateways of elaborate design, still patched in places with brilliant tiles, or with fragments of painting adhering to the walls, open into neglected gardens of rank luxuriance. But the most imposing monument of this avenue, which was known as the "Chehar Bagh," is the great Madrasseh i Shah Hussein, or college for the education of dervishes. The exterior walls on either side of the lofty portal are relieved by panels of faience, and the windows are of latticed wood. The pointed arch of the deep recess in which is the entrance is decorated with the stalactite forms familiar in Arabian art. The lower part of this recess is panelled with white marble, and above with rich and intricate designs in tile-work; the door itself is incrusted with silver richly wrought. The beautiful dome of shining blue, with a running design of yellow curving arabesques, has lost half of its coating of faience, and one of the golden balls on the top. They are believed by the citizens to be of solid gold, and the story goes that one of them was stolen by its guardians and sold to an English tourist. Within the entrance are fruit-stalls and samovars, where tea is dispensed to the faithful. I afterwards visited the interior, and saw the students poring over their books in the cloistered niches, or sitting with their kalyans around the tank under the tall poplars of the court. This great avenue was once the "Champs Élysées" of Ispahan, where the rank and fashion of the city flocked on summer evenings, and congregated about the cafés and in the tea-gardens, some of which still survive. But now, many of the great trees have been cut down for firewood, the stone fountains are broken, and much of the curbing has disappeared. There are mud-holes and ditches in the roadway, and the tanks are morasses choked with tall reeds, rotting vegetation, and thick green slime, among which the frogs pipe in ceaseless and melancholy chorus. Still beautiful in its pathetic and hopeless decay, no spot in the world could appeal more touchingly to the imagination, for what is left is sufficient to show that it was once the perfect flower of Persian art.

At the end of this avenue we cross the river by a long bridge. Although this is the age of bridge-building, when miracles have been wrought in iron, one must go to Ispahan to realize that a bridge may be a work of artistic beauty. Curzon says, "One would hardly expect to have to travel to Persia to see what may in all probability be termed the stateliest bridge in the world," and "its entire length is 388 yards; the breadth of the paved roadway is thirty feet." This is the bridge of Ali Verdi Khan, and it still triumphs over time and decay, built as it is of solid masonry, with nearly a hundred pointed arches supporting an arcaded gallery. The broad boulevard still continues on the other side, with its broken conduits, its great shells of ruined palaces, mounting gradually the slope of the desert plain towards the tall purple crag of precipitous and striking outline, which towers above the landscape as Arthur's Seat rises over Edinburgh. It was noon and intensely hot as we turned into the path on the left, which borders the river. The broad and stony but dry bed of the stream was carpeted for a great distance with the stamped cotton prints, fresh from the dyers' vats along the banks, which are now so familiar in our own markets. They are spread out to dry in the sun, and to the highly colored landscape they add a foreground of vivid and startling color, of which rich Venetian red is the key-note. Beyond this are a distant blue line of water, a fringe of poplars, and the turquoise domes of Ispahan, and over all the profound blue sky.

Passing the decaying palace of the "Aineh Khaneh," we ford the river and halt in a lovely spot, high above the water and shaded by great trees. Here the tents are pitched, and, leaving my companion to rest, I set out to explore the neighborhood.

Before us, across the river, stands the stately Aineh Khaneh. In front of the main fabric, with its square mass of yellow stone, pierced by latticed windows, adorned within and without by tile-work, and by crumbling and smoke-blackened frescos, projects a lofty pillared hall or loggia, open on all sides but one to the wind and the light. Its flat roof rests upon slender shafts of cedar, with bases formed of sculptured marble lions.

The ceiling retains much of its original color and its glittering decoration of glass mosaic. An army of tents, the encampment of a Persian general, stands on one side, above the water, and in the background rise the serrated and purple crags. Near the palace stands a single towering pine, the only black note in this matchless landscape. Continuing along the bank, we come to a second stately bridge, crossed by another long avenue, starting from the great square in the middle of the city, and finally losing itself, like the first, among ruins in the desert plain beyond. This bridge is called the Pul-i-Khaju, and although less than half the length of the other, it is, to my mind, a much more beautiful and decorative feature in the landscape. Like the first bridge, it is two stories in height, built on a platform, which descends in a series of steps to the water on either side; this substructure is cut by channels through which the water flows under each arch. But the original and novel features of this bridge are its hexagonal towers at each end and in the middle, which give rise to unexpected and picturesque angles. In these expansions of the upper story are richly decorated chambers, formerly used as cafés, and the whole bridge is gay from end to end with colored tiles. The platform on the east side is still, as in old days, a favorite resort and lounging-place in the afternoon. Veiled women, wrapped in long blue garments, still look down from the upper windows on the life below. Men are bathing on the steps, or sitting with tea-glasses and water-

PUL-I-KHAJU BRIDGE, ISPAHAN

pipes around the café at one end, while gayly caparisoned horsemen clatter over the pavement of the bridge and up the avenue which leads to the city.

Let us follow them under the battered gateway, which replaces some former monumental entrance, and we shall find ourselves in another boulevard, shaded by chenar-trees and poplars of great height. The border of the canal, save for the occasional sloughs, answers the purpose of a sidewalk. The palaces and gateways which formerly adorned it have been replaced by more modern and paltry structures, or by long walls. The oldest trees have been cut down, and a double avenue of ancient rose-trees beneath them has also disappeared. From the upper end of this street a series of narrow lanes, passing at one place under a gate flanked by round towers, leads into the labyrinth of bazaars, and gradually, as we advance, the noise and bustle increase till we reach an opening by which we enter the Meidan, the great open square, or rather plaza, which is the very centre of the city's life. This open space is 560 yards in length by 174 in breadth, (to use Curzon's figures). Flanked at intervals along the sides and at both ends by imposing and beautiful architectural fabrics, symmetrically planned with an eye to cumulative effect, it still remains an enduring monument of the departed glory of Ispahan.

At one end of this square, or parallelogram rather, and occupying the central space, stands the great "Mosque of Lutfullah." The arched portal, at the bottom of which is the entrance, is in a recess which bows inward hexagonally, leaving space for a tank in front. Above this portal, and set at a different angle, is the higher entrance of the inner sanctuary; and the dome, between two slender minarets, rises above the great pile. The entire building is covered with mosaic of beautiful faience. Even the stalactite-work within the pointed arches is also coated with tiles. About the entrance are panels of the same lustrous mosaic, but finer and more elaborate in detail, resembling in rich and restful harmony of color the ancient prayer-carpets, where blue and yellow designs are relieved upon a dull black ground. A low parapet of white marble fences off the space in front of the entrance. On fête days, when crowds and processions are passing in and out, and richly caparisoned horses are grouped in front of

ENTRANCE TO THE GRAND BAZAAR AT ISPAHAN

the low marble wall, this spot has the charm of a picture, in which the moving groups of men and horses are outlined in light against the great blue pile in sombre shadow. At the opposite end of the place a lofty tiled gateway, flanked by highly decorated and recessed walls, opens into the great bazaar. A tank in front reflects all this splendid color, and the angular and unexpected masses of shadow cast by the multitude of colored and faded awnings projecting from the walls, as well as the crowds about the margin and the shops on each side. On my first entrance into this square I was accosted in good English by an Armenian shopkeeper from Julfa, where the European colony resides, who offered to show me something of the city. Together we stroll through the bazaars, entering the sunlit courts of the great caravansaries, fascinating in their wealth of color and detail, back again into the crowded corridors, which are less gloomy than usual, as the vaulted roofs are often whitewashed and adorned with rude painted arabesques, and sometimes with great mural pictures, representing mythological subjects and battle scenes. An all-pervading odor of ripe fruit fills the air, for it is now the height of the season, and the fruit-stalls are overflowing with melons of every size and color, and with piles of magnificent muscatel grapes and crimson pomegranates. All Persia is strewn with melon rinds just now, not only in the cities, but along the mule tracks in the desert. The aroma which hangs about the cook-shops gives evidence that the citizens of Ispahan have a high standard of culinary excellence, and the steaming saddles of roast mutton or lamb, with the outer crust done to a delicious brown, and daintily cut into fantastic patterns, would grace the table of any Parisian restaurant. In one of the most crowded spots, at the intersection of three different thoroughfares, under a lofty dome, a group of men are sitting in front of a number of large trays containing viands of appetizing and seductive aspect. One has the appearance of a pudding garnished with jelly and geometric designs of colored fruits, another seems to be a highly decorated species of "pilau." We learn that they are the remnants of some rich man's feast, and are the perquisites of the chief cook, sent here for sale.

In the long copper bazaar, with its deafening din and clatter of metal, we come to the door of a crowded and tumultuous café, through which the verdure of a garden beyond invites repose. While we are waiting for our tea, a well-dressed Persian, accompanied by one or two followers, saunters in. He has a rather brutal but good-natured face, and his long, light overcoat is of the most fashionable tint. He salutes my guide, who tells me that he is the chief executioner, the Monsieur Deibler of Ispahan, and upon our solicitation he seats himself at our table, and enters into conversation with my guide. In the course of a light and airy discussion of the popular methods of "working off" the victims of justice employed in other countries, he evinces a critical appreciation of the neat despatch with which the guillotine does its work, and is most keenly interested in the process of electrocution, the last fairy tale of Western science. But his face clouds up as he complains that his business has been "very bad" of late. It frequently happens, to explain this state of things, that when a criminal has been condemned, a number of merchants club together and buy him off by offering a large sum of money to the prince as a ransom. The released culprit then becomes their slave for life. On the other hand, when nothing interrupts the course of justice, the executioner arrays himself in crimson garments, and, being a tender-hearted man in spite of his roughhewn face, he is obliged to fortify his nerves with strong drink before he can give the fatal stroke of the sword. He then places the head of his victim in a tray, and makes the round of the bazaars, thrusting it into every shop, and, according to custom, each merchant is obliged to put down a piece of money, thus swelling his receipts to what is often an important sum.

THEODORE CHILD

October 25th.—All day the tent has been littered with bric-à-brac, embroideries, inlaid boxes, metal-work, and strange little souvenirs, for which we have bargained and haggled with the itinerant merchants, who bring their treasures in saddle-bags and on donkeys. They are hanging about the kitchen tent, and ingratiating themselves with the servants. No sooner do we dispose of one than another turns up smiling and salaaming at the tent door. We are anxious to get away in spite of the open hospitality of our kind friends at Julfa, for it is now certain that this spot is unhealthy, and the nights are becoming bitterly cold. Although there seems to be not even a suspicion of dampness in the clear air, for we have carefully examined the exterior canvas of the tent as well as the grass around us late at night and before sunrise, and found everything quite dry, yet there must be some malarious influence at work. Each one of us has felt it in a different way; the servants and muleteers have all had touches of fever, and the health of my companion has become strangely affected, so that we are both looking forward to the purer air of the high ridges which we shall cross on the way to Shiraz.

NOTE.—*Mary, November 2d.*—It was here in this rock-bound desert that Mr. Child felt the first approach of the fatal illness which soon developed into typhoid fever. In response to my urgent appeal for help, addressed to our friends at Julfa, nearly forty miles from our last camp, and carried by a runner from the village, a medical assistant was at once sent. Although he rode at full speed for the whole distance, he arrived too late, and my friend died as we were carrying him by easy stages to Julfa, but, happily, unconscious of suffering.

FROM ISPAHAN TO KURRACHEE

I

The kindly and sympathetic welcome which I found at the mission did much to render more endurable the painful circumstances attending my return to Julfa. Had I brought the cholera itself with me it would have made no shade of difference in the warmth of my reception, either by Dr. Bruce* or by the ladies of his household. Whatever arguments may be brought forward, justly or unjustly, against the utility of foreign missions in general, there can be no shadow of doubt as to the beneficent results of their work in Persia. During the recent epidemic at Tabreez the Medical Department of the American mission, then under the direction of Miss Bradford, did noble work, and it was to her constant care and untiring energy, as well as to the devotion of our Armenian friend, that two of our party owed their recovery from Asiatic cholera. And after hearing so many sensational histories of Kurdish atrocities from Europeans along our

* I feel that I may, without committing any indiscretion, mention Dr. Bruce by name, since he has been so long identified with Julfa, and every recent work on Persia has added something to his fame. Curzon says: "This mission is under the control of the well-known and greatly respected Dr. Bruce, of whom it may be said that he is as good a type as can anywhere be seen of the nineteenth-century crusader. In an earlier age the red cross would have been upon his shoulder, and he would have been hewing infidels in conflict for the Holy Sepulchre, instead of translating the Bible and teaching in schools at Julfa."

route, a new light was thrown on that subject when we met at least two American ladies connected with the mission who had travelled about among Kurdish villages regardless of exposure, healing their sick, and striving to better the condition of their women. Whatever sect they may belong to, the men and women who have devoted their lives to this cause have shown themselves to be absolutely fearless in the discharge of duty; their record is one of self-sacrifice and pluck, and they represent most worthily the church militant.

Mr. Rabino, the active head of the Imperial Bank of Persia, says, in a letter from Teheran: "I enclose you various letters and reports from the American Presbyterian missionaries, for whose courageous and devoted labors I, an Englishman and a Catholic, can find no words to express my admiration. Their hospital was positively the only organization for the help of this terribly visited city." To supplement his statement it is hardly necessary to add that these modern Templars have had no incentive in the shape of pecuniary gain, no stimulus in the guise of social success, and not even the poor reward of publicity. Their names will never be inscribed in the Court Gazette of any local four hundred; and the press of their own country, occupied with the conduct and bearing of its social leaders, the presence of royalty, and other matters of vital importance, has no space to chronicle deeds which, if performed by another race and in another age, would have been held worthy of undying fame.*

* In the same letter Mr. Rabino says: "It may interest your readers to learn that Sir Joseph D. Tholozan, K.C.M.G., who has been the Shah's physician for over thirty years, and a student of cholera for nearly fifty years (he is a Frenchman, and was formerly an army surgeon), has, after long reflection and study, come to the conclusion that the real centre or focus of cholera is not India but Central Asia—*i.e.*, Samarcand

Julfa, November 5th.—Julfa is a suburb of Ispahan distant about three miles from that city. Originally an Armenian settlement, it is still the headquarters of that Christian sect, and it is also the residence of the European colony of Ispahan. Although the Julfa Armenians are accredited by some travellers with most of the vices appertaining to Christians, and with but few of their virtues, yet the faces one meets in the lanes of that leafy retreat have an intelligent and friendly character which one does not often encounter in the bazaars of other cities, and the fact that so many of the villagers speak excellent English or French shows the influence of the missions. It was now advisable, for many reasons, to make an early start for Shiraz. The leading physician

and Bokhara. The epidemic from which we suffered first appeared at Meshed; coming from Afghanistan, it crossed the Caspian to Baku, and also came to Teheran about the same time. Tabreez received the infection from the Caucasus a few days before us. There were practically but two European doctors in town to attend to the community: Dr. Ooling, C.M.G., of the British Legation, who rode in from the country almost every day and sometimes at midnight, and Dr. Basil. We of the bank had a hard time of it: of some one hundred persons, including thirty soldiers, we lost ten (two Europeans). Our young fellows behaved splendidly, nursing our sick day and night, attending to them under the most painful circumstances, closing their eyes, burying them, and reading the prayers for the dead. One of our staff, a young Parsee, was all over the town attending natives, for which he received a gold medal from the Shah and the title of Khan."

Rev. Lewis F. Esselstyn says, in his official report: "Some twenty or more Europeans died in Teheran. Some independent estimates place the total number of deaths in Teheran at 13,000, while equally good authority places the number at 20,000; perhaps something between the two would be nearer right. Following cholera, there was considerable typhoid of a mild form and dysentery. Cholera has been very severe. Some cases have been fatal in two hours from the start, and many in twelve. On August 25th [1892] I made the following statement: 'There have been 5000 deaths in Meshed and 12,000 in Tabreez.'"

ON THE "CHEHAR BAGH," ISPAHAN

of Julfa had marked on my pocket-map a number of villages where cholera had broken out along the "chapar route." * There were rumors of quarantine—more to be dreaded, perhaps, than the remote chances of infection. It had become too cold at night to sleep in the tents, which were left behind, and we were to "put up" at the chapar khanehs or at the caravansaries along the road. In order to avoid the infected villages, and consequently the danger of quarantine in the desert, it was advisable to follow a somewhat unfrequented route, which in this country sometimes entails unexpected adventures. It would be quite incorrect to convey the impression that a journey across Persia is attended by any unusual risk or exposure. In ordinary times, and in the cool, bracing weather of spring or autumn, few trips could be more agreeable, and one may carry along an unlimited quantity of portable comforts. But in this case the circumstances were exceptional; the attitude of the people had not been particularly friendly to Europeans since the fall of the "tobacco monopoly." Added to this, cold weather was approaching, and there was some chance of being snowed up in the passes should one be delayed by quarantine. And, above all, after the loss of my companion, which had fallen so heavily upon me, I could not, alone, look forward with that keen interest and happy anticipation to the life on the road with which we had set out together, but must carry with me instead an unending regret that he could not have lived to reach India, and accomplish what would have been, beyond a doubt, his crowning work.

* Chapar route, the main line, provided with "chapar khanehs," or Government post-houses, and with roomy caravansaries for travellers. This is also the line of the Indo-European Telegraph, where shelter or assistance can always be obtained at the stations.

II

Mayar, November 6th.—The caravan now consisted of seven animals only, three mules and four horses, not counting the donkey which the chavadar brought for his own personal use. This new chavadar, Hadj Ali, had contracted to take me to Bushire in twenty-one days, exclusive of the brief halt at Shiraz or other delays on the road. He was not prepossessing, being wall-eyed and of hang-dog aspect, as well as slovenly and ragged in his attire. Although he seemed quiet and tractable enough at Julfa, where the contract was made, it soon appeared that he was the possessor of a most disagreeable temper. His ebullitions of wrath may have been due to the circumstance that he was thwarted in his original design of being the sole master of this caravan and its movements. We had been advised long before that when a chavadar is engaged in this way, he always expects to stop when and where he likes, and to take rather more time on the road than he has contracted for. Carapet, a young Armenian of good family, who had started with us when we first left Ispahan, and had shown himself to be thoroughly trustworthy in any emergency, had also undertaken to cook, since no one of good repute had presented himself to perform that function. It is true that a cook who was anxious to go to Bushire, but whose reputation and appearance had prevented us from engaging him in the first instance, had hung about till the last moment, and had then found a place in another caravan going the same way. Had it been possible, I would have taken another route rather than traverse the same stretch of country again. There was no other way, and we pressed on in order to sleep at Mayar the first night. After passing

LOWERING LUGGAGE FROM THE HOUSE-TOP AT DAWN

Marg we had the light of a full moon for the rest of the way, and, finding the chapar station occupied by the other caravan, we went on to the great ruinous caravansary of Mayar, near our old camping-ground. The baggage was heaped pell-mell on the stone ledge within the gateway, and, as it was too late to think of dinner, we mounted the winding stairway to a prison-like cell above, swept by the cold night wind which blew through the narrow embrasures; but, wrapped in blankets, we were soon sound asleep.

Kumisheh, November 7th.—The chapar khaneh which we reach early in the afternoon is worthy of a description as a type of its class. A smaller and more cosey edition of a caravansary, it promises greater comfort. Around the clay wall of the court-yard is a row of lozenge-shaped openings, where the horses can put their heads in and reach their fodder; an enclosed plane leads to the roof, where two small rooms, opening into each other, are built over the gateway. In this instance the doors can be closed, which is unusual, and on the terrace outside Carapet begins his culinary career, assisted by the chief functionary of the establishment, whose Astrakhan cap is decorated with the badge of his office. From the balcony above the street there is a view over drab-tinted clay roofs to a steep crag a mile or so beyond, which, from its color and texture, appears to be fashioned of the same substance as the town. While Carapet is proceeding rather diffidently with his preparations for dinner, as if doubtful of his success, a long caravan passes through the street below. It is the same which started just before me from Julfa, and which had occupied the chapar khaneh at Mayar last night. Behind this caravan rides Hussein the cook on a donkey. He is the man whom we had refused to engage when we first left Ispahan, and, seeing us on the terrace above, he steers his donkey into the gateway. It seems that he has lost his place with the other caravan, and, having hired his steed of our chavadar, he hopes to follow us to Bushire.

Maksud-Beggi, November 8th.—In order not to stop at Yezdikhast, the first on the list of infected villages, and marked on the map with two stars, doubly to be avoided, I had intended to pass by Maksud-Beggi to Aminabad, some hours farther on, and so get by Yezdikhast on the following day. But not being as yet on my guard against the machinations of the new chavadar, he managed by various delays and pretexts to arrive here rather late in the day. In the discussion which follows he first exhibits his unamiable temper. But the chief of the village and the man in charge of the caravansary, who both seem to be of respectable standing, intervene; and as they all assure us that it would be impossible to reach the next station before night, we conclude to make the best of it here. We select a cell a shade less begrimed and sooty than the majority, and are soon comfortably installed, while the chief, who has consented to sit for his portrait, settles himself just outside the door. As a model he does not prove a success, for his attention is constantly distracted with counting out copper coins, writing letters or receipts, and transacting the business of scribe in general to the community. The other caravan now comes in, and instead of dining alone, as I had anticipated, I have the joy of sharing their good cheer in a cell which has been quickly converted into a civilized dining-room by the magic means of a well-set table, carpets, and gay hangings which hide the blackened stone, folding armchairs placed in front of the blazing fire, and, most important of all, the charm of congenial society.

Yezdikhast, November 9th.—Hadj Ali smooths matters over by promising to take a short-cut to Shiraz, by which we hope to avoid the other cholera villages and the dreaded quarantine.

The approach to this place is a succession of surprises. The town, a compact and yellow mass of crowded dwellings, appears to rise abruptly, and close at hand above the level plain which we are crossing. All at once a profound ravine opens in front of us, and perched high up on the summit of the yellow cliffs on the other side are the houses which we saw from the plain. Descending steeply to the pebbly floor of this ravine, which is an ancient river-bed, we turn to the left and ride along under the perpendicular ledge. There are filthy pools along the bottom of it, and black, slimy stains descend the rocky wall from the rickety wooden balconies and projecting windows of the town above us. If the people overhead are dying of cholera, they are surely very quiet about it, and there is no sign of life at any of the windows. We come to the chapar khaneh on the other side of the ravine. It is locked up, and a little farther on the ravine opens on to a broad river, which we cross by a bridge, and enter an imposing caravansary of the time of Shah Abbas.*

In this way we avoid entering the town. The river is bordered on both sides by vertical cliffs, and from the gate of the caravansary, looking across the bridge, we get the most striking view of Yezdikhast. The long ledge on which it stands is pierced by many caves and openings along the top, and from a distance it is difficult to make out just where the town begins, where the caves become windows and doors. They are accentuated in many places by jutting windows and crazy-looking balconies propped by sticks, at a great height above the stream below. This long rock ends in a thin wedge where the ravine on the other side enters the river-bed. Separated at the other end from the main range of cliffs by a species of drawbridge, it can easily be made as inaccessible as a vulture's nest perched on a crag, and the dark streaks which stain the cliffs below heighten the resemblance to a roosting-place of those scavengers of the desert.

It was at this caravansary that Houssein first became incorporated into our caravan, in the capacity of cook, and made his début with a remarkably successful curry.

Dehgadu, November 10th.—Hadj Ali's chief assistant is a grotesque, bandy-legged negro, whose buffoonery makes him the joy of the caravan. When we are on the march, and he is perched on the top of a pack-mule, crowning

* Shah Abbas the Great reigned in the seventeenth century.

like a Gothic gargoyle the very apex of the piled-up baggage, he sings by the hour, and with more trills and falsetto quavers than Yvette Guilbert. When he is tired of singing he tells stories with monkey-like grimaces and pantomimic action. Nobody understands his dialect, but all laugh, for his gayety is irresistibly contagious. Then he falls asleep, and lags behind, swaying violently, till he is awakened by a fall, from which he always picks himself up unhurt. At daylight we leave the caravansary, and crossing a field where peasants are gleaning, follow along the base-line of the great cliffs which wall in the valley. Ravens are wheeling and croaking above, and, as we begin to ascend the cliffs, coveys of partridges rise whirring from the path. Another table-land, crossed by a range of bleak hills, stretches before us when we have mounted the cliffs, and, looking back, the river valley seems to have sunk out of sight, and Yezdikhast appears to be on the same unbroken plain. We are at an elevation of nearly seven thousand feet, and the air, though invigorating, is cold and chilly. The only objects of interest during the long day's march are the glimmering snow-fields of Kuh Alijuk, another seven thousand feet above us. We meet no sign of life on the road, but late in the afternoon we sight a herd of antelopes or gazelles scampering away in the distance and showing their white tails. The village of Dehgadu, where we expect to pass the night, finally appears in the distance, scarcely distinguishable from the stony hill-side on which it stands. Outside the walls and near the gate there is a long, yellow patch dotted with dark figures, from which we infer that the inhabitants are winnowing their grain. As we approach, the dark figures begin to run towards us, agitating their arms and implements of labor, and some of them are shouting. Although it is not usual for Persian rustics to take such unnecessary exercise, we pay no attention to them, being wrapt in vague speculations as to what manner of lodging we shall find here. In a moment they have surrounded Carapet, who is riding some rods in advance, and have begun to belabor his horse with their wooden pitchforks. My first impulse is to draw a revolver; and Carapet, in his wrath, slips off the cover of my rifle and reaches it out for me. Carapet is a boy who

QUARANTINE GUARD AT DEHGADE

might be "quick with the trigger" on slight provocation, and by the time I have got the thing safely under my arm our assailants have turned their attention to my horse, abstaining, however, from attacking our persons. My situation on this curveting and frightened beast, who was too tired to run, and had not the nerve to stand still, began to be somewhat unsafe as well as embarrassing. It is needless to say that these gentlemen constituted the "sanitary committee" of Dehgadu, and that we were quarantined for having passed by Yezdikhast. Since Western civilization has set the example, Europeans have no right to complain if these people see fit to enact the sorry farce of quarantine in a village of mud huts. We managed, by backing our horses, to keep clear of the crowd until the arrival of the chief, who explained with formal politeness that these people were brutes, and had exceeded his orders. By this time the baggage animals had arrived, and the villagers led the way to a barren field about half a mile from the walls. Here the chief and his assistants hastily scraped away the straw and débris from a hole in the ground, uncovering a spring of filthy yellow water; and while beasts and men drank copiously, they brought armfuls of sticks and built a bonfire. During all this time I had never ceased to threaten and remonstrate, egging on Carapet to put it into forcible and profane Persian, and fortifying my position with the fact that they had actually attacked the caravan. We swore that if they did not take us in we should ride across to Dehbid, on the main road, and wire to the legation at Teheran. Under ordinary circumstances diplomatic interference would have been tardy and ineffectual, but in this case I felt confident that our cause would be taken up at once. Our situation while the issue was pending was not enviable: there was no other shelter within eight farsakhs (over thirty miles), we could not find the road at night, and the hills on this side of the main route were said to be somewhat unsafe after dark. Added to this, it was becoming bitterly cold in the waning daylight. We unloaded the horses, and opened a tin of beef and a bottle of whiskey. After a brief consultation among themselves, the chief and some of the others went off to the village to have another conference, leaving us squatting over the fire. They presently came back and offered us the freedom of the town, only begging for a written certificate of good conduct, and a little whiskey for the chief's father, who was sick unto death. I chose for my quarters the room over the town gate; and while the baggage was being hoisted and dragged up a broken and ruinous stairway by these knights of the pitchfork, others brought firewood and provisions, limited as usual to bread, chickens, and eggs. Our aggressors now showed themselves as zealous in promoting our comfort as they had been before in driving us off, and it was with some little difficulty that we finally prevailed on them to leave us alone for the night.

Dehgadu, November 11th, 6 A.M.—All the masculine part of the population, and some veiled women as well, have turned out to see the start; and while we are on the roof packing the baggage and inciting Hadj Ali to action, we look down on a long line of upturned faces. The owners of these faces are propped lazily against the opposite wall, watching our every movement, and paying but slight attention to the discourse of a ragged and paralytic old fanatic seated on a dungheap, who is alternately haranguing the crowd and cursing us with uplifted hands.

November 12th.—The long stretch of country which now lies before us proves to be the most desolate and cheerless on the road to Shiraz. The only soul we meet on the way is a ragged, grizzly bearded Kurd, who had evidently sighted our procession from afar, and was waiting for it to come up; he addresses a loud and plaintive monologue to us, at the same time pointing to a long line of beetling cliffs which rose above the path. This oration, being translated, means that there is a dying man in a hut somewhere among these heights, and he beseeches us to go up and see him. This we declined to do, not having implicit faith in his statements, and he then begged for money with which to purchase medicine. As it did not then occur to me that there was no pharmacy in the neighborhood, I gave him two "krans," and we left him, roundly abusing us for not giving him ten.

The lateness of the hour indicates that we must be approaching the end of the seven long farsakhs (I say long, because every traveller soon discovers that there are both long and short farsakhs), and the yellow walls and castles rising from the plain show that we cannot be far from the haven promised by Hadj Ali. But all these architectural wonders are but deserted ruins. A lonely and isolated pile near the foot of a steep ridge which seems to bar our farther progress is pointed out as the caravansary. Carapet has galloped on to see what sort of quarters Hadj Ali had chosen for us; by the time I reach the building Carapet has concluded his inspection, and returns with an air of hopeless dejection. The caravansary proves to be but a crumbling shell, tenanted by a tribe of nomadic Kurds, who are camping out in its ruins; every cell is occupied by their families. Men, women, and children, cattle, goats, and chickens, are huddled promiscuously together in the dirty cells behind the tattered remnants of black tents which cover the arched openings, and the air is filled with the choking fumes of dung fires. One or two caravans are encamped outside. The only place where we could by any possibility sleep is a deminutive cell on the roof, open on three of its six sides to the wind. This time Hadj Ali had overstepped the mark; he had reached the "end of his tether," and I waited for him to come up, intending to remonstrate so effectually that he would be more careful in future. Feeling confident that he was master of the situation, he received our mild remonstrances with aggressive insolence, and even went to the length of threatening Carapet with his stick. This led to the sudden downfall of Hadj Ali, and although he called loudly upon his two assistants for help against the infidel, they paid no attention to his outcries. People who live in Persia say that there are good chavadars as well as bad ones, men whom you can intrust with any amount of property, but we did not have the good-fortune to fall in with them. Those whom we had, however, were not the worst of their kind, but they were brutes for the most part, possessed of a certain degree only of animal cunning. Our situation, for which Hadj Ali was in a measure responsible, could not be called a dilemma, for there was no alternative, no other shelter for many miles, only the little cell on the roof. The appearance of the crowd which now poured out of every nook and corner of the ruin was not reassuring, particularly as my baggage contained considerable coin and plunder of various kinds; and the cold was increasing, as the wind blew straight down from the snow not far above us.

The old beggar who had met us on the road with the legend of the sick man now came in, having followed close behind, and he seemed to be one of the head men of the tribe. The petty pilferings to which our baggage had been subjected in various places had made it advisable to engage the chief of the village, or of the caravansary, to watch outside the door at night, so we now selected the most responsible-looking man to mount guard. As the stairway which led to our eyrie became a ragged cliff half-way up, the baggage was hoisted on to the roof by means of the cords used for tying it on the pack-saddles, and with the aid of all the able-bodied men available. When it had been deposited in the cell, and the gaps blockaded with boxes and closed up with rugs.

there was barely space enough for my camp-bed and Carapet's mattress. It was impossible to have a fire there, as there was no outlet for the smoke. Hussein installed his kitchen just outside the arch opening into the stone niche overlooking the court of the caravansary, and built a fire of brushwood at the threshold. It was now the turn of the sick and the lame; my inadequate medicine-chest was dug out from its retreat, and I could but regret having come to this country without having taken the degree of M.D., and being thoroughly qualified in practical surgery as well. By way of additional precaution, the night was divided into two watches—I was to take first, and Carapet the second; but it was a physical impossibility for that youth to keep awake, and we both ended by sleeping the sleep of the just till dawn. The good people gave us no trouble, and we left at the first red flush of sunrise. Ice had formed during the night along the margin of the stony brook which flowed past the gateway.

Asupas, November 13th.—The route to-day descended by a steep pass into a warmer zone. The village, seen from above, appeared to be grouped about a citadel, and surrounded by trees near the margin of a river. Persia is the home of illusions, and the citadel proved to be but a mud house a little higher than the others. In order to reach the chief's house we descend from our horses at a low gateway, and after traversing a maze of barn-yards, and ascending steps to a higher level of flat roofs, whence we can look down into the other huts of the village, where the women are working at their looms weaving "kelims," or striped carpets, we cross by a shaky bridge of sticks and clay to the chief's house. The baggage is carried all this distance by porters. A large room, quite open to the sky at one end and at the adjoining corner, is swept out and placed at our disposal. The chief is a handsome, genial man of forty or thereabouts, clad, like the other villagers, in a faded blue blouse. There is but little prospect of privacy, as both he and the other members of the family, including the children and the family dog, a small greyhound wearing a frayed and embroidered blanket, make continual incursions to ask what we need, prompted in part by curiosity, and also by genuine hospitality. At our appeal he provides blankets and mats to serve as portières at the openings. In the morning he tells us that his men are bringing in a wounded wolf which had been killing their sheep. The poor brute has a broken leg, and is dragged reluctantly along by a rope tied about his muzzle; knowing that he is doomed to die by slow torture, I ask permission to finish him with a rifle ball. Our chief mounts a thin, wiry Arab, takes his Martini, and, preceded by the greyhound bounding in front, escorts us for an hour or more, pointing out at a pool near a steep cliff the spot where he had shot a brigand from some neighboring Kurdish tribe a fortnight before, and his two comrades had escaped among the rocks.

Mayun, November 15th.—We ascend another wild pass by steep and winding path, where the dust rises in clouds, and then down into a series of deep gorges walled in by great bastions of blue-black slate; the valleys and hillsides leading up to the cliffs are dotted with thickets of tamarisk, and low, thickset thorn bushes. Through the last valley runs a deep mountain stream beneath a dense growth of tangled jungle and brakes of tufted canes. The air is close and heavy under a brooding November sky. At the unpromising village of Mayun we are received by the governor of the district and the local chief, sitting with scribes and servants in a sort of open hall on carpets and rugs of white felt. In the adjoining room, which has three arched openings, servants are making tea in a huge samovar, and heaping wood on the fire which blazes in the chimney. Although I protest against soiling their clean white rugs, they place a chair for me in their midst, and tea is brought in cups of fine porcelain. Outside, in the dirty enclosure, two superb Arab horses with fine slender legs are tethered to the wall. One of them, a dapple-gray, stands on his hind-legs and fights with the groom, hitting straight out from the shoulder. Our hosts offer us the adjoining room, which seems rather too open for the season, and we finally settle down in a small, black, cavern-like place in the yard. The governor thinks we must have an escort through the next stretch of country, to which I demur, knowing that it means backsheesh, and feeling confident that we are sufficient in ourselves. As I looked at this governor, it becomes apparent that a slight change of raiment would make a "boulevardier" of him, and my opinion is strengthened when he asks if we can spare him a bottle of cognac. At dawn he comes to take leave of us. A little farther on we are intercepted by three horsemen, who come on at a tearing gallop and rein up suddenly in front of us. These gentlemen are the promised escort, which I hoped the governor had forgotten; but "one glance at their array" is sufficient to show that they are worthy of their hire and of great artistic value. One of them is the governor's little son of twelve or thirteen, mounted on a slender and spirited black horse, like one of the trained "Alezans" at the Hippodrome. He sits very erect, with an air of great dignity, and carries a fine double express rifle, marked with the name of a famous Bond Street firm. His harness is elaborately decorated with silver-work. An older man, armed with a Martini rifle and showily gotten up, rides behind him, and they are followed by a pict-

MOSQUE DOOR AT SHIRAZ

uresque and rakish trooper. Here the stream, which has become a deep river, swirls and eddies round a willow-fringed curve under frowning walls of purple slate. On all sides rise the towering battlements of rock, some crowned with needle-like pinnacles, others with flat, table-like summits. We are entertained with more histories of brigands, which harmonize with the scenery. This time two of their villagers were killed in an affray with Kurds from the neighboring heights. Our escort were greatly interested, but, I fear, politely incredulous when told that one "professional" in our country had made a fortune by holding up express trains, and had successfully defied the State militia.

Shiraz, November 19th.—Most of the famous panoramas of cities extolled by travellers are said to "burst upon the eye," and Shiraz proves a shining illustration of this well-worn expression. As in an artistically arranged diorama, where one is led on through dark passages to the dazzling climax, so here, after winding for long hours through gloomy mountain corridors, between walls of ever-increasing height, one comes suddenly upon a gap, a notch, in the seemingly endless series of cliffs. Following the course of the torrent, the road descends abruptly to the notch, where the stream is walled across by a great dam of masonry, and Shiraz lies far below us in an emerald-green plain, illuminated for a moment by a long track of light from the west. The road passes under a high gateway built against the cliff on one side, communicating with various arcaded structures higher up among slender cypresses, recalling the way-side chapels of Italy. A steep paved causeway littered with bowlders descends to the plain, where a broad avenue, flanked by orange gardens and bordered by venerable cypresses, with a shining blue dome at the end of the vista, leads into the city. Across the plain rise the purple mountain barriers which lie between Shiraz and the sea. At the gate I found the negro who had been sent on the day before with a letter announcing our arrival, and at the bottom of the hill the two gentlemen who had charitably offered entertainment to the men and beasts of this dusty and weather-beaten procession. A short walk takes us to the gate in the long garden wall enclosing our host's residence—a low, bungalow-like structure, with a broad white-pillared veranda. A tank in front reflects the lurid November sunset, the dark cypress spires, and the white columns, as well as the brilliant masses of autumn flowers; among them are many-hued chrysanthemums, and such late roses as have been spared by the frost. Men in white flannels are playing in the tennis-courts. At the dinner which follows the famous wine of Shiraz is on the table. From the conflicting opinions of different travellers, I had been led to expect something like a heavy and cloying liquor, but my verdict would be that it is more akin to old port, with a suspicion of marsala.

III

Shiraz, November 20th.—The most characteristic features of this city, which has been in a way the Florence of Persia, as Ispahan was its Rome, are the old and neglected gardens surrounding the decaying pavilions and garden-houses of its ancient rulers. Persia explains both Mogul India and Moorish Spain, for in both countries the landscape-gardening seems to have followed the canons of Persian taste. Many who have not been in Persia are familiar with the gardens of the Generalife in Granada, or, better still, the palace gardens of Agra and Lahore, where one may find the same stone-curbed canals, bordered with flowering shrubs or by avenues of cypresses, where even the designs of the inlaid tiles and of the arched colonnades differ from those of Persia only in some minute details. One of the most attractive of these old pleasure resorts is situated on the slope of the mountain behind the house. Dark masses of foliage rise above the wall and the gate by which we enter, and just inside is a great tank, now dry and dusty, which once reflected the ranks of tall cypresses, together with the successive terraced platforms, all decorated with mosaic tiles, which lead up, like long flights of steps, to the principal pavilion standing high on the hill-side. A stream of water once fell in rippling cascades over slabs of fretted marble into this lowest reservoir. But all is now in ruins: the water-courses are dried up; the supporting walls of the terraces have crumbled away in many places, leaving only heaps of bricks, among which gleams here and there the vivid blue glaze of a tile. One or two slender minarets still retain their glittering surfaces of porcelain. It may have been in this very spot that Hafiz borrowed much of the imagery which gives such color to his verses that they seem still fresh and living to us moderns. Both he and the poet Sadi, his great rival in fame, lie buried in garden tombs not far off. As Emerson says, "the cedar, the cypress, the palm, the olive, and fig tree, the birds that inhabit them, and the garden flowers, are never wanting in these musky verses, and are always named with effect." This garden, like those nearer the city, is still the resort of the fashionable youth of Shiraz, who delight in displaying their superb horsemanship on the roads which lead to it, and one often encounters picnicking parties of veiled ladies in some secluded nook, where their rugs are laid on the russet carpet of fallen leaves. There are always groups of young men looking down from the

CARAVANSARY AT SHIRAZ

higher galleries above, over the ruined terraces and the tree-tops below, and many of them have scrawled their names in the Persian characters on the mouldering stucco of the alcoves. They seem to ride out here for exercise, and to enjoy the view, as their Italian brethren climb the terraces of San Giusto at Verona. Many of these young fellows, who probably represent the *jeunesse dorée* of Shiraz, have an air of greater refinement than is usual in the northern cities; their handsome horses are carefully groomed, and their trappings and saddle-cloths, often of immaculate white felt stitched in arabesque designs, although quiet in effect, are faultlessly correct.

In the city there are many picturesque nooks and corners, and a few elaborately built and imposing bazaars. One cannot convey in words an idea of the beauty, both in color and "motif," of the crumbling panels of tiled mosaic which adorn the outer walls of the old "Madrasseh" and of some of the mosques. The offices of the Indo-European Telegraph Company occupy a fine old palace; the garden in front is entered through an arched portal, from which a narrow canal, bordered by flagged walks, leads to the entrance of the building; the gardener, probably for his own domestic needs, had ornamented one of these walks by a border of cabbages, with highly decorative effect. A dado of marble, with lions sculptured in low relief, runs along the front, above which are old latticed windows of rich and intricate design. Here let me say a word in regard to the interior decoration, not particularly of this palace, although it applies to it as well, but of several, of which I remember one at Tabreez occupied by this same company. I refer to the artistic value of the fireplaces in the general scheme of decoration. The low and graceful pointed arch has a sort of penthouse projection half filling it above, to favor the

GARDEN AT SHIRAZ—SUNSET

escape of smoke, and the panel of wall surrounding it, as well as the dado on each side, is delicately painted in arabesque of dark blue and gold. I could think of no more apt simile than the brilliantly illuminated frontispiece of an old missal.

The last night of our brief halt at Shiraz was made memorable by a dinner, at which most of the gentlemen connected with the telegraph service were guests, and one of the youngest of them had the gift of song, both grave and gay, sufficient to move a far larger audience than was formed by his appreciative colleagues. He had just volunteered to fill the vacant post of Dehbid, and this was the eve of his departure. Dehbid is the highest and coldest station of the Indo-European line, and the last incumbent had died from exposure while on duty in the snow.

My neighbor at the table had been summoned up there in the depths of winter, and had helped to dig his grave with his own hands under the drifts. From this it may be inferred that the lives of these men are not altogether free from risk and hardship.

Khan-i-Zinian, November 21st.—A change in the administration of the caravan was effected while the baggage was being loaded at Shiraz, and in place of the negro another man turns up, who is part owner of the animals. He is a little, weazen-faced old man, wearing a blue wadded cap, bordered with Astrakhan, and his chin is decorated with a startling fringe of white and orange beard, the orange tint being due to the ineffectual application of the henna dye. Hadj Ali at once takes up the thread of some former dispute with his coadjutor, who has a shrill, high-pitched voice of his own, and a manifest intention to have the last word. The morning sky is black and threatening when we leave Shiraz and begin the ascent of the hills; and as I walk on ahead, out of sound of the bells, I can still hear the wrangling voices of the two chavadars. Rain begins to fall, driven in our faces by a cold wind, as we enter a barren valley among the hills. High above the dark slopes which rise on all sides gleams of snow appear through the rifts in the clouds. The road soon becomes too muddy for walking, and it is not easy to hold the reins with stiffened fingers. Late in the afternoon we reach the great caravansary to which we had been looking forward as a refuge from the wet and cold, but, to our dismay, every cell is occupied, and only after a period of long waiting in the sleety rain Carapet finds a dirty cell, which is nearly filled with bales of cotton. With great difficulty two men are found to remove a few of the bags from the top of the pile, and so make room for the baggage. Under the circumstances cleanliness must wait, and without sweeping out the accumulated dust of ages wet sticks are brought and a fire is soon roaring in the chimney. The dust which surrounds us is forgotten in the joy which follows the successful process of thawing, and the reaction produced by hot whiskey accompanied by the appetizing fumes of Hussein's curry. Out in the darkness a muleteer is singing in a full rich voice, and the plaintive cadences of his song are strangely suggestive of the Malaguenas of Spain.

November 22d. — It is foggy when we leave our quarters in the morning, but there is a mellow glow behind the fog which presages a fine day. A clear sunrise follows, and the passing figures of men and animals are outlined with orange against the violet mist, which hides all of the mountains excepting their dazzling white crests, which tell sharply against the exquisite pale green of the sky. A long descent into a valley brings us at noon to the telegraph station of Dasht-i-Arzen, which seems to be locked up and deserted. Now we climb the first and highest ridge of the "Kotals," at least the highest point of our route, which is some 7400 feet above the sea. The newly made road which we follow to the top winds through a forest of low and spreading oaks, with considerable undergrowth; the dry brown leaves still cling to the trees, the sunshine is hot, but the mud in the road is frozen hard. From the summit a view opens downward through the branches of the trees over what may be called, with regard to its climate, tropical Persia. Long parallel ridges, with some oblique spurs, hide the gulf, which is really but a few miles distant as the crow flies. A corner of a lake, half hidden by a shoulder of rock, lies below us, and the forest which clothes the mountain on which we stand begins to look fresh and green again. In a few hours we shall overtake the summer.

Here the famous descent begins known as the "Pass of the Old Woman," and it is certainly steep. Of course it is far easier to walk, as the ground is completely covered with rolling pebbles and bowlders, except where the path crosses a slope of rock, and there the feet of countless animals have worn deep furrows in the stone. From a convenient resting-place, half-way down, there is a bird's-eye view of the great caravansary of Mian-Kotal, standing on a rocky slope dotted with groups of horses, mules, and merchandise, and one may look down into the crowded court-yard within. Here, while strolling about a few yards from the walls, I came suddenly upon a wolf trotting carelessly up the hill with his tongue lolling out, dog-fashion, but he turned and bolted at sight of a European costume.

CARAVANSARY OF MIAN-KOTAL

November 23d.—There is no longer any chill in the night air. The road downward continues through the forest, now dense and green, over loose stones and débris, to the plain, which has a park-like appearance, with scattered groups of great trees. In the long ridge parallel with that which we have just descended there is a gap, through which we approach another descent called "Kotal-i-Dokhter," the Pass of the Daughter. Here the road is paved with great blocks of slippery stone, and there are in places deep furrows or troughs filled with mire, which have been cut by the laden animals in their endeavors to avoid the slippery pavement. I had begun to think that the height and steepness of these famous stairways of stone had been exaggerated, when all at once the narrow causeway turns a sharp angle and plunges seemingly down a precipice. It is a giddy depth into which we look down from the low parapet, and beyond rises with almost perpendicular lines a mighty black wall of rock. The paved causeway winds down with short, sharp turns, corkscrew-like, floored with irregular, pointed, and polished bowlders, on which it is not easy to walk, with slabs of stone crossing it at intervals, after the fashion of Roman roads. To keep one's balance without holding on to something is difficult, and yet Carapet had the "gall" (to use a Western word adopted in Persia) to ride my horse down to the very bottom of the descent. Compared to this pass, the "Gemmi," down which no one is allowed to ride at the present time, is as an avenue floored with asphalt. But to those familiar with the glacier passes of the Alps, or the higher rock peaks, I must admit, at the risk of weakening the force of my statement, that this would seem but an easy promenade. Once down in the valley, under a sun which burns with ever-increasing force as we descend, the road becomes irksome to the last degree. strewn with bowlders and pebbles like the bed of a mountain torrent. Gnarled and ancient rose-trees shade the path in places, and the stunted thickets are alive with song-birds. We pass the end of the lake which we had seen from above, leaving on the right some modern bass-reliefs sculptured on the face of the rocks, and, crossing a marshy river, we enter upon the plain of Kazerun—a long, narrow plain of clay, diversified only by a few thickets of stunted thorn-bushes, bounded by the two parallel walls of the Kotals; that on the south, already in shadow as we approach Kazerun, is serrated or notched along the top with strange regularity as far as the eye can follow it. Vertical fissures, beginning near the top and apparently of great depth, descend to the plain. Every one has seen by the road-side a clay bank cracked and split open by the sun, and nature seems to have duplicated this process here on a grander scale. Kazerun, with low red walls and a fringe of date-palms rising from its gardens, resembles an Egyptian village. We are directed to a garden villa, and entering an archway under the house we pass at once from the blinding glare of the road into the cool green gloom of an orange garden. The trees are of such size and their foliage is so dense that only a few slender rays of sunlight filter through and sparkle like gold coins on the black soil. We are free to camp out where we will, and select for a dormitory one of the upper rooms, with a door opening on to the flat roof, commanding a wide view of the plain. When the windows are thrown open the leaves almost shut out the sky, and one might pick the oranges from their stems. Hadj Ali wanted to take the animals to a caravansary some distance off, but as this place is known to be the Capua of muleteers, and to have an irresistible seduction for them,

THE PASS OF THE DAUGHTER

he was first made to promise that at 4 A.M. he would be on hand. Five o'clock came, but no Hadj Ali. A messenger was sent to find him, and then Hussein by way of emphasis. It was after eight when he finally appeared, quite indifferent, and evidently "spoiling" for a row. His wish was gratified, and this time there was a prospect that we might finish the journey in peace without him; for, dropping his coil of rope, he started for the town, shrieking and gesticulating in a perfect frenzy of rage. He soon thought better of it, however, and, returning to his duties, gave us no more trouble, although I could hear his grumbling voice far behind as he ambled along on his donkey, venting his discontent meanwhile on his long-suffering partner.

Kamarij, November 24th.—Here we put up in a great ruinous house like a fortress. The men being away at the mosque, negotiations are conducted from a distance with the women of the household. The baggage is hoisted up the winding stair to a sort of open terrace, surrounded on three sides by the fortress-like walls of the house, and the other looks down into a dirty enclosure or stable-yard. Of many strange bedrooms which I remember, this is one of the most unique. A row of doors, none of which will shut properly, deeply recessed in the thick wall, open on to this terrace; there is also a door at one end; over all these doors are arched openings, through which the wind blows. The ceiling of this long, narrow room is also arched, and, like the wall (that part not occupied by doors), bears traces of former magnificence in the shape of stucco mouldings of delicate design; but all is black and bituminous with age and smoke. Now the men are coming back from afternoon prayer, and, followed by all the male villagers, precipitate themselves up the stairs in order that they may miss no detail of this "circus." Hussein entertains a crowd of them in the adjoining kitchen when he opens the canteens and begins preparations for dinner, while a sufficiently large number remain to inspect my personal belongings, and to study at close quarters the singular habits of their owner. Some of the doors are finally closed, and means are devised to stop the other openings with carpets, so that a little privacy may be obtained.

Daliki, November 25th.—From Kamarij, after a slight rise, we descended another 1200 feet in most precipitous fashion by winding stairways worn in the rock, but fortunately unpaved, to the plain of Konar Takhteh, where we arrive in the mid-day heat. It was only too evident from the subterfuges of Hadj Ali to insure delay that he had laid his plans to pass the afternoon in slumber; but my intention was to sleep at Daliki, and after a short halt to rest the animals we move on. I had now made nearly all the journey from Shiraz, as well as from Ispahan, on foot, excepting only those portions of the route which traversed dusty and monotonous levels. In this way it was easy to gain time by running down the "short-cuts," and thereby earn the leisure to smoke and meditate and marvel at the surrounding desolation. Down the last of the Kotals to Daliki was, if not the steepest, certainly the hottest and dustiest stage of the journey. The tea in my felt-covered flask had become tepid in the sun, and being made with brackish water it was doubly nauseous, so that the sight and sound of a roaring blue river racing through the gorges below was uncommonly welcome. But the river proved mockingly elusive and difficult of access, as the dusty grooves of the road followed along the heights, and at times quite away from the course of the stream. Choked with the limestone dust and parched with thirst, I can hardly believe in my own good-fortune when the road turns suddenly downward through a shady glen to the very margin of the water. It proves to be as salt as the Dead Sea itself, but happily not too salt to bathe in, and from this point on the heat of the sun is tempered by clouds. Following the gorge made by the river, over a great paved bridge guarded by a ruinous castle, along high cliffs of blue slate, across marshes, and winding upward through another ravine, we halt in the topmost notch, and look westward into a sunset of purple and gold across a vast plain dark with palm groves; long streaks of water behind the thickly planted stems reflect the orange of the sky. There are no more Kotals, the sea lies beyond, and only a short descent leads down to Daliki. The landscape surrounding the post-house, which stands amid thickets of low and spreading date-palms, watered by rivulets threading among their stems, seems doubly attractive after the arid and treeless ravines above; and the deep-toned after-glow, now fading into twilight, adds the fascination of mystery. Here at last it is warm; we shall burn no more wood, and the very sight of quilted coverlets and blankets is oppressive.

Borasjun, November 26th.—From Daliki we follow the edge of the plain, and on our left rise the fissured walls of the Kotals. The road is crossed by rivulets which spread out into miry pools bordered with black and iridescent mud, from which a strange, fetid odor exhales. Near the foot of the hills are a few rusty derricks, sheds, and other appurtenances of the petroleum industry. Carapet has gone on, as he has friends in the camp, and presently I find him seated at table among a group of Russian engineers in the chief tent. They had been prospecting for oil for three years, but without success. There are channels of warm water crossing our route from hot sulphur springs and other mineral sources. Many of the people we meet on the road are Arabians from the opposite coast, wearing wide turbans of some striped material. The enormous caravansary at Borasjun is certainly the finest I have seen in Persia. Built within a few years, it was evidently designed for security, and is a fortress as well as a hostelry. Within is a splendid suite of rooms for the governor or other travelling officials of high rank. A stone's-throw off is the telegraph station, where I am again to enjoy the ever-ready hospitality of the "Indo-Europeans." A telegram from Bushire has just been received announcing that a steam-launch will be sent to Schiff at a few hours' notice. This means that owing to the forethought and courtesy of the British Resident, as well as the kindness of our consular representative, I shall be spared a journey of twenty miles across a steaming salt marsh, and so be able to catch the British India steamer now due at Bushire. The official in charge of the telegraph house tells me, as we dine by candle-light on the broad veranda, that this is the hottest station on the line; although an Armenian and a native of the country, he does not speak of its summer climate with pleasure. The apparatus is in the adjoining room, which is so constructed that although open to the wind, the sun can never reach it, and the operator sits in grateful obscurity. But for nine months the climate is most trying; the mercury often stands at 120° Fahr.; the walls of the room are so hot he can scarcely bear to touch them: and while at work he has the floor flooded with water to the depth of several inches. And yet it is only a few days from Dehbid!

A hard white plain lies beyond Borasjun, and after a time the serried ranks of date-palms cease, and only a few plumed sentinels rise here and there among dark clusters of tamarisk-trees. Since leaving the mountains a new shrub, like a species of gigantic milkweed, has appeared along the road-side.

Bushire, November 27th.—The last vestige of vegetation disappeared some hours beyond Borasjun, and there was not even a fringe of grass along the borders of the salt pools, but still no sign of the sea appeared in front of us. Within the limits of vision there was nothing but the far-extending level of dried mud, darkened in places by cloud shadows. But by way of variety this desert of crusted mud soon became an equally infinite extent of wet mud. First crossing a few pools of mire, the horses were soon splashing along ankle-deep in black slime, and the road disappeared. We were obliged to hail a passing peasant to guide us to Schiff. The prospect was not encouraging. If the influence of the tide was felt so far inland, what was there to prevent a tidal wave from washing us back to the hills? But the salt flavor of the breeze showed that we could not be far from the shore, and soon a line of low sand-hills tufted with waving grass rose above the horizon; and then Schiff itself, only a roofless stone ruin, with a few masts of boats rising behind it, and a group of fishermen silhouetted against the sky. The steamer is lying far out from the beach, as the water is shallow, but the crew are already on shore and waiting for us. It is but a few minutes' work to transfer the baggage to a fishing-boat, while we ourselves get out on the shoulders of the men. The lateen-sail is hoisted, and, leaving the caravan to continue round the bay, we run alongside the launch. Comfortably ensconced among the cushions under the awning, while the boat is steaming rapidly across a rough green sea, I have leisure to enjoy the last view of the Kotals, rising above the horizon behind like a far-reaching fortress wall; and there is not a shadow of bitterness or regret in the reflection that I have no longer any use for them. Bushire has no harbor, but only an open roadstead, where a few steamers are pitching about in the rough water; but it is still the chief port of the south, as all the freight from India and much of that from England is carried up into the interior by the road which we had descended. The high, closely packed houses of the town, with latticed windows and often with projecting upper stories, give it something of an Arabic character, which is borne out by its floating population of gulf Arabs. There is already a flavor of India in the air, and at the entrance of the British Residency, which stands on the sea-front, a group of tall and martial-looking Sikhs, handsomely uniformed, are mounting guard.

The Resident, on whom I called, had recently been appointed to this post, after a long and distinguished career in India. The kindness of our representative had provided rooms furnished with every comfort for a long stay, including a cook and servants, and he had made most accurate guesses as to the nature of my tastes in the matter of luxuries; indeed, it would be impossible to imagine hospitality more complete or more gracefully extended. But the arrival of the steamer next day prevented me from imposing too long on his good nature. The gray, stormy weather which prevailed at Bushire seemed to strangely affect and almost totally obliterate the local color of this ultra-Oriental seaport, as if it had borrowed for a time the climate of Brittany.

IV

Steamer "Occidental," November 29th.—We are leaving Bushire, and steaming slowly out into the gulf. Hussein and Carapet came down to the pier with me, and the baggage, increased by a number of small packages

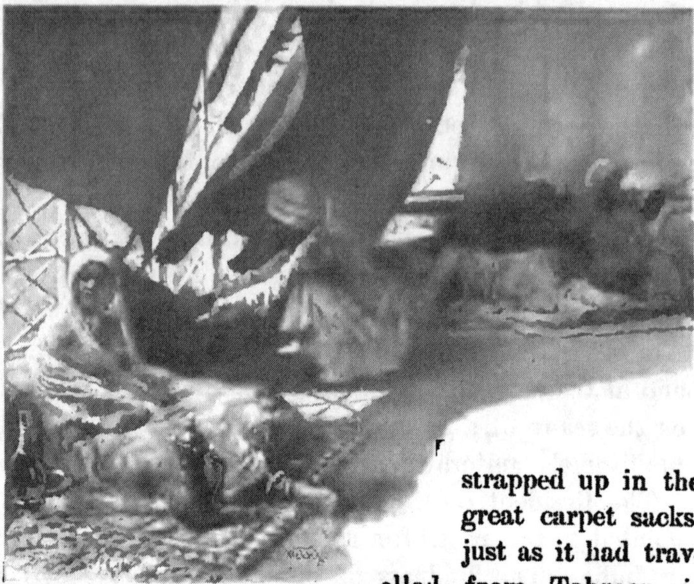

UNDER THE AWKINGS

strapped up in the great carpet sacks, just as it had travelled from Tabreez, is pitched into a lateen-sailed lugger, or "buggalow." Two custom-house officers, two "hamals," or porters, some small vagabonds, and a white-bearded old beggar who trades on his indistinct articulation, are all clamoring for more "krans," while the boat waits for the mail-bag and the first officer. When this functionary is on board, sail is hoisted, and we run three miles out to the steamer under a lowering sky and through rough water. A white Angora cat tied to a bench among the baggage seems to be in the throes of seasickness. As we approach the ship, steering through a swarm of boats and lighters crowded with vociferating Arabs and Persians shouting at the mob on deck, who are howling back at them, we have great difficulty in forcing a way through, and there seems to be no room on the quarter-deck for one more passenger, and none on the forward part of the ship, crowded with a double row of horses. After vain attempts to reach the gangway on the leeward side, we drift round the stern into the seething and bumping jam of boats, and a rope-ladder is let down for us, while the luggage is hoisted and pushed up the side of the ship and over the rail. There is not a European on board save the officers. Canvas screens shut off the small quarter-deck from the forward part monopolized by the horses. As the exportation of Persian and Arab horses is the principal business of the gulf ports, and the boats of the British India line being the only regular steamers on the coast, their decks are like floating stables. Most of these horses are landed at Bombay, and transferred to the Arab stables in the quarter known as Byculla, where they supply the demand for polo ponies and for the cavalry service. Double awnings and canvas walls make a dim twilight on the after-deck, crowded, like the rest of the ship, with Indians, Beloochees, and Arabians. A part of the deck is taken up by an Indian Nawab, chief of a frontier stronghold in Beloochistan, and his retainers. His Highness, a grizzled and weather-beaten old warrior, and blind of one eye, which is quite hidden by a fold of his loosely wound turban, draped in a striped mantle, or "abya," such as one sees in Palestine, is squatting over his hookah, and one of his hirsute followers is busily engaged in keeping the coals aglow in a small furnace from which the pipes are lighted. The chief's interpreter, a handsome black-bearded native of Scinde, arrayed in a stunning coat made from an imitation leopard-skin rug, now comes forward, and in formal and precise English explains that the Nawab wishes to know whence I come, whither I am going, and what is my mission in India. His Highness is not much wiser than before when these things are explained to him, but he asks many questions about America, whether the caste system is in vogue there, and whether it is as large as Britain. . . .

5.30 P.M.—While I am busy in my cabin opening valises and hand-bags the hubbub and uproar increases among the boats, which are swinging and bumping together under the round window; men are running wildly down the gang-way, and descending by ropes past the open port; the screw begins to revolve, the boats and lighters drop astern, their crews wildly struggling to keep clear of the ship, and we are off for Kurrachee. Here, on the ship, Persia ends and India begins, with the Portuguese stewards from Goa, the Indian cooks, the Nawab on deck with his hirsute staff, the swinging punkas down in the saloon, and the perpetual curry. At dinner the captain and the officers, all young men, fill up the table, and one might travel far without meeting more genial company; the captain, an enthusiastic "aquarelliste" and amateur photographer, understands instinctively the necessities of the artistic vocation, and proves to be a most faithful ally. While we lie smoking after dinner in deck-chairs on the only vacant space, which is between two of the cabin skylights, we are conscious of a persistent and monotonous tapping, which at first seems to come from the machinery, but is traced to the mahogany roof of the skylight, where the Nawab, enveloped in a pink check shroud, is peacefully dropping off to sleep. Two of his attendants are rapping his extended joints, thereby promoting slumber: this is the percussion system of massage treatment practised in Beloochistan, where it has been known for ages. Verily there is nothing new; but when this discovery was proclaimed by the wise heads of Paris all the world flocked thither to swell their coffers. One of the Nawab's followers is a pale, sad-faced man, of a distinctly Moorish type, wearing a white rag of a turban wound after the fashion of Tangier, and a pair of dilapidated "European shoes." This man has a history. He was in the service of Yakoob Khan, late Emir of Afghanistan, and now a state prisoner at Rawal-Pindee (India). After the political events which led to the downfall of Yakoob he remained some time in India, but finally returned to Cabool disguised as a begging dervish, to see his wife and child. He was discovered, and sentenced to be blown from the mouth of a gun. He dug his way out of prison and escaped to Beloochistan, and here he is again, a pensioner of the Nawab.

Lingah, December 1st.—The landing at the chief port of Laristan is not devoid of interest. There is a heavy surf, and the small harbor or basin has a narrow entrance. But in the chief officer's boat, which is lowered the moment we come to anchor, one cannot but feel perfectly safe. We land at a crowded beach, for the bazaar of the town extends quite to the basin, where a line of quaintly built boats is drawn up on shore, and the remaining space to the breakwater is filled with larger vessels—Arab dhows, or bungalows, like those in which Sindbad the Sailor made his historic voyages and discovered strange things. Such high-sterned galleys have never sailed in Western waters since the days of Columbus, and, what is stranger still, turbaned Arabs are still building these antiquated but seaworthy vessels on the beach, where hammers ring, and there is a smell of rosin and of shark's oil, with which they smear the timbers. They are the "plunging boats which beat from Zanzibar," in the Salsette boat-song interpreted by Kipling.

Leaving the low yellow walls of the town and the dark palm groves behind, and threading a way among the crowd of Arab sailors and "longshoremen" which throngs the beach strewn with baskets and vegetable débris, with

BOATS SEEN FROM THE DECK

bags and coils of rope and bundles of bamboo, we reach the boat, and, waiting for a favorable moment, shoot through the narrow opening of the breakwater out into the roaring surf, which is now running high, and but for the timely aid of our commander, the first officer, we should have been swamped or washed back on the beach.

Bunder Abbas, December 2d.—A day of rain, of tropical downpour, and the awnings are weighted with water. The Nawab and his little court are suffering much discomfort. Their charcoal furnace on the quarter-deck cannot be kept alight, and there are no more hot coals for the "hookahs." All day long we are surrounded by a crowd of boats and barges. A quaint high-pooped pinnace, a survival of ancient days, is drifting aimlessly about, unable to discharge its cargo of eight horses, all busily eating from their nose-bags, with intervals of squealing and fighting. This ship has a high stern cabin open on all sides, and filled with coffee-bags and nameless rubbish well water-soaked, like the crew. Late in the afternoon the sky clears, and a lofty purple range of rocks becomes visible beyond the town. Long wreaths of vapor still hang on the lower slopes, and there are momentary glimpses of snow-topped heights beyond. Other ranges appear to the east and west, and against the sunset is outlined the low and craggy island of Ormus, the once famous mart of Eastern commerce. Rays of orange-tinted light shine through the openings between the awnings and their pendent canvas screens. There is a rattle of dice; his Highness, squatting on a clean straw mat, is playing a queer little game with some new-comer. In the middle of his carpet is placed a square-armed cross made of red cloth, and the arms are divided into squares by white lines, on which are placed a few little cones of red and white ivory. The rattling is done with four or five long boxes of yellow ivory. On either side of the Nawab squats a line of his long-haired and loose-turbaned followers, intent on the game. No one seemed able to explain the object and end of their game, which will remain forever a mystery. Many new passengers have come on board, the horses threaten to invade the quarter-deck, and the Nawab is obliged, in order to maintain the integrity of his domain, to place a guard at each end of the space, with orders to resist all attempts at invasion. Most of the new-comers are Hindoos and Indians of varied castes. The cabin next mine has sheltered a constantly changing population of yellow people. A few hours ago it was occupied by a semi-European, or Eurasian, with two Indian servants. He has gone, and among the new occupants is a rather handsome young Indian girl, with a baby; she wears a sort of transparent half-mask of some gilded and glittering material, after the fashion of Scinde, and never shows her face in public. My cabin opens into the dimly lighted saloon, where the punkas hang motionless over the tables, for the weather has changed since last night, when the mercury stood at 84° Fahr. in the captain's cabin on deck. Swarthy Portuguese stewards are laying the cloth; a grim gray twilight shows through the ports of the rounded stern, and two shrouded Mussulmans are saying their prayers on the only vacant space between the two tables, fenced in by my surplus baggage. Down the stairway leading to the deck blows the west wind, laden with a pungent odor of stable, and with flying straw and chaff. Above, on deck, the crowded horses are all blanketed, and eating comfortably from their bags; great haunches of meat hang from the awning-poles overhead. Somewhere in the bow the cry of a muezzin is heard, and in the clear space astern a group of Moslems are praying in unison, while an occasional red ray from the stormy sunset gilds the kneeling figures. At night we leave Bunder Abbas for Jask.

In former days Bunder Abbas was of greater commercial importance, but of late other avenues of trade have been opened up, although it is still the focus of several caravan routes leading to the interior cities, and through them to Central Asia and Afghanistan.

Jask, December 3d.—Only a long sandy point is visible from the deck across the bay, which curves to the left, following the line of a distant mountain ridge. We cross the surf, and land on the beach near the group of low buildings surrounding the telegraph station. The town itself is seven miles away. As we walk up to the settlement the air is hot and close, although there is a light sea-breeze. A few low bungalows, inhabited by the telegraph staff, are grouped about the offices, and there are several plantations of stunted young trees, which do not appear to thrive in the sandy soil. A number of deserted bungalows were once occupied by soldiers sent by the Indian Government, but they are now ruinous, and their compounds overgrown with weeds. The place looks like a forsaken cantonment in India, and the bungalows themselves might have been brought from that country. Jask owes its present importance to the Indo-European Tel-

HORSES ON DECK

egraph Company. There are two submarine cables, one of rubber and one of gutta-percha, from Jask to Bushire, and one cable from Jask to Kurrachee. There is a station at Charbar, 200 miles from Jask, and another at Guadur, 112 miles beyond Charbar. From Jask two land wires run, each a complete circuit, to Kurrachee, carried by one set of iron poles, made by Siemen. The cable formerly went from Jask to Guadur, but now goes straight to Kurrachee. There is also a station at Ormarah, and one at Sonmeanee, near the Indian frontier, but now dismantled. Morse's alphabet and recorder are used.

Muscat, December 4th.—Having been sole occupant of a two-berthed cabin, hardly large enough to hold my baggage, and littered with wet sketches, it was with something like dismay that I saw the arrival of a European who was to share it with me; but he proved to be excellent company, and I was the gainer in the end. He had been making a scientific invasion of some remote province, and was now on his way to Simla, in order to report.

The landlocked harbor of Muscat, shut in by dark-hued and richly colored volcanic crags, rising precipitously from the purple and glassy water, in which their long reflections waver, seems almost unreal in its pictorial and scenic arrangement. Like a vision of Claude Lorraine, each bold promontory and ragged peak is crowned with a little castle or watch-tower—a gleaming white or yellow note in the dark landscape—dark, although flooded with the warm light of a tropical sunrise; and even at this early hour the air is hot and steamy. Behind the town rises a still higher pinnacle of splintered rock, and a larger castle of Portuguese origin seems to have climbed up from the massive white houses below. High up on a cliff at the entrance are perpetuated in white letters the names of several famous vessels which have visited the port, and among them the United States steamship *Brooklyn* is conspicuous. The long, square façade of the Sultan's palace, with a line of balconied and latticed windows, or "mousarabies," overlooks the placid basin where his rusty steam-yachts lie at anchor. The flotilla of caravels and galleys, resembling those in the battle-scenes by Venetian painters in the Doge's palace, which surround the

ON THE BEACH AT LINGAH

steamer, is crowded with naked blacks, whose brawny shoulders glisten in the sunshine.

We descend with infinite care into a narrow and crank canoe floored with straw matting, and are sculled to the landing. A black guide offers his services, and we wander out of the town, passing through the grateful shadow of a deep gateway, where the soldiers of the Arab guard, wearing wide, loose turbans of some striped material, lounge on the benches. Their ponderous matchlocks are hung on the walls behind them. We have no concerted plan, and care not which way we turn, for all is new to us, but hardly changed since the days of great Caliphate of Bagdad. A sandy road through a suburb of huts built of canes, palm leaves, and matting leads into a deep ravine with perpendicular cliffs on each side. There is a sound of music, and farther on a dance is just beginning. The floor of this open-air ball-room is like a tennis-court, and the low wall surrounding it is crowded, like the rising ground beyond, with gay and laughing spectators. All are Africans or Arabians *—"Sidis" they are called—and the dancers are mostly women. Many of these ebony sirens are not uncomely, and look excessively good-natured. They are richly and daintly costumed; many wear transparent masks of gold lace like the women of Scinde, which half conceal their faces, and heavy clinking anklets, with other ornaments of gold. The dance begins like a sort of promenade, accompanied by much clapping of hands. My shipmate's knowledge of Eastern tongues enables him to chaff with these ladies, and insures a welcome. We are even invited to take part in

* I have used the term Arabians to denote the inhabitants of the peninsula of Arabia and its adjoining islands, as the word Arab is so often applied to all races from India to Morocco.

the festivities. When we return, by another path, to the city, under the straw awnings of the bustling fruit market, we stroll through the spice-scented gloom of the narrow streets shaded by the projecting latticed windows, and along open arcades where weavers are manipulating threads of scarlet and gold at their looms, to the little shop of the postmaster. He is a grave and well-educated "Baboo"—*i.e.*, Bengali—representing the modern element of Muscat, and we sit down to have a chat with him.

The ponderous gates to the Sultan's palace across the street now swing open, and a guard of soldiers preceding a group of richly dressed courtiers comes forth. It would not have surprised us had the Grand Vizier Mes-

BLACK SIRENS OF MUSCAT

rour suddenly stepped into this ninth-century foreground with a message from the Caliph, and just then our guide says that the Sultan's brother, who is the centre of the group, wishes to speak with us. He is under the impression that we have come to pay our respects to the Sultan, and, only too willing to embrace the opportunity, we send our cards. After a brief delay we are ushered into the court-yard, accompanied by the postmaster, who kindly offers his services as interpreter, and mount the great outer staircase to a long and narrow whitewashed room. A range of arm-chairs standing on a ledge raised above the floor extends entirely around the room. Both of the longer walls are quite taken up by the open windows, through which blows the soft tropical sea-breeze, and the glare of intense light reflected from the orange cliffs which rise just beyond a strip of deep blue water under the windows of the seaward side fills the room with a strange glow. The sole ornaments are a few old European and American clocks. The Sultan enters with a throng of gray-bearded ministers and a little boy richly costumed. His Highness seats himself at one end of the room, and his followers sit down in the long row of chairs at his left. He is a handsome young fellow, with a clear *café au lait* complexion and curling black beard; quietly dressed, his sole ornament is a gold-mounted and jewelled dagger. He is a brother of the Sultan of Zanzibar. This Sultan is a "camera fiend"; he knows all about the Eastman Company, and wants the address of the best maker in Paris. One of his dreams is to visit that city, renowned for its hospitality to Eastern potentates, and from the evident gayety of his nature one might infer that he would not suffer from *ennui;* but he explained that the state of his little kingdom would not permit a long absence at present. The interview was now concluded, and after drinking in prudent measure the sweetened liquid proffered in tall glasses, we took leave of his Highness and went to the British Residency. Here tall Indian servants, with regimental badges on their turbans, stand at the doorway. The sea-breeze sweeps through the open rooms, across a balcony of great depth, furnished also with divans and arm-chairs. As at the Sultan's palace, the balcony looks down into the water, which mirrors a great wall of dazzling and glaring rock, with a castle clinging to its face, and so near that we can feel the heat thrown back from its surface. Through a narrow triangular gap the deep, dark blue of the outer sea is visible. In summer this place is a furnace, situated as it is almost on the northern tropic, and even now the temperature recalls that of Bombay in April. The captain joins us at lunch, and we all go out to call on our consular representative. As the tide had ebbed when we reached the captain's boat, we rode out to it on the backs of the Lascar sailors.

Those who have seen the "barren rocks of Aden" rise from the glassy bay when there is no wind at sunset can readily understand how Muscat looked in the intense color of its setting as we were pulled out to the ship. The deck now has a decided list to one side with its increased human and equine freight; there is no room to walk without stepping on the outstretched toes of the reclining multitude or the fingers of children sprawling among them. What was before open space is now packed with a dense mass of brown and yellow humanity, in which every race of India might seem to be represented. They lie on the benches, on their piles of bedding, boxes, bundles, and crates, while the interstices are closely packed with smaller articles, baskets of highly scented fruit, guavas and bananas, water-pipes,

MUSCAT FROM THE HOUSE-TOPS—SUNSET

"chatties," and coffee-pots. A strange and musky odor, like the smell of a Bombay street, intermingled with whiffs of smoke from the hookahs, and a faint aroma of attar of roses, now pervades the ship; and beautiful are the effects of light under the awnings and canvas screens when the afternoon sunshine lies in long patches, cross-hatched with the violet shadows of the netting, on the deck, and brown faces alternately reflect the golden light of the west and the cold blue tones from the water. Among the new passengers is a young Hindoo from the Punjaub with his servant; he is a scientist in government service, and in addition to his own specialty has found time to become a promising electrician. He has a round, jovial face, is constantly laughing and displaying a fine set of teeth, and looks about twenty-five years of age. His costume of gray frieze is European, and he wears a flat black velvet cap. This gentleman is a welcome addition to our circle, and without apparent effort gives a spurt of renewed life to the after-dinner talk. The little vacant space on the quarter-deck, of which the captain's chair is the centre, now becomes a sort of "cenacle" when the lanterns are lighted, and our Hindoo friend ranges joyously from one topic to another, expressing himself in sonorous and correct English, rolling his R's, and prefixing each statement with "you see, sir," which contrasts finely with the Scotch and Irish accent of the others. I think we began with Edison's latest inventions and what is being done by rival electricians; but just now he is reading Darwin and Herbert Spencer, and from these points of departure, in an airy, optimistic, half-mocking vein, he flutters lightly on like a butterfly in a garden, through the realms of speculative science: from Emerson, Carlyle, Professor Fiske, by easy transitions, to Bellamy's socialistic millennium, Buddhism, Theosophy, Longfellow, and we are let down at last to the hard present with the Presidential election, Gladstone, Parnell, Home Rule, and the Chicago exhibition. Having touched upon Indian art and the Art idea in general, he became inspired with the beauty of the tropic night, the wake of fire streaming behind us, and the "larger constellations burning" overhead. Of course he cannot be taken as an average example of the way England is educating India, but the wide-spreading turbans of that country often shelter active brains. . . .

It was almost with regret that we sighted the low sandhills of Kurrachee, and steamed up the narrow canal among the uncouth iron monsters of progress — towering cranes, rattling steam-dredges, and shunting trains of freight cars. In the deafening uproar from the mob of Indians and Parsees which now invades the deck it is almost impossible to take leave of our friends the officers. There is a momentary glimpse of the Beloochees, rallying round their chief, now armed with their guns and "tulwars," which had been restored to them, and we descend into a lateen-sailed boat, which takes us to the iron sheds of the custom-house. We presently emerge, and are swallowed up in the roaring and struggling throng of cab-drivers, hitherto kept at a distance by the clubs of the police.

LAHORE AND THE PUNJAUB

I

ONLY a few months ago, when all Paris had flocked into the streets to welcome the officers of the Russian fleet, and on the gala-night when an act from the *Roi de Lahore* was given at the Opera, by a coincidence noted at the time in the columns of the *Figaro*, the last Maharajah of Lahore lay dead in his hôtel near the Champs-Élysées. He was the last of the sons of Runjeet Singh, and after the death of his father, and when the Sikh war, followed by repeated uprisings, had ended with the total defeat of Shir Singh, the power of the Sikhs as a nation was broken, the Punjaub annexed by the government of India, and Lahore ceased to be the capital of a kingdom. These events took place in 1849.

The young Maharajah was invited to take up his residence in England as a guest of the nation, and the first Lieutenant-Governor ruled in his place. Although the Sikhs gave ample evidence of their prowess at the battle of Chilianwala and in other engagements, they have since remained firmly loyal to the British "Raj,"* and it is to-day generally admitted that the suppression of the mutiny a few years later was mainly owing to their support, as well as to that of the other Punjaubi regiments. Upon entering India from the north one is made aware of the

* Vernacular for government.

importance attached to the maintenance of the frontier in a permanent state of defence by the predominance of the military element. The "troopers" now land their passengers at Kurrachee; and along the railway to Lahore, at intervals of a hundred miles, there are "rest stations," provided with soldiers' quarters, adjoining the railway buildings.

In the event of the long-looked-for invasion from the north—now more of a shadowy phantom than ever, since the success of Sir Mortimer Durand's mission to the Ameer of Afghanistan—Lahore, being a rapidly growing railway centre, would become a most important point of distribution and base of supplies. It is only nineteen hours from Peshawur in front of the Khyber Pass, through which most of the Moslem conquerors found their way to the great treasure-house of India, and it has direct railway communication with Quetta, commanding what is believed to be the only other practicable entrance.

The railway to Quetta starts from Ruk Junction (on the Northwestern Railway), and the distance is two hundred and eighty-nine miles. Quetta, surrounded by thirty-eight miles of fortifications, including small detached forts commanding different positions, and provisioned for an eight months' siege, is considered as practically impregnable. The two or three other passes in this section have no thoroughfare for artillery, and the Bolan Pass can be easily defended by a small number of men, as there are narrow passages between steep walls of limestone where only three or four can ride abreast. The railway now goes on to New Chaman, only one hundred miles or so from Candahar.*

* Latest advices from India state that the Ameer during the recent negotiations decided to allow the railway to be extended several miles into his territory beyond New Chaman.

It was definitely settled during the recent negotiations at Cabool that the jurisdiction of the Indian government should include this point.

The ostensible object of Sir Mortimer Durand's mission was the settlement of certain questions relating to portions of the frontier hitherto left undefined, and which were a fruitful cause of disputes, as well as to promote a better understanding between the two powers. If one may judge from the tone of the press, the results of this conference have given much satisfaction in India, and an added sense of security, while the Ameer, on his side, may well congratulate himself on the importance attached to his friendship. He is also the gainer by six lakhs* of rupees, to be added to his annual subsidy of twelve lakhs, and it has been proposed to decorate him with the Order of the Bath. It is generally understood, however, that he did not offer to make any concession in the matter of railways, and the consideration of this delicate question was postponed to a more convenient season.

Although the Ameer seems to appreciate the advantages which may accrue to him from friendly relations with the Indian government, he also values his position as an independent sovereign, and, like the Sultan of Morocco, is not over-anxious to be brought into closer contact with powerful neighbors.

With the Ameer as an ally, Afghanistan becomes a formidable breastwork against any advance from the north, and he probably realizes that in the event of a Russian occupation of India he would not long be able to maintain his present independent position. Now that he is reorganizing his army according to Western stand-

* A lakh at the present rate of the rupee is somewhere in the neighborhood of $30,000.

ards of efficiency—arming it with machine-guns and other improvements, and has gone deeply into the manufacture of war material at his extensive factories in Cabool under European direction *—Afghanistan is becoming a power to be reckoned with in any case. It is noticeable that the men who have met and conquered the Afghans in former days, as well as in recent campaigns, speak with marked respect of their military prowess. Such average specimens of these surly hirsute sons of Anak as one meets in the bazaars of Delhi or Lahore enable one to realize that they are excellent fighting material, and they look as if they might have descended directly from the primitive men of the stone age. These nomadic Afghans and Pathans from the hills of the frontier are, for the most part, peaceable peddlers of " notions," Cabool grapes, and other fruit, or they are horse-dealers and camel-drivers. Like the Persians, they are lighter in color than any race of India, but ruddy, deeply sunburnt or tanned, and begrimed with dust. Their national costume is far from graceful or elegant, consisting of a mass of dirty-white cotton drapery, loose, flapping skirts, a well-worn sheepskin coat, and a dark turban, called a koola, which has once been blue, loosely twisted around a pointed cap covering a fringe of shaggy hair.

Many Afghans, Pathans, and Beloochees now take service under the English colors, and some regiments are mainly recruited among these cutthroats of the borderland. These fellows need a lot of training before they can be got into proper shape, but it is precisely this element which gives to the Indian army its peculiar stamp, its appearance of disciplined, business-like ferocity. The

* Some of the Martinis made at the Cabool factories were recently tried on the ranges at Peshawur, and, according to the India journals, were found to be quite satisfactory.

GATE OF THE MOSQUE VAZIR KHAN

Afghans and Pathans have a reputation for dash and pluck akin to that of the Irish, although they are said to lack the steady, staying qualities of the Sikhs. While it is usual to undervalue the elements of physique and initiative in these days of machine-guns and smokeless powder, these qualities must ever play a prominent part in border warfare among the rugged defiles and winding passes of the northern frontier. These men of the north, while they can be regarded only as a part of the floating population, and are encountered in every large city of India, are yet numerous enough in the streets of Lahore and Amritsar, or Mooltan, to give a decided tinge to the character of the crowds. When we analyze these crowds in detail as they pass through the bazaars, we shall find that the most pronounced, the most conspicuously local types, are the Sikhs. Up to the time of the annexation they were the ruling class, although far from being the strongest numerically. Originally a military race, both by inherited tradition and by natural tendency, many of them have become cultivators, since the opportunities for active service are few at present, but a large number of them form the "corps d'élite" of the Punjaub army. A Sikh regiment on parade is a spectacle which offers some novel points of difference when contrasted with the *matériel* of most European armies with which the unprofessional observer may be familiar. When first seen in the distance they present the appearance of a long scarlet band of uniform thickness, supported by slender black lines; as they approach they are seen to be unusually tall, black-bearded fellows, uniformed in red tunics, and with great red turbans which increase their apparent height, while close-fitting black gaiters accentuate the thinness of their legs. Whoever has watched the drill of the Grenadier Guards in London may form an idea of the precision which seems to be the standard of the Sikhs. They may be, perhaps, a shade more rigid in their "good form," with an appearance of greater effort, due to the fact that European discipline is as yet to them like a strange garment to the wearer. The observer will not be slow in realizing that he has before him not only a different race, but a different specie of the human animal. As in Europe there does not exist at the present day a strictly military caste, the conscripts who people the casernes are drawn at haphazard from workshops, farms, and from the slums of cities, and do not impress one, save in the case of a few bodies of picked men, as having any special aptitude for the calling of arms. These men, tall, sinewy, and athletic, supple and feline in their movements, are evidently endowed with a peculiar fitness for their vocation, and look as if little were needed to arouse their traditional instincts. In the average regiments of the Punjaub no men are taken under five feet six inches in height and thirty-three inches round the chest; in some regiments none under five feet seven; but judging from the strapping fellows in the Sikh regiments, their standard must be still higher. Although the Pathans and Sikhs are usually given the first rank for soldierly qualities and bearing, the "Goorkhas," of Mongolian race, from the hills of Nepal and Assam, are nearly if not quite as efficient.* Being of small and wiry physique, they do not make such an imposing appearance on parade, but they are fine mountaineers, full of fire and pluck in action, and at such times, when their innate ferocity comes to the surface, their officers often have dif-

* An officer who has held with honor and distinction several of the highest positions in the service has just added in a note, "I think it is a toss-up between Goorkhas and Sikhs for the first place, Pathans coming third."

ficulty in restraining them. What is known as the "Bengal army," including the old Punjaub frontier force, comprises sixty-five battalions of infantry, of which the greater part are Goorkhas, Sikhs, and other Punjaubis, two mountain batteries kept for small expeditions (with mules), and twenty-three regiments of cavalry, of which nine are "lancers."* Each of these regiments is com-

* Roughly estimated, the Bengal army is constituted as follows:

Cavalry.—Twenty-three regiments, composed of 14 light cavalry, 9 lancer regiments. Of these 4 only are called Punjaubi cavalry, though the composition of the rest includes a large number of Punjaubis. Nineteen regiments with 8 troops each (152), classed thus:

	Troops
Hindostani Mohammedans from Bengal	28
Punjaubi Mohammedans	26
Independent tribes from beyond northwest frontier—*i.e.*, Pathans	3
Border tribes within British territory (Pathans), Mohammedans between the Indus and the Khyber Pass	12
Sikhs (Punjaubis)	39
Dogras (Punjaubis)	12
Hindostani Rajpoots	8
Hindoos from Bengal proper	24
Total	152

Infantry.—Sixty-five battalions, of which 16 only are recruited from Bengal, the Northwest Provinces, and Oude. Nine are pure Sikh regiments; 13 Goorkha regiments; 27 Punjaubi regiments. These 27 Punjaubi regiments are generally half Hindoo and half Mussulman.

Artillery.—Two mountain batteries with mules.

The term "Punjaubi" as here used includes Pathans (trans-frontier and cis-frontier), (all Mussulmans), Punjaubi Mohammedans, Sikhs, Dogras (Hindoos).

The Indian army at present consists of three main forces—the Bengal, Bombay, and Madras armies. The Bengal army is quartered in Bengal, Assam, the Northwest Provinces, and the Punjaub, while Quetta, for some reason, is garrisoned from the Bombay army.

These different divisions have just been made into army corps, all under one commander-in-chief in India—*i.e.*, the Bengal, Madras, Bombay, and Northwest Frontier forces.

PUNJAUBI INFANTRY

manded by English officers—the commandant, two "wing commanders," four wing officers, of whom two act as quartermaster and adjutant, and one medical officer. Next come the native officers—eight "subadars" (ranking as captains), eight "jemadars," sixteen buglers, and eighty others (havildars and naiks), and then the rank and file, eight hundred sepoys. In the Punjaubi frontier force nearly all regiments are dressed in mud-colored kharki drill, blue turbans, blue or kharki knickerbockers, and white gaiters, while five regiments of Sikhs wear red coats. The British officers seem to live for the most part on excellent terms with the native officers, addressing them always (in the Hindostani equivalent) as Sir, although the subadars actually rank below the junior subaltern. All these men are volunteers or enlisted men, and the terms of enlistment are peculiar. The period of the first engagement is three years, after which the sepoy may claim his discharge if there is no prospects of hostilities. and even within that time it is often granted for adequate reasons. Each sepoy gets seven rupees a month, with a gradual increase after three years' service and good conduct. Out of this he has to pay for his own food, which costs him three and a half rupees per month, but he receives thirty rupees on enlistment to help purchase his uniform, and five rupees annually to keep it up. He has also two suits a year provided by government, besides blankets and other articles, and he has also a chance to make a little money by musketry prizes and in other small ways, although he does not usually manage to save much of his pay.

The total annual cost of a native regiment, including the pay of the British officers, and all other expenses, is well under two lakhs of rupees, and it may be considered the cheapest infantry in the world. The "sowar," or native trooper in the cavalry, is rather more of a swell than the infantry sepoy, since he must be a capitalist before he can serve the "British Raj." He has first to deposit two hundred rupees towards the purchase of his horse, and his pay is thirty-one rupees per month, out of which he has to find everything. Thus the regiment mounts itself, and none of the horses belong to government. The position of an ambitious young officer, especially if he be desirous of passing into the staff corps, entails steady work, for in any case he has to become an accomplished linguist. As Hindostani only is spoken in the regiment, he must pass the "higher standard" in that language, with written exercises in a character resembling the Sanscrit; "Urdu," which is written in Persian characters; and if there are Pathans in his regiment he is expected to pass an examination in their dialect, as well as to learn something of the Punjaubi dialect, which, however, is a "voluntary."

The native officers have either risen from the ranks or are more rarely commissioned directly from the Viceroy if sons of deserving men. In the long list of camp-followers attached to each regiment many peculiar vocations are represented, such as sweepers, water-carriers or "bhisties," a Mohammedan moollah, a Sikh priest, and a Hindoo priest; also two native schoolmasters, one to teach English and the other Hindostani. Most of these enlisted men are farmers, recruited in the country and in villages, and never in towns; they are allowed to visit their homes at stated intervals, with free passage by rail, and in other ways their servitude is rendered comparatively light; there are also liberal pension arrangements, and each regiment has its own reserve. Many of these regiments, besides the Sikhs and Goorkhas, have achieved distinction in foreign campaigns, and among others the

Bengal Lancers, who served in the Egyptian war. We happened to be on a steamer which was one of the first to pass through the canal when it was opened to traffic after the close of hostilities, and while strolling about in Suez in the company of an officer of the Madras army we chanced upon a couple of these troopers. My companion was anxious to inform himself as to the part they took at the battle of Tel-el-Kebir, having the glory of the Indian contingent at heart. He proceeded to question them in Hindostani, and they answered as if on the witness-stand. According to their statements, corroborated afterwards in Bombay, it was they who had routed and cut down the flying remnants of Arabi Pasha's army. A few days later, while we still lingered on at Bombay, in spite of the October heat—for the city was new to us then, and full of a strange exotic charm—the troop-ships arrived with all the Indian contingent, and during the fêtes which followed we had the opportunity of admiring their agility and skill in lime-cutting, tent-pegging, and kindred sports. We afterwards met them larking about fraternally with kilted Highlanders and Goorkhas, or squatting over the camp-fires in their company.

Whether the "sowar" belongs to the blue-coated cavalry of the Punjaub, or to the "lancers," in faded blouse and carelessly wound turban which have seen honorable service, he is never without a certain wild picturesqueness, which suggests a not remote relationship to the Bedouin, and when off duty he falls easily into the elastic and supple attitudes of his race.

An authority on military matters is said recently to have favorably compared a Bengal Lancer regiment with the Lifeguards and other bodies of the finest cavalry in the world; while, according to the *Times of India*, another

GOING TO THE REVIEW

unimpeachable judge, who has had the best opportunities of forming an opinion, pronounces any good regiment of Indian cavalry to be quite equal to the Cossacks of the Imperial Guard.

II

One may reach Lahore by through express from either of the two great ports of western India, Bombay and Kurrachee. The journey from Bombay, the most interesting of the two routes, as it passes through such cities as Baroda, Ahmedabad, Ajemere, Jeypore, and Delhi, can be made in less than sixty hours, and covers 1328 miles of railway. On the other hand, the route from Kurrachee, which is much shorter, being only 821 miles, has only one important city on the way, Multoon, although one may stop, as the writer did, at Kotree, and visit Hyderabad (Scinde) across the Indus. But he will have to leave his comfortable divan in the railway carriage at 2 A.M., and finish the night on a lounge in the waiting-room of the station. Let us suppose, then, that he adopts the latter plan, having arrived by steamer at Kurrachee. His baggage is opened in the great iron sheds at the landing, where the examination, although rigid as a matter of form, is lenient enough except in the matter of liquors and fire-arms.

Just outside the custom-house he will find a long row of "gharries," of the species known as landau, each provided with a pair of smart and generally well-conditioned horses. The red-turbaned "gharry wallahs," or drivers, are even more demonstrative here than elsewhere, for fares are low and competition keen; they will come to blows over his luggage, which is usually awarded to the victor. As one is driven along the straight and dusty avenue thronged with bullock carts and wagons conveying bales of cotton and other merchandise to and from the docks, he will realize that while Kurrachee is a keen commercial rival of Bombay, it still lacks much of the charm of the older city. Everything in the way of architecture is as yet new and raw; the gardens, filled with dense tropical growth, appear to have been recently planted, for the cocoanut and other palms are stunted, and many trees lean away from the sea, as if tired of struggling against the winds. There are none of the tall and graceful towers of foliage which adorn the coast farther down, for this is the beginning of the comparatively desert country of Scinde, and glimpses of pale sand-hills may be seen beyond the tree-tops. Yet there are flowers everywhere, and morning-glories twine over the ornamental iron fences and trim hedge-rows. There is a travellers' bungalow near the business centre, and a hotel near the railway station of the cantonment, where guests are lodged in various detached and galleried structures provided with doors which will not shut, as is usually the case in Indian hotels; but this is a feature to which the new-comer soon becomes resigned, and it cannot always be said to imply negligence on the part of the managers, for the wood of doors and sashes shrinks with each dry season, and swells again with the monsoon weather.

After the silence of unprogressive Persia, there was a sense of companionship in the snorting of the iron horse, and the rattling and jolting of the long freight-trains, which were continuously manœuvring a few rods from the back doors of this establishment. The stranger in India will be impressed with the fact, and still more potently should he have had any recent experience of eastern Europe and the Turkish Empire, that this government does not occupy itself in the least with the concerns of the casual traveller: whatever his nationality may be, he is free to come and go as he likes; nothing is said about passports, no printed form is brought to him to be filled out with his age, profession, etc., and he is not followed by gensdarmes or haunted by spies; he is not obliged to register himself at a police station, and he may sketch, photograph, or do anything in reason. In short, there are none of the arbitrary and fussy little restrictions and annoyances which are the rule elsewhere. There are certain fortresses in the north, and even at Lahore, where he may not sketch without permission, which could probably be obtained without difficulty, as it would seem in any case that much is left to the common-sense and discretion of the officials. Aside from the fact that Kurrachee is a rapidly growing port and a distributive centre, expected by its sanguine citizens to leave Bombay far behind, there is little to interest the stranger beyond its winter climate, which is a shade cooler than that of Bombay. One does not need an overcoat, nor a "punka" on the other hand, and there is no chill at sundown or in the morning air. Away from the crowded hive where the native population quarters itself, and which has much of the teeming and dirty picturesqueness of similar sites in Bombay, as well as the same close and musky odors, the European city, if wanting in the architectural magnificence of Bombay, is at least planned and laid out on the same generous scale as regards space. The banks, public buildings, and government offices are massive, rectangular, arcaded structures of pale yellow stone, each standing alone in a waste of gravel, or planted, each like a country-house, in its own grounds; but there are a few streets where the shops stand close together and elbow each other as in European towns. The new "Scinde Club" may be taken as an example of the Indian club-house in general. The spacious lunch-room on the

A LAHORE STREET—MORNING

first floor may be left open to the sea-breeze or closed by glass screens, and this apartment opens on a wide terrace. The reading-room is as solemnly quiet as that of a London club; there is a conservatory or fern-house, sleeping-rooms for members, and everywhere an atmosphere of substantial comfort and luxury. In the park which lies at the end of the fashionable drive, there is a circular plot of greensward surrounding a tank with an ornamental iron fountain in the centre; the edge of the water is defined by a border of vivid white and yellow flowers in pots, which tell forcibly against the dusky thickets of low cocoa-palms. A well-dressed Mussulman, standing on the turf near the fountain, had spread his prayer-rug on the grass, preparatory to his evening devotions, conversing meanwhile with his two friends, who are lounging on an iron bench across the gravel walk. He then concentrates his thoughts on higher things with the air of rapt self-forgetfulness which all Mohammedans command at such moments, resuming the conversation when the brief function is over.

The writer's time in Kurrachee was largely taken up with preparations for the trip inland and with interviewing English-speaking servants, who came provided with written characters more or less fraudulent, as any "munshi" can write a first-class recommendation for eight annas, and Kurrachee is proverbially a bad place to start from in this respect. We elected to start for Lahore on the night after the troop-ship *Crocodile* had arrived and had disgorged her floating population. There are two stations at Kurrachee, the city and the cantonment, and as most of the new-comers were lodged in the neighborhood of the latter station, which was just across the road from our hotel, it seemed wiser to take our chances at the city terminus, particularly as the railroad superintendent had posted a notice advising that course. Notwithstanding the confusion and chaos of steamer trunks and porters, we managed, with the help of my fellow-traveller, who was going on to Simla, to find an empty compartment, and by the time the train was taken by storm at the upper station we were comfortably extended on our divans. This rush of travel only lasts for a day or two after the arrival of a trooper or a mail-steamer, and at other times there is plenty of room in the first-class sections.

The line which runs up to Lahore, communicating with the south of India by way of Delhi or Ferozapoor, is now known as the Northwestern Railway (broad gauge), and follows the line of the Indus River for the greater part of the way. At Ruk Junction the military road runs northward to Quetta and the frontier of Beloochistan, and at Musserabad another military route, following the Indus to the northeast, makes a shorter alternative route to Peshawur by way of Rawal-Pindee.

Hyderabad, the principal town of Scinde, lies just across the Indus from Kotree station, which we reached at 2 A.M. Having concluded to stop over and visit the city, I got down with my baggage, expecting to find Motee, the newly engaged servant, on the platform. Not finding him among the sleepers in the third class, I made myself fairly comfortable in the waiting-room of the station, trusting that he had been carried on and would turn up the next day. The station-master, whose acquaintance I made in the morning, very kindly took me down to the landing on his "trolley," or hand-car, and detailed an employé from the freight-office to accompany me to Hyderabad. Along the bank of the river, bordered by a dense growth of date-trees, lay moored the "Indus flotilla," a line of white double-decked river steamboats. Some of them formerly ascended the river to Mooltan, but the service has been discontinued since the building of the railway. A large steam ferry-boat, crowded with deck passengers, took us across to the high sandy bank opposite.

Seen from this point, the shelving red bank, dotted with camels, bullock-carts, and carriages, with venders of fruit and sweetmeats, the broad yellow flood and the distant palm-fringed shores, recall in their general features the environs of the Nile at Ghizeh. Hyderabad itself, only a short drive from the bank, has but one main thoroughfare, and its appearance seems to indicate a greater degree of poverty than is usual in towns of similar size and importance. Persia has stretched a long arm across the Indus, for the pale, rose-tinted mud walls of the houses, the tombs of the Ameers, high-domed, and walled with porcelain, and the sloping towers of the citadel would all be in keeping with any Persian landscape. There are one or two excellent schools for natives under government supervision, which were founded by Sir Jamsetjee Jeejeebhoy. In one of the little side alleys, where we had been attracted by the never-failing lure of bric-à-brac, and in an unpretentious little house, we found a merchant prince who dealt in marvels of needle-work. He was seated, when we entered, against the white wall at the door of an inner chamber, behind a lofty and most imposing "hubble-bubble" mounted on a silver stand, after the local fashion. While his servants unfolded pile after pile of embroideries and curtains, he entertained us with his impressions of the remote localities which he had visited, and talked to us of London and Madrid, of Paris and Zanzibar, and Cape Town, and of the store under Shepherd's Hotel, from which he derived much of his revenue; but what impressed us particularly was a command of French and Spanish rare among Hindoos.

At Kotree, upon returning to catch the mail-train, Motee

reappeared in a most penitent frame of mind. His friends at Kurrachee had given him a magnificent "send-off," and at the moment when the train had stopped on the previous night he was sleeping off the effects of extensive libations, and had been carried on a few hundred miles.

The compartment which now fell to my lot had a species of piazza, where we could place a camp-stool and enjoy the landscape. At sunrise, after a chilly night, we cross the Indus by an imposing suspension-bridge; the stream is both wide and rapid at this point, and in the middle rises a rocky island crowned with a ruined fortress, ornamented with panels of blue faience. A broad metalled road winds along the opposite shore of the river, under a fringe of tall date-palms, and the town of Roree, on the other side, rises steeply from the water; its lofty balconied houses of red clay and the angularity of its outline recall the cholera-smitten town of Yezdikhast, on the way to Shiraz. It is one of those places where one is tempted to stop and look about; but to yield to this kind of temptation is seldom expedient or wise, for the chances are that should one find a travellers' bungalow, it would probably be at a distance of several miles from the spot which attracted him, and destitute of either cook or larder.

Beyond Roree we enter upon far-stretching plains floored with white clay, sprinkled with groups of dusty, waving tamarisk-trees, with here and there a marsh covered with dense low bushes and thickets of yellow jungle-grass, with tall plumes bending before the wind, and there are occasional mud-holes and pools of yellow water. All is vast, melancholy, and monotonous. At long intervals a thin cloud of dust indicates a distant road and passing bullock-carts. Everything in the compartment is covered with a layer of fine dust, which is blown up from the embankment and sifts through the window-sashes. This is the usual character of the landscape which borders one of the great rivers like the Sutlej or Indus, and it is not devoid of a certain sterile grandeur, like the approach to the sea on some desolate northern coast. First the villages and cultivated fields cease, and then comes a broad tract of waste lands, alternately clayey or sandy, dotted with forlorn and stunted tamarisks, looking as if they had passed much of their life under water. Then there is often a wide extent of clay and sand dunes, which has all the illusion of a desert, with its apparent limitless horizon and its mirage. Then all at once the ground slopes abruptly down to a broad river-bed of sand or gravel under the high trestle-work of the railway, and far below a few thin blue channels of water seem to lose themselves in the glaring waste. What at first appeared to be the opposite bank dotted with low bushes proves to be a long island, beyond which is another waste of sand and water. In the season of the monsoon all this territory is often covered by the yellow rolling flood.

III

It is night when the train runs into the great fortress-like station of Lahore, built with an eye to possible military necessities; the arching expanse of glass roof, and the multitude of gas-jets twinkling dimly in the smoky gloom aloft, suggest a somewhat reduced edition of Charing Cross Station; this chance impression is strengthened by the brilliantly lighted news-stand and book-stall of Wheeler & Co., well furnished with light literature, from the period of Ainsworth to the fatalistic Tolstoï, and by the "nickel-in-the-slot" machines. But there is a note of piquant contrast in the three tall Indian falconers, with great buzzard-like hawks, nearly as large as eagles, which strugglingly balance themselves on the shoulders or turbans of their masters, who stand on the platform environed by portentous piles of bedding, and hunt in their clothing for "pice" to pay the luggage coolies. A few Europeans are pacing the platform in heavy ulsters. Upon the steps of the bridge which crosses the tracks to the other side of the station a party of "Rewari" ladies, with plump brown arms incased in rings of glittering metal, with swinging skirts and heavy anklets, richly costumed and pungently perfumed, are stooping down, intent upon scraping up a mess of some brown, greasy edible which they had spilt upon the steps. A railway official in uniform is conversing with the mob of third-class native passengers carrying strange packets of every conceivable shape; they are confined like prisoners behind the cross-bars of a strong wooden grating, and presently, when the train is ready the official turnkey will let them loose. So intermingled are Europe and Asia that it is not easy to determine which is the discordant note—this underground railway British book-stall, and the sign of "Bass's Ale," or the hooded hawks and the brown ladies with the tinkling anklets. Outside the station carriages are numerous, and you may go to your hotel shiveringly in an open barouche labelled "first class," or get into a shigram, which closes like a coupé, but is labelled "second class," avoid the risk of a chill, and court the risk of being turned away from the hotel "for want of room," as every hostelry is crowded at Christmas-time.

There is no lack of hotels at Lahore, considering the smallness of the transient population, and, as usual, they are all situated in the civil station, as the European settlement is called. These hotels offer no points of difference in their outward appearance, save their conspicuous signs, from the bungalows of private citizens, which are planted at intervals along the broad avenues. As the European suburb is unusually large, these highways, shaded by tall trees of the tamarisk family, have a rather wearisome sameness, and this impression of monotony is partly due to the sombre hues of the foliage. Journeying along in a shigram, at some distance from the outer walls of the Indian city, towards the quarter called Anarkali, we follow a road bordered by tall banana-trees. In the early morning the ground is white with hoar-frost, and most of the huge leaves which arch over us are brown and shrivelled; the dull red rays of the rising sun

AN OPEN-AIR RESTAURANT, LAHORE

slant through the mist or silvery-gray vapor which lies along the ground. The sight of this tropical but frost-bitten luxuriance does not seem quite in accord with one's preconceived notions of a climate where there are at least eight months of hot weather, where the season of burning winds and wet "tatty mats" begins in March, preceded only by few dull and languorous days which follow the cessation of frost. These rose-tinted rays of light, the silvery mist behind the fresh green or dull gray of the leaves, have a strange charm, but there is a suggestion of malaria in the damp, raw chill, largely due to the plentiful irrigation, which turns every field or garden-patch into a stagnant pool. While the English community of Lahore, as elsewhere in India, has elected to live away from the native city, and while the original nucleus of this settlement was planted, for sanitary and other reasons, far from the city walls, it has gradually filled up the intervening space, so that the usual neutral ground, or no man's land, has ceased to exist. In the crowded suburb of Anarkali, which we must traverse in order to reach the post-office, the bazaars extend out from the city gate to the European civil lines. This quarter, where the architecture is chiefly Indian, with that yellow and stuccoed suggestion of Portuguese influence which still survives, is given over for the most part to "Europe Shops," kept by English-speaking natives, Eurasians, and occasional Parsees. These shopkeepers are mainly clad in what might be called an adaptation of the European dress to Indian needs, and in their shops and warehouses everything in the way of clothing, household articles, jewelry, furniture—new and second-hand—as well as provisions, wines, and other luxuries, can be purchased usually at rates as cheap as in England, for there is close competition. As the government has not yet resorted to a tobacco monopoly (which is a dangerous experiment in Eastern countries), almost every variety of tobacco and cigarettes may be found in the show-cases of these shops—Vanity Fair, Old Judge, as well as Egyptian, and the Kaiser and Hind cigarettes of Malta. The cheapest, and naturally most popular, cigars are the Trinchinopoly and Manila cheroots, which are good and remarkably low in price. In every little "medical hall" kept by an anglicized native there is always a stock of the standard remedies, such as quinine, phenacitine, and antipyrine, put up in convenient shape, and often these packages bear the label of some well-known American firm. Fortunately for the health of a community which supposes itself to be possessed of common-sense, the sale of these simple remedies is not, as in Austria and some other Continental nations, restricted by law, and a physician's order is not necessary for the purchase of a box of quinine pills.

A significant feature, not only of Lahore, but of every other large community in India, is the abundance of second-hand shops crammed with furniture of every description, smart and new or broken down and decrepit, which naturally results from the periodical migrations to which people connected with the civil or military service are frequently subjected. As they are liable to be sent at brief notice to the remotest parts of the great empire, it is seldom worth while to transport all their household effects with them, at great expense, over thousands of miles of railway or by camel and bullock trains. Few English names appear on the signs in this suburb, but "Cheap Jack" and "Cheap Shop" are considered by the native merchant to be of lucky omen, and "Europe Shop" still holds its own in popularity. "Budruddin Hassan" suggests by association of ideas the trade of the pastry-cook, and in front of one shop, of which the exact location is not

CARVED BALCONIES

now quite clear to the writer's memory, there is a piece of very delightful English which reads thus: "All kinds of Syrup, Jelly, Pickles, and Medicine Selling Company." Over these shops and lower stories there are often balconies of carved wood, such as one sees within the walls, and they are usually occupied by young ladies of the nautch-dancing sisterhood, who are keenly alive to the value of a scarlet or a yellow blossom in their blue-black hair, but unfortunately some of them do not realize that the effect of rice-powder on a transparent brown skin is rather disastrous. The principal street from the city gate, where great trees and dusty thickets occupy the space once filled by the moat, and where there is a crowd of small traders, snake-charmers, fakirs, and showmen with tents and booths throughout its entire length to the opposite end, where it merges into the European quarter.

gives one the impression of a sort of Oriental Bowery. Beyond this there is more space and greensward enclosed by low rails, and the principal post-office, with empty mail-vans standing outside. Every morning, before the early mail is distributed to the public, a trooper in scarlet uniform gallops from the post-office to Government House with the mail-bag for the inmates. In this vicinity are situated most of the principal municipal and government buildings, the Mayo School of Arts in connection with the Art Museum—and few similar institutions in any country can boast of a finer installation, or one more in keeping with its main object, the encouragement of Indian industrial art. Here are the churches—one of which was once the tomb Anarkali, a favorite of the Emperor Akbar; and the cathedral, which is Gothic, like many similar edifices in India, is quite as much at home in its environment as are the Greek temples of London. The tomb intended to perpetuate the memory of Anarkali is not the only instance in Lahore of that thrifty disposition of the modern Romans to utilize these monuments of a more poetic age. Upon one occasion when in quest of information I was directed to the office of the railway superintendent, and found him installed in the tomb of some worthy of Persian ancestry, to judge from the noble arch incrusted with tiles which rose above the recess in which his employés were at work; and there are several other examples of equally successful adaptations.

The principal English shops and warehouses are not often situated in buildings constructed especially for commercial purposes, but in the ordinary domestic bungalows standing alone in neglected compounds; and as the bulkier articles, such as trunks, perambulators, or household furniture, are kept outside on the verandas, one might fancy that these temples of commerce were all dwelling-houses, and that the inmates were forever on the point of moving out or of just getting settled.

Government House, the seat of the Lieutenant-Governor of the Punjaub, stands in attractive grounds near the fine park known as the Lawrence Gardens, on the outskirts of the civil station. The flower-beds and parterres which adorn the public and private grounds in this neighborhood are more luxuriant and varied than the winter gardens of the Riviera. In the early morning, as well as at night, they are much frequented by jackals, which show their appreciation of them by trotting about in couples through the shrubbery. An open-air fête had been held in one of these gardens in the afternoon, and when the last guests had departed, many of them in furs and ulsters, and while we were standing before the chimney fire within, the conversation was interrupted by the howls of a band of these nocturnal ramblers just outside the doors.

IV

A tramway line, which passes the railway station and the rows of little tenements built for the employés, runs on through a long street where the "cheap eating-house" flourishes, and between the shops of artisans, dyers, and tinkers, ending at the city gate. This edifice, one of those stuccoed sulphur-tinted monuments of the Georgian order which at one time were sown broadcast over the length and breadth of India, gives access to a narrow winding street, flanked by tall houses. A great deal of business and gossip is going on at all hours in this street, and the little shops are of that universal type which prevails in all Moslem countries, from the Atlantic to the Great Wall of China, and which existed in all probability in Pompeii as in modern Venice. From a cavernous arch at the end

MINARET OF THE MOSQUE VAZIR KHAN

we emerge into the square facing the mosque of Vazir Khan; like the great place at Ispahan, it contains little to remind one of Europe, and the transition from the trim avenue, the horse-cars, and the red pillar post-boxes at intervals is strangely abrupt. The mosque is almost purely Persian, but for the two jutting windows on each side of the tall and deep recess above the entrance. The entire front of the gateway is a brilliant mosaic of the kind known as "kashi-work," and the four massive towers, as well as the façade of the inner court, repeat the same scheme of blue and yellow and faded green. Age has but mellowed the tone of the whole edifice, and the great Persian letters of the inscription over the main entrance are still resplendent in vivid turquoise blue.* The frescoed walls within the niche, of which the ornamentation above is less deeply indented than in the Persian examples of similar work, have taken on a rich bituminous and smoky tone like an old painting; and the dado above the square platform on each side of the steps, which is of marble, once white, threaded with slender black lines forming interlaced stars and hexagons, has been toned by age and the contact of many garments to a golden brown. The venerable Mussulmans privileged to pass their lives on the steps and the lounging-place on either side may be seen there at any time of the day, and after an absence of several years I recognized the same faces among them. They constitute a species of club, or rather an Oriental "Cercle des Decavés," and are seemingly content to sit and see the world go by without taking a very active part in its endless movement. When not asleep or otherwise employed they appear to be absorbed in vague speculations upon the infinite, but, like their European imitators, are doubtless dreaming of mere material things. It is their custom to begin the day with a sort of dress parade—a minute investigation of their tattered raiment. Having completed their inspection, they proceed to select a sunny exposure if in winter, or when the hot winds blow they retreat into the dim brick-vaulted corridor

* "Remove thy heart from the gardens of the world, and know that this building is the true abode of man."

provided for their comfort by the munificence of an imperial Vizir,* and proceed to do nothing. A few of the elect, whose heads are well thatched with a shock of black hair, and with faces tanned to the color of burnt sienna,

TAILOR'S APPRENTICE, LAHORE

have literally gone to the dogs, and grovel in the dust at some distance from the steps among the canine frequenters of the sacred spot; their unique garment being of the same color as the ground, they are scarcely distinguishable from it. If they are professional mendicants, as they seem to be, they pursue their calling in a gentle and unobtrusive manner, and without the aggressive energy displayed by their brethren of Naples.

There is, in truth, a good deal of life and movement to be seen from the crumbling steps of Vazir Khan; there

* Built in 1634 by the Vizir of Shah Jehan.

are two domed edifices which may have once been tombs or fountains, but which now shelter various trades beneath the rude thatched awnings projecting from their eaves. Tailors and tailors' apprentices stitch all day at piles of dilapidated garments in their shadow, and cobblers busy themselves with heaps of dusty old shoes, and in the middle of the square there are open-air restaurants, where great kettles of tinned copper stand upon platforms elevated above the ground and surrounded by rough benches; sooty frying-pans sizzle on little clay furnaces, and the keepers of these restaurants sit enthroned among their cooking utensils and diligently fight the swarms of flies with long-handled brushes. In the

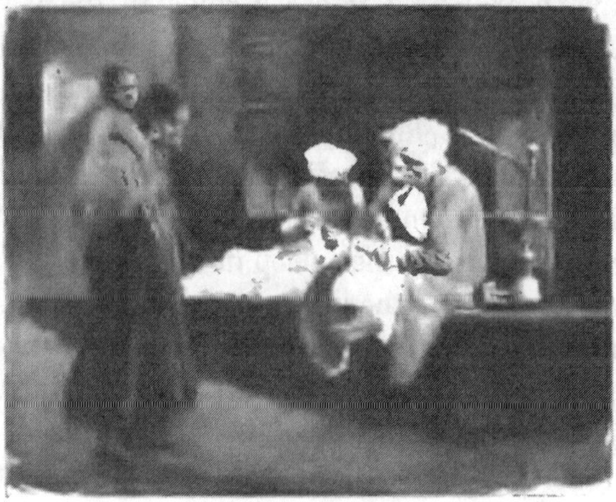

TAILOR SHOP, LAHORE

middle of the day the benches are crowded with customers, who have the appearance of being peasants from the outlying country, or Pathan peddlers; and most of them being voluminously swathed in white, they look not a little like the patrons of similar places in Morocco. A great deal of horse-shoeing and veterinary practice is carried on in one corner, under a great tree, and there is always a sound of hammering and clashing of metal from the smoky arches behind. Occasionally two men drag up a struggling ram to the corner steps of the mosque; having seated themselves, they proceed to divest him of his fleece, and after finishing their work confide their own heads to the barber, who plies the shears under a straw awning close by. The great open court of the mosque is seldom thronged except at noon; a few school-boys con their books under the eye of a master in one corner, and an occasional beggar strolls in, and stretches himself out to sleep on the pavement among the pigeons. To those who have been reared in other lands, in the fear of the stern sacristan and the autocratic suisse, there is something broadly democratic in the faith of Islam as it is practised to-day. While in most countries still under Mussulman dominion the unbeliever is rigidly excluded from the mosque,* the humblest of the faithful may find there a refuge from the weather, sleep in the protecting shadow of its cloisters, and bathe in the water of the tank. Without descending again into the square, we may pass through the long corridor and down the little steps at the end, and we are in the gayest street of Lahore; in its display of carved and weather-beaten wood-work, of balconies and jutting windows, each house exhibiting the individual taste and fancy of its designer, it is probably unequalled in any city of the East. The dark brick wall of the mosque, relieved by brilliant panels of unglazed tiles, and pierced by a window here and there, shadows for some distance the

* The stranger is made welcome to-day in any of the mosques of India, and there are but few where he is even expected to don the traditional slippers.

street, which expands beyond into a little square, littered in the afternoon with the baskets of small hucksters, and the sunny wall of the house which rises across the way is a thing to study and to enjoy. Its oriel-windows are delightfully irregular in size and shape, and the intervening spaces, from the eaves down to the ragged little shop roofs and tattered awnings, once gaudily painted with intermingled combinations of arabesque designs, gods, and animals, have been toned to a mellow golden hue by the sun; dilapidated cane mats hang at some of the windows, and the shadow of a great tree flickers on the wall in the afternoon.

A few steps farther on and the wealth of old woodwork becomes fairly prodigal; the side streets, as well as this main artery, give one the impression that each householder has vied to outdo his neighbor in throwing out these crowded ranks of beautiful windows, and in covering every inch of wall with decoration and with color. Where the windows do not project they are made interesting by complicated stucco mouldings, by panels of painted flowers, by courses of glazed red and blue bricks, and they usually open upon a long wooden balcony, high enough for one to sit and look down through the interstices of the wooden gratings. Even the under sides overhanging the street, and the brackets, are richly painted, and often mirrors are inserted in the centres of elaborate rosettes. Peacocks of tinted stucco perch on the white domes of the windows, and peacocks of painted wood, twisted into the shape of brackets, uphold the rows of great square "moussarabies." At one end of this marvellous street there is a perspective of golden domes, and at the other end tower the lofty minars of Vazir Khan. Beyond the group of gilded domes, and near the extreme end of the street, there is a house front most lavishly decorated by the painters' brush. A corner of the largest window was tenanted by a young lady, doubtless a professional beauty in her world, for she certainly had the calm assurance of bearing characteristic of the order. At certain hours of the day she held a little salon or *conversazione*, languidly keeping her place in the corner, while the turbaned heads of her guests could be seen leaning back against the window-sill on the other side. A companion usually joined her, and sometimes they would both trip

DYER'S SHOP

swiftly down the steep stairway to the street, and after exchanging confidential remarks with their friends the shopkeepers across the way, which left them in a state of choking and inarticulate mirth, they would climb into one of the crazy one-horse vehicles known to the Anglo-Indians as the "jingling Jimmies," and drive hurriedly off. On these occasions they appeared in elaborate street costumes, with transparent shawls of delicate tissue worn loosely over the long silken tunic, microscopically embroidered, and the ankle-tight silk trousers, which here replace the swinging skirts of Rajpootana. The Jumma Musjid, or Great Mosque, rises beyond an open desert space near the end of this street. Its four tall minars of red stone are its most striking feature, and near by is the imposing domed mausoleum of Ranjeet Singh, and the entrance of the great fortress enclosing the royal palaces. Parts of them were built during the reigns of Akbar and Jehanghir, and other portions completed by Shah Jehan and Aurungzebe. High up on the red fortress walls above the moat there are square panels of brilliant tile-work, with yellow elephants, horsemen, and figures of warriors and gods on a blue ground. There are beautiful things within the walls, as in the deserted palaces of Agra and Delhi, marble preciously inlaid with flowers of colored stones, and in the "Shish Mahall" the glittering Persian mirror-work.

But chapters might be devoted to description which, after all, would convey to the reader's mind but an inadequate idea of this decayed splendor. One would have to go very carefully over the ground to form the vaguest conception of how the place once looked, as it is so encumbered with barracks, magazines, and "public works" buildings, and in the innermost retreats, once sacred to the emperors, the red-coated British private now smokes his pipe when not on duty. The old gardens in the neighborhood of Lahore, such as "Shalimar," where ancient mango-trees are still green and vigorous, where the marble terraces are weather-worn and broken, the canals choked with weeds, and where only a few mouldering gateways still retain patches of lustrous "kashi-work," have a charm which they may have lacked when freshly laid out in the days of Shah Jehan.

Perhaps the most impressive of all is that which surrounds the grand mausoleum at Shah Darrah, beyond the river Ravi. There are alleys of wild palms, orange and mango trees, and forgotten corners near the broken walls where tall yellow canes have sprung up. It would be impossible to forget the first impression of the lonely mausoleum, the vast extent of tessellated pavement, overgrown with dry grass, and the four lofty minars at the corners; from the high level of the terrace the landscape, which stretches away on every side, is empty and objectless, but bathed in the tranquil afternoon light it gives one the illusion of eternal summer. In the short winter the sunny days are full of glow and color; as few of the trees lose their leaves, there is but little to suggest decay, and the charm of this and of other gems of Indian landscape is free from that somewhat depressing quality known as sentiment in painted interpretations of nature.

COURT OF THE MOSQUE VAZIR KHAN

V

It is seldom that two cities of almost equal size and importance, such as Lahore and Amritsar,* are placed so near together, for the distance between them is but thirty miles. Amritsar, being the cathedral city of the Sikhs, is in its way a great religious centre, as well as an important commercial entrepôt. It is a "city of polemics," and is often chosen as a tilting-ground where wordy tournaments take place between the professors of diverse creeds, where those who have gathered to discuss in a spirit of calm and temperate investigation the merits of each respective faith often end in fierce controversy. Of late Christians and Moslems have been hurling defiance at each other, and as a sequel to one of these philosophical debates, the Mussulman controversialist ended by working himself into a frenzy, and threatening his opponent with dire and endless punishment. Amritsar seems to have more of the bustle and roar of commerce than Lahore. The narrow streets, darkened by tall brick houses, made picturesque with ornate windows like those of Lahore, are crowded with heavily laden bullock-carts and buffalo "teams," blocked with long camel trains, jammed with droves of donkeys, and among the hurrying crowds one discerns a new element in the tall, gaunt men with Mongolian faces, wrapped in long wadded gowns, and wearing fur caps and high boots. They abound in certain "serais,"† where they may be seen at prayer on the broad platform in the middle of the courts, as in the caravansaries of Ispahan, or wandering about in the bazaars with dazed and distracted mien, as if stunned by the din

* The population of Lahore at present is 176,854; Amritsar, 136,766.

† Caravansaries.

of the city. They are evidently of a different breed from the stout, squat Mongolians from the hills one meets in other northern towns, and have probably come from Toorkistan; one connects them instinctively with Central Asia, because of their samovars and loose-sleeved wadded kaftans.

At the end of a narrow and crowded lane one comes suddenly upon an open space, and from the railing at its edge lies the far-famed Lake of Immortality, enclosed by palace walls and screened by verdure, with the "Golden Temple" rising from an island in the middle. But before descending the steps the profane visitor must halt at the police station, and select a pair of slippers from the pile provided for the use of strangers. The uniformed Sikh policeman who is detailed to accompany each visitor first points out a large sign with parallel columns in many languages, enumerating at length the things which one may not do on hallowed ground. The sanctity of the place could not have been more jealously guarded when the Sikhs were the ruling power. From the border of the tank, which lies in the afternoon shadow, the Golden Temple gives one the impression of a glittering jewel, or of some rare old Byzantine casket wrought in enamel and studded with gems. Small and compact, glowing with color and scintillating with light, its mirrored image reaching far down into the purple depths of reflected sky, it has at first sight a glamour of unreality, like an opium vision of De Quincey, or the "pleasure dome of Kubla Khan." Two colors predominate, the gold of the upper part and the clustered domes, and the white marble of its base, toned and softened by the faint color of its inlaid flowers; the curtained doors and windows add flashes of scarlet. In its environment of deep-toned dusky purple sky and water it has the intensity of a luminous point or focus of

STEPS OF THE MOSQUE VAZIR KHAN

light, and the dark masses of foliage behind are of great value in the landscape.

An advanced state of æsthetic culture may, it might be admitted, prove a drawback to complete and unreasoning enjoyment of this and of similar things in India, particularly if one is biassed and hampered by preconceived notions of what is correct according to the canons of conventional good taste in matters of classical, or of Renaissance, or Gothic, art.

The lake is surrounded by a tessellated marble pavement, varied in pattern, and shut in from the noise of the city by white palace walls, with balconies and window-seats overlooking the water, and by great trees. On one side there is a wilderness of dark foliage belonging to distant gardens; among the trees are a few gleaming kiosks and domes, and rising above them are three tall towers, the more distant of which is of massive form, and decorated with panels of tiles and mosaic. Along the inlaid pavement of the margin groups of priests, worshippers, and fakirs of an order peculiar to the Sikh religion are slowly pacing, and discoursing, let us hope, of higher things, and not of the "pice" which they have extracted from their confiding followers. Sometimes we come upon a priest or pundit seated under a tree or on a little marble seat at the water's edge and deeply absorbed in a ponderous book. Near the foot of the steps by which we descend there is usually a school-master seated on the pavement, surrounded by a circle of small students. A few artisans who manufacture wooden spoons, combs, and other souvenirs of the shrine are allowed to ply their trades in shady corners around the tank, and the great baskets of the flower-sellers heaped high with roses and other flowers, among which great masses of odorous yellow jasmine predominate, add a note of

ENTRANCE-GATE TO THE GOLDEN TEMPLE OF AMRITSAR

yellow and orange, recalling the color of the temple. These merchants are for the most part busily engaged in weaving long chains of the fragrant yellow blossoms, which are bought by the pilgrims as offerings.

In order to reach the island sanctuary one must pass through a portal which is in itself a palace, covered, like the temple, with plates of embossed and gilded copper, with inlaid marble and painted panels, and through great doors of silver which give access to the causeway leading to the temple. Here everything is of polished white marble—the pavement, the low latticed parapets, and the slender chiselled columns supporting gilded lanterns. Along this causeway passes continually a throng of worshippers and pilgrims, making the journey on their knees from shrine to shrine. Within the temple, under a canopy of crimson velvet and on crimson cushions, sits the priest reading with monotonous intonations from the sacred book, and facing him at a little distance sits a circle of the devout under the central dome, which is enriched, like the walls, with faded color and with mosaics. Through the open doors, partly covered by scarlet portières, streams the blue light from the rippling water. Pigeons fly in and out over the heads of the worshippers, and there is always a noise of cooing and of wings. When one returns by the white causeway bordered by gilded lanterns through the silver gates to the mainland, he sees before him another and higher temple, with golden domes, and from a gallery in the second story, where behind red curtains and awnings there is a glimmer of color and tarnished gold, the Granth * is read in the morning to the accompaniment of strange music played by an orchestra seated below on the mosaic pavement and in the shadow of tall trees. At this hour banners are hoisted on the two flag-staffs which rise from the court. There is much which is impressive in the ritualism of the Sikhs, and it is free from a certain element of Hindoo worship which strikes Western observers as being grotesque or barbaric. The influence of the Greeks in northern India is now believed to have been both slight and transient, and it would be going quite beyond the mark and venturing fathomless depths to attempt the tracing of any connection, however remote, between this open-air school of Sikh philosophy and those of Greece. But the more modern race seems to have inherited the taste of the older one in the matter of poetic surroundings.

While painting within the precincts of the temple I had excellent opportunities of studying the ways of the people. The chief of the temple police, who often accompanied me and pointed out the things of interest, was a

* The sacred book of the Sikhs.

fine type of the martial Sikh—erect and rigid in his bearing, with a bristling fan-shaped black beard, and huge snowy turban, partly concealing his ears. I soon divined that he had a lingering hope of being handed down to posterity on canvas, so I presented him with a sketch of himself when we parted, by which he was much gratified, but at the same time somewhat puzzled and perplexed. As the canvas was small, I was obliged to leave out his hands.

FLOWER-SELLERS IN THE GOLDEN TEMPLE

which, I fear, he considered an unaccountable oversight. The folding easel and camp-stool, which were at first regarded with polite curiosity and afterwards with gradually increasing mistrust by the devout promenaders, gave rise to rather an amusing incident. I noticed that passing couples and groups of priests and fakirs would gaze intently at those unusual objects, and then pass on, talking earnestly together. Two of them finally stopped, and upon looking up I saw that they were having an animated discussion with my servant, who reluctantly interpreted what they were saying. It seemed that they had taken exception to the unfortunate camp-stool, for by some law of their religion nothing of the nature of a chair was allowed within the enclosure. I at once folded up the camp-stool, and the maker of wooden combs who was working close by offered me the box in which he kept his tools as a substitute, while the gharry wallah went out to the carriage and brought back the cushions. The two priests seemed quite satisfied when the letter of the law, if not its spirit, had been fulfilled, and courteously allowed the easel to remain when its mysterious mechanism had been made clear to them. Some of the fakirs, of an order peculiar to the place, wore tall pointed caps, bristling with a war-like panoply of steel blades and sharp-edged rings, such as formerly encircled the steel casques of the Sikh warriors, and are now twisted into the red turbans of the Sikh infantry. Two little girls who stopped to look on were daintily and elaborately arrayed in holiday dress, and the elder, nine or ten years old at a venture, leading her little sister by the hand, wore a turquoise ring on each of her ten brown toes. All these personages, pacing slowly and noiselessly along the tank, with always the same background of illuminated water, are like the figures in a decorative frieze, and one cannot but

SCHOOL OF THE GOLDEN TEMPLE

question whether another shrine exists so happily surrounded, and where all discordant elements are more completely shut out. The impression which one receives at first, and which remains in one's mind as a lasting souvenir, is that of a blaze of color and of light, in which nature has furnished the complementary notes, the purple of the sky, and of the water ruffled by long wind streaks of azure, and the dusky green of the foliage, which so enhance the value of the white and gold and scarlet: and at the same time the knowledge that every architectural detail which meets the eye is of costly and precious workmanship does not detract from the charm.

But there is one incongruity, one slightly jarring note, and that is the obtrusive brick clock-tower which dominates the enclosure at the entrance. Built in a style which might be termed Early New England Gothic, it must have reminded many an American wanderer of the fire-engine house in his native village, or the ambitious but inexpensive church-tower of sanded wood. Far from being intended as a gratuitous insult to the Sikhs, it was most probably a generous donation on the part of the European community, meant to serve as a perpetual object-lesson in architecture, and as a dignified protest against barbaric excess of ornament.

The religion of the Sikhs originated about the end of the fifteenth century, and according to Mr. J. A. Baines, to whom we are indebted for the admirable census of India (1891), "was due to the teaching of one of the most influential sectarian leaders of a quasi-unitarian revival amongst the lower classes of Brahmanism"; and although mainly Brahmanic, the Sikh religion shows traces of the influence of Islam. Mr. Baines further says: "The political objects of the Sikh leaders obscured the doctrinal, and culminated in the establishment of the kingdom of Runjeet Singh. In the present day peace has relaxed the bonds of discipline, and the distinction between Sikhs and the rest of the Brahmanic community is mainly ritualistic. . . . For example, it was found by experience that at the census the only trustworthy method of distinguishing the creed was to ask if the persons in question repudiated the services of the barber and the tobacconist, for the precepts most strictly enforced nowadays are that the hair of the head and face must never be touched, and that smoking is a habit to be absolutely avoided."

To go deeply into the distinguishing marks of these bewildering castes and their subdivisions would perplex an ethnological expert, and the casual amateur is too often distracted by the sensuous outward beauty of things to enter deeply into such questions of abstract analysis.

A PAINTER'S IMPRESSIONS OF RAJPOOTANA

I

On some maps of India the territory which is entirely under British rule is tinted red, while those states still under the sway of native potentates are indicated by a wash of yellow, and it is at first something of a surprise to find this tract relatively so large. In the western part of the empire there is a great triangular space, having its base along the valley of the Indus, and its apex reaching southward to the tropic; within this space are situated the contiguous dominions of several of these rulers, and they are the states which show fewest results of European influence. Bikanir lies in the northern part of this tract, separated from the English strip along the Indus by the Bikanir Desert; southward lie Jodhpore and Jussulmeer, and then Oudeypore; while to the eastward are Jeypore, Alwar, Gwalior, Patiala, and many others; the important state of Cashmir lies far to the north; southward, and well within the tropic, Baroda; and in the Deccan the great state of Hyderabad. These scattered principalities, and many smaller ones, comprise all that is left of the "India of the Rajahs," where the feudal age and its customs still survive to a greater or lesser extent, and they acknowledge to-day the suzerainty of the Queen-Empress, as they once did that of the Mogul emperors. The prince, whatever his title may be—Maharajah, Guicowar, Nizam, or Rao—governs his kingdom and administers justice much as his fathers did before the advent of the English; the representative of the viceregal government, or indirectly of the crown, is styled the Political Agent or Resident, and while his official position might be compared to that of a foreign minister at a small European court, it is relatively more important and complicated. He is in effect the political adviser of the governing prince, and through him are transmitted the wishes or commands of the imperial government, which, although they may reach the prince in the shape of polite suggestions, are not to be disregarded. In many states the position of this official personage, this power behind the throne, may appear to be a sinecure, but it may become, without a moment's warning, a position of grave responsibility. Upon the Resident devolves also the duty of looking after his countrymen who come within the borders of his jurisdiction. Not that he is supposed to keep a hotel for globe-trotters, although he never lacks guests, nor is he officially obliged to take any notice of strangers; but he always knows what Europeans are within his borders, and what they are doing. While there is no apparent system of "espionage," and the stranger, of whatever race or nation, is free to come and go at will without of necessity coming in contact with any official whatsoever, there is a provision, and a very clever one, for the entertainment of the casual stranger, which is sufficient for most emergencies. It could be made, without any official action being apparent, exceedingly difficult for any one considered objectionable, or whose motives were liable to suspicion, to find a night's lodging or a "square meal" in most native states. With the exception of Jeypore, I cannot remember any other capital of a native state provided with a hotel, and the "traveller's bungalow" is usually maintained by the Rajah, and is often unprovided with cook or khansamah. This measure, whether intentional or not, is cleverly calculated to keep out European tramps or vagabonds, who do not usually travel accompanied by cooks and servants, while at the same time any one with respectable credentials is sure at least of being well received.

These states of Rajpootana do not seem to suffer from the plethoric excess of population which weighs upon other districts. Since the government has begun to look seriously after the material welfare of its subjects, and has practically abolished war, pestilence, and famine, which were nature's methods of keeping a just balance hitherto, the rapid increase of population in other parts has already become a matter of serious concern, while Rajpootana, and especially the section northwest of the Rajpootana-Malwa Railway, is still a sparsely peopled, half desert country. It is here in these remote states that the ancient prestige of kingship has most completely escaped the levelling tendencies of the age, while at the same time the rising generation of princes are more or less under the influence of Western ideas. The Indian Rajah of to-day, while politically a vassal of the central government, which guarantees to him the autonomy of his state and the continuance of his dynasty, seems actually to enjoy more personal independence than any European sovereign. The cares of state do not weigh so heavily upon him, and he has more time to indulge his personal tastes and to cultivate "fads." This also means a larger opportunity for culture of a higher class if he is disposed to avail himself of it, and there is no reason why he should not begin life as an Eton school-boy, if it is thought best for him, and take his degree at Oxford or elsewhere. A prominent Rajah has just received the degree of LL.D. at Cambridge, and has donated a large sum to the university for the purpose of founding a scholarship. When he returns to his own country and becomes the chief of the state, he may resume at once the mode of life of his predecessors, and remain conservative in the matter of religious observances, immure himself in the impenetrable privacy of his vast and many-windowed stronghold, overlooking the desert from the summit of a rock, or he may build himself a new Italian villa furnished in whatever happens to be the spirit of the latest London art craze, and cultivate a wider social world. Thus we may find in these rulers an infinite variety of type and character, from the strict conservative who is the most complete existing survival of the feudal age to the equally picturesque example in which the feudal age is overlaid with a thick and glossy nineteenth-century varnish. There is the horsy Rajah whose passion is the turf, who imports English jockeys and grooms,* and there is the polo-playing Rajah, and the one who has translated Shakespeare into Hindostanee, as well as the other whose greatest literary feat was the translation of the Queen's *Journal.* There is also the fine old conservative who has but one wife, and slays his tigers with his own hand. These little kings have an easier and a much more royal life than their less fortunate confrères in Europe, where the kingly vocation is hedged about with doubt and uncertainty at present. They are not troubled as yet with socialists, nihilists, or with dynamite, which they regard only as a useful plaything for blowing up rocks and making a noise. The uncensored free press of India has little influence over the masses of their subjects, for the most part loyal to old traditions, but illiterate, and those who can read have scant respect for the

* As early as the beginning of the seventeenth century the Emperor Jehanghis prided himself on his English carriages and horses.

querulous fault-finding of Babu journalists. The modern Rajah has become a prominent figure everywhere. One meets him gazing abstractedly at the passing crowd of rastaquouères and tourists from the steps of the Grand Hôtel, and wearing usually a pair of patent-leather shoes with side elastics, which mar the effect of his otherwise correct attire, or sitting in front of a café at the absinthe hour when he is out of business, or giving a dinner at an open-air restaurant on the Champs-Élysées. We meet him at Aix-les-Bains or at Homburg, and we hear of him in London or Long Branch. We have seen him in lavender and gold turban sitting in a box at the Hippodrome, while the dashing cortége of Roman princesses drove past in chariots. He has the privilege, denied to European sovereigns, of leading at will a double existence, and when he leaves his work in India he has Europe for a playground. The papers from time to time teem with stories of his freaks, his fêtes, and extravagances. Of the reverse side of his life, especially from a political standpoint, those gentlemen of the civil and military service who have been Residents could tell many tales, which it would be unwise to repeat here, as they might mar the effect of the picture. So long as things run smoothly on in his dominion he has little to fear from any disturbing outside elements, and in any case the worst which could happen to him would be a diminution of his salute by one or two guns.*

* The relative importance of a prince is indicated by the number of guns in the salute accorded to him by the government.

II

JODHPORE IN 1887

It is a difficult journey from any quarter to Jodhpore, and cannot well be undertaken without assistance from the Maharajah, as there is much sand, which is best crossed by camels. — *Murray's Guide to the Punjaub*, ed. 1883.

How to get to Jodhpore, and in the event of our getting there should we find any shelter more hospitable than the cold ground, were questions which we tried in vain to solve, until we chanced upon a copy of the Rajpootana-Malwa Railway Guide, in the book-stall at Ahmedabad station. According to that largely circulated but not always reliable authority, it was merely a matter of rupees—six and two annas, first class—and the intervention of the Rajah would be quite unnecessary, as the Jodhpore State Railway, starting from Marwar Junction on the main line, had just been opened.

The second and more momentous question was satisfactorily solved, after having written to the station-master of Jodhpore, and having received in reply a postal-card, stating that there was a dâk bungalow and a khansamah. Upon investigation it appeared that this little railway had two trains a day—one up and the other down; and, as elsewhere in India, both of them either started or arrived at unseasonable hours. We could not take the mail-train from Ahmedabad without waiting twelve hours at Marwar Junction, and the only alternative was to take the "mixed" or slow train, chiefly patronized by natives of the country, who, as we soon learned, were all hurrying to avail themselves of the cheap and comparatively expeditious mode of travel now placed at their disposal by his Highness, assisted by the great British Raj. We were obliged, perforce, to follow their example, pass the night in the train, and get out at the junction at 5 P.M., there to await the departure of the Jodhpore train, an hour later. As we rattled on through the golden green of guava orchards and thick plantations we saw but little change in the landscape since our first visit to India, several years previous. But the monkey population seemed to have largely increased. A correct

WATCHING THE TRAIN

census has not yet been taken, but by-and-by the slow-moving but thorough British Raj will discover that the number of these white-bearded and sacred brigands triples every year, and will consider the necessity of transporting some of them beyond the seas in the interests of the guava culture. We had ample opportunity as the train went on for the study of this guava culture in its different phases. In one orchard the trees were full of the long-tailed marauders: the patriarchs, often of great size and strength, and endowed with supernatural activity, were ripping off fruit—leaves, branches, and all—with no gentle hand, and throwing them down for the benefit of the little ones, while farther on we passed a whole tribe fleeing before the enraged husbandman, not giving themselves overmuch trouble, but easily leaving him and his water-skin out of sight in a few long bounds, and taking refuge like a flight of locusts in the next orchard. But they seemed to enjoy life withal, and those that had finished their day's work and earned a little leisure came down to the embankment and sat in rows to see the train go by, the big ones looking meditatively down at us while the children nestled in front.

In the dry chill of a December morning, and in the dim blue twilight between the waning of the moon and the first flush of dawn, we found ourselves surrounded by our baggage on the platform confronting the clustered white domes of the station at Marwar Junction, which rose up pale and ghostly in the wan light, looking more like the sanctuary of a Moslem saint than a railway junction. Following our "boy" and the baggage coolies, we crossed the tracks to the opposite platform, where we could just make out another train. This train was not yet made up, and the temperature being uncomfortably low outside we settled ourselves in the station-master's office, where we beguiled the time with hot tea, and with watching the Babu ticket-seller doling out third-class tickets to natives at his little window, a function accompanied by much bullying and browbeating on his part, and vexation of spirit on theirs. Every piece of money which he took, after being well tried and rung, was often as not flung back in the face of the humble passenger, accompanied by a volley of abuse if he was not quick enough in getting out his change from the bulky hoard of copper "pice" tied up in the end of his turban or in a fold of the waist-cloth; and one could not but wonder at the patience and resignation with which they all received the insolence of Jack-in-office. When no fault could be found with the money he threw their tickets at them, and slammed down their change with such vehemence that bits of it rolled off on the floor. At last the station-master, tall and spectacled, in a flat black velvet cap and an English sack-coat, from which a quantity of white cotton drapery escaped and floated loosely about his thin, bare legs, came out to unlock the door of the compartment we were to occupy; and after installing ourselves as the train crawled slowly out at sunrise, we began the day with a substantial "chota hazri" from the store put up at the Ahmedabad bungalow. For the greater part of the way the line seemed to have no embankment, and to consist of a single track laid down in the desert, with the merest sketch of a road-bed. The country was not a desert of the sandy sort, but only a waste of gravel, for the most part treeless, except for rare and scattered thickets of gray thorny bushes, or distant clumps of trees indicating the position of a village. Where the plain did not merge into the sky the horizon was a range of low hills, varied by occasional isolated peaks, with sharp volcanic outlines, which dwindled as we approached them into brown, mound-like eminences of no great height. On the top of every telegraph pole was perched a hawk, a kite, or a buzzard, always motionless; and, in truth, the rate of speed at which the Rajah's train crept slowly over the sixty-four miles of gravel was not likely to interfere with their digestive meditations.

When we reached a village, or even a flag-house, with a collection of mud huts in the background, we made a lengthy halt, and when the engineer met an acquaintance we came to a stand-still; and on all these occasions the gaunt, jackal-faced village dogs trotted alongside for miles, looking wistfully up for the chance bone or crust of bread, or they ran on ahead and barked at the engine. These capricious halts did not, as might be supposed, subject us to the risk of collision, since our train comprised the company's entire rolling-stock. A dapper little Thakor or princeling of some sort entered the other compartment of our carriage at one of the way stations, and his crowd of retainers got into third-class carriages some distance off. As he stepped out at every station to issue orders to his people, we had several opportunities of observing him. He was a fair type of the Jodhpore swell, young, with a budding mustache, and hair brought down in a large glistening curl over each cheek. His small pink turban, dainty as a lady's breakfast-cap, was cocked jauntily on one side, and he wore a caftan of striped and rainbow-tinted silk; he kindled a fresh cigarette at each station, and his little air of insolent swagger was quite in harmony with the rakish set of his turban and his aggressive side-locks. It is now a long time since these mediæval swashbucklers have had a chance to exercise their hereditary calling, but a little taste of guerilla warfare would not come amiss to them. At one of these stations, where he had sent a servant to look for a clean handkerchief among his luggage, the train had to wait until it was forthcoming. The conductor, a native having a few words of English at his command, looked in at the window from time to time, and evidently took a deep interest in our welfare, for he seemed much concerned when he learned that we had no acquaintances in Jodhpore, but felt relieved when I explained that we had notified the khansamah at the dâk bungalow of our coming. Towards noon we sighted a long, steep ridge of rocks with

PALACE WINDOWS, JODHPORE

scattered white buildings on the top, and others gleaming among gardens on the plain; and as we drew nearer we saw that the white spots on the ridge were part of the vast pile of architecture erected centuries ago by the Rajahs of Jodhpore, and placed like an eagle's nest on the very summit of this inaccessible crag. When we reached the station, which resembles another saint's tomb with white domes, it was at once evident that the arrival of the train was still the event of the day in this hitherto isolated capital, for a large part of the population had assembled outside, and was looking eagerly over the fence—a long line of brown faces, with well-oiled black locks curling over their ears, with mustaches and beards, all having the piratical upward tilt affected by the Rajpoot order. Nearly all were in white, with dashes of red and gold; women and children filled up the interstices, and behind them stretched a plain of glaring red sand, back to the gray line of battlemented walls which hid the town. In the faint shadow cast by a few young acacia-trees which had been recently planted in the sand groups of fiery little horses were tethered, and slender camels with the double saddles in vogue here, all decked out with yellow and scarlet harnesses and saddle-cloths, with strings of blue beads, charms, and gaudy housings; there were also bullock-gharries with tented domes of faded red, and a large barouche, superannuated and dusty. Two low square buildings of dark stone like the station, and likewise painfully new, stood a little farther down the sandy track leading to the town. One of them was the bungalow; and having gathered our belongings, and intrusted the various packages to baggage-coolies, we hurried across to our quarters; for the glare of noon here, even in December, makes any shelter seem inviting. The little prince was driven away in the barouche, surrounded by a compact mob of men, some running in front and some behind, all carrying swords and guns. The tall camels, each with a pair of swaying riders, and the procession of slower-moving bullock-carts, followed in the rear. We were met on the veranda by a smirking and salaaming khansamah of a debased Rajpoot type, who announced, as he lifted the cane mat which hung over the door, that tiffin was ready.

The bungalow, being brand-new and clean, was not uninviting, but, as usual, our quarters were not overburdened with furniture — two "charpies," or native bedsteads, guiltless of any covering whatever to conceal the nakedness of the net-work of stout tape on which the traveller is expected to lay his weary frame; for he is still supposed to carry his bedding whenever he goes far afield into "Mofussil" districts—to use the current phrase for whatever is beyond Calcutta and Bombay. In the middle of the room stood a square table holding the "tiffin" and two or three chairs. A door at one corner opened into the bath-room, furnished with a decrepit wash-stand, a brass basin, and a wooden tub which had seen service long before the existence of this bungalow: all bath-rooms which I have seen in India, whether in private houses (with few exceptions) or in hotels, are of one uniform pattern. There is a chunar, or cement floor, and the space where the tub stands is fenced off by a low parapet of cement, on which a row of round and unwieldy pots of red clay stand in depressions. They are too bulky to lift, and exhibit an unpleasant tendency when molested to slop over on the wrong side and pour their contents over one's shoes, so that it is safer not to go near them. From the front veranda (for there was another veranda, on to which a door opened at the opposite end) a landscape of red sand lay before us, bounded by the line of gray walls; one or two massive and sombre-hued trees rose above the wall, and over all the distant castle built upon the rock. We were awakened early on the following morning by the deep and guttural croaking of the ravens, which strutted about on the veranda or sat on the door-steps. The ceaseless cawing of the ubiquitous crow we were already accustomed to, but the sudden rasping croak of a raven uttered a few yards from the sleeper's ear has quite the effect of an alarm-clock.

Having ascertained that there were no carriages to be had for mere lucre, no Parsee livery-stable, and not a vehicle of any sort, I left the "mem sahib" on the veranda, and proceeded on foot to hunt up the Political Agent, and to take in the town on the way. It was not a long tramp through the sand to the nearest gate, and the mystery of the silent gray walls and what might lay behind them would have stimulated one to far greater exertion. Within the gateway there was deeper sand, a few large trees, some ruinous shells of masonry, and rough stone walls masking the gardens behind. Taking the most promising of two or three narrow streets which began at this point, we kept on in the shadow of fortress-like houses, often of red stone, and sometimes white-washed. The rare balconied windows usually projected over tall pointed gateways, and through many of them we entered, first asking of the gate-keeper, or whoever we happened to encounter inside, permission to look about the court-yard, and we invariably met with courtesy.

The façades fronting on this outer court are decorated with the usual wealth of delicate stone tracery, and often the story above, resting on plain and massive arcades, is one continuous latticed gallery, projecting well outward, relieved by ornate little windows at intervals. In one quarter a few groups of palaces surrounded a large tank.

One of them, built of red sandstone of exactly the same color and value as the sand in front, seemed to me then—and will always seem, for I have kept a study of it—a marvellous combination of massive simplicity and graceful, but not excessive, decoration. The walls, which rose directly from the sand of the road, save for a species of ramp in front, leading up to the high Persian arch of the entrance, were unrelieved below by a single ornamental detail, while all the decoration was lavished on the projecting windows above. The great central window over the gate had the curved cornice* or window-cap characteristic of the later Mogul style, the panels were filled in with beautiful stone lace-work, while on either side were slender bay-windows of varied forms. Through the open gate below the green foliage of the garden made a pleasing note in the expanse of red. The beauty of this façade was greatly enhanced by the fantastic shadows thrown on the flat wall by these various projections. Beyond this building the road passes under a sulphur-tinted arch, forming part of a house lavishly sculptured and frescoed. We had ascertained by inquiry that there was as yet no "Residency," and that this road led to the camp where the Political Agent was living in tents. Presently it led us into what looked like the outskirts of a country fair or a colossal travelling show. Booths and tents became thicker on both sides; there were itinerant merchants, sweetmeat-sellers, grooms leading blanketed horses, an elephant or two divested of their gaudy overcoats, and busily tucking away vast quantities of forage; a number of riding-camels were tethered in one place, and pompous chamberlains in scarlet-and-gold liveries strutted about with tall silver maces. Over the tops of

* Alluded to by Fergusson as the Bengali curved cornice.

the tents a showily decorated and galleried wooden structure, like the grand-stand at a race-course, rose in the background. We were directed to the tent of the Political Agent, where I sent in my card by the bearer. Should one's first initiation into tent life have been in Palestine, he may remember that it was fairly comfortable; in Persia, both comfortable and decorative; but not until he reaches India will he find its highest development, and it is within the limits of possibility that he may come to regard a house, which has always the same outlook from the windows, and which cannot be folded up and set down again in a new landscape, as vastly inferior to a tent. A canvas corridor led into the grateful obscurity of the inner sanctum, where a double roof kept out the glare and the heat of the sun.

I found the Agent sitting at a table littered with books and papers, and although in this instance an introduction of some sort would have facilitated matters, our mission was soon explained. He rode over on the following morning to my quarters, while I was sketching in the town, and in the afternoon one of the Rajah's carriages came to take us to the castle. The two syces who ran in front to clear the way had work to do, for Jodhpore streets were not intended for wheeled vehicles; and, fortunately for the Jodhpore world, visitors do not often invade its narrow bazaars, for all business seemed to be suspended during our transit, and we felt like apologizing to the citizens for disturbing the placid current of their daily life. As there was no pavement even of the most rudimentary sort, the wheels sank noiselessly in the deep sand, and much shouting and brandishing of sticks were necessary to warn the people of our approach. The crowds dissolved noiselessly in front, and the various units of which they were constituted backed up in rows against walls and doorways or the parapets of water-tanks, forgetting for a moment their Rajpoot dignity, their traffic and gossiping, but placing themselves so as to have a good view of us; the little milk-white bullocks, humpbacked and sacred as they were, had to be ignominiously hustled off on one side, often at great risk to their slender hind-legs; droves of donkeys, loaded with sand or stone or firewood, were driven down side alleys or up on door-steps; and sometimes a philanthropic Brahmin would swoop down in front of the horses, regardless of peril, to rescue some heedless puppy from the wheels. Through the dust in front we could discern frightened camels rearing and bucking, and finally bolting off with their riders, while nothing could induce the buffaloes to stand their ground and face the onset of the running syces, shouting: "The sahib comes!—he comes! he comes!"

We halted in a small open square near a water-tank surrounded by temples. Here we had to get down, as the causeway which led up to the castle was too steep for the carriage. At the beginning of the ascent we passed under an outer tower guarded by soldiers, between heavy gates thickly covered with long spikes, and closed by an enormous bolt fully two feet in length. The road, becoming steeper as we mounted, was paved with slippery slabs of stone, and in many places the sloping ledges had been smoothed over, leaving a natural pavement. Parties of dashing cavaliers, arrayed in brocade or fine muslin, each with his little turban so placed as not to hide the handiwork of the Rajpoot barber, galloped or trotted past us, keeping their seats with jaunty ease in spite of the treacherous stones. At the top of the first rise a tall yellow gateway spanned the road, showing a patch of deep blue sky under the arch, and overhung by the jutting red windows of the palace. A sharp turn to the right brought us to the inner barbican of the citadel and the entrance of the palace itself; a few old palanquins and dilapidated elephant-howdahs were piled up on the ramp in front. Within the shadow of the arch we found a museum of antiquated fire-arms: matchlocks and shields were hung on the guard-house walls, and there were curious swivel-guns and mountain-batteries, formerly carried on the backs of elephants and camels—rows of musket-barrels, six or eight in number, strapped down on a thick plank, so that they might be fired at once, but it must have taken patience to load them in the face of a charging enemy. From the group of soldiers and retainers lounging within the recess of the gate-tower, or lying stretched at ease on charpies, a carelessly dressed fellow, who seemed nevertheless superior in rank to the others, came out and offered to do the honors of the palace. But there was a lurking drollery in his manner, which seemed to say that he was playing the part of guide mainly for his own inward entertainment. When we saw him the next day, blazing with scarlet and gold, riding at the head of the Rajah's cavalry escort, we congratulated ourselves on not having offered him backsheesh, which, however, he would probably have pocketed as part of the farce. Beyond the gate we came to a battery consisting of a row of extraordinary pieces of ordnance, which must have been as old as the Spanish Armada at least; these guns were fashioned in the likeness of crocodiles, marine monsters, or crouching tigers, and mounted on dilapidated and decaying carriages. One or two of them, more conventional in form, were of enormous size.

From the edge of the terrace, which was simply a platform of the natural rock, and without rail or parapet, we looked down full four hundred feet, past the white backs of wheeling vultures, on the flat roofs of Jodhpore, and

CASTLE OF THE RAJAHS OF JODHPORE

far abroad over the barren plains. Directly below us were the tanks, two squares of intense blue, reflecting the sky overheard; and as we turned back, the great red palace, a vast collection of grated stone windows, seemed to hang above us like tiers of ornamental bird-cages. A few steps led up to an open court, or rather terrace, overlooked on three sides by the latticed cages. According to report, some hundred ladies of the late Rajah's household are still sheltered behind these perforated prison walls, but they gave no sign of their presence. The pavement was partly covered by a faded but beautiful old carpet; and crossing an elevated marble platform, we entered by a low door of repoussé silver-work the wilderness of courts and cloisters, of narrow corridors and pillared halls and little boudoirs, where the delicate stone tracery of the windows softened like a filmy veil the light of the vast canopy of sky and the far-reaching desert landscape. One long dim chamber, with two richly furnished beds, was hung, walls and pillars alike, with old portraits of the emperors and the kings of Delhi, by native artists. We came out at last in a small marble court at the top of the palace, which was partly open to the sky, and which had been a favorite sleeping-room of the old Rajah. Mirrors, more or less tarnished, were fixed in the walls on every side, and suspended from the roof by chains hung a swinging bed of heavy silver, on which were piled the embroidered cushions as they were left by the last occupant, but now frayed and dusty with time and neglect. When we returned to the city, through the many gates, down the slippery causeway, stopping again and again to enjoy the changing panorama, and found the carriage waiting in the square among the temples, the sun was already sinking; and as we drove back through the red sand of the city the passing figures of people and the tall camels, each with a pair of riders sociably swaying in unison, one behind the other, with the same rhythmic and regular movement, loomed up through a haze of golden dust, which shone like an aureole behind their heads; the silhouettes of those in the track of the sun were quite enveloped in the glory of light, while those nearest us and in the shadow reflected the pale violet and lilac hues of the eastern sky. The streets were as free from the noise of traffic which one is accustomed to associate with a crowded quarter as the waterways of Venice: our wheels made no noise as they sank in the sand, there was no sound of footfalls, so that the voices of the people chaffering, laughing, or disputing were preternaturally clear and distinct; and when for a moment these sounds died away, the silent hurrying figures seen through the haze, mingled with the pungent aromatic smoke of the brush fires, seemed like dream-people, intangible and unreal.

The market-place, a vast parallelogram of sand in the centre of the town, is enclosed by low white arcades, entered by four gates, and swarming with life on two or three days in the week. From this point one has the most impressive view of the castle. Just beyond the arcades rises the steep bare precipice, defended in places by castellated forts; the precipice merges into a white wall of colossal height, partly of masonry and partly the rock itself; and above the wall rises the castle, like a compact walled city, with pointed spires of temples, tall battlemented towers, and its multitude of red latticed windows. It looks as impregnable as the Matterhorn, and even a scaling party of Swiss guides would find work in reaching the base of the great walls.

The western wall of the city touches a range of scarred and sombre volcanic rocks, and a rough and stony caravan track which left the metalled road at this point and led up into a deep gorge was a favorite resort of ours just before sunset. When we pushed on to a little pass between gaunt black cliffs like the crater of a volcano, and could look down through a ragged notch towards the setting sun, a desert of sand stretched before us, bordered by dark ranges of desolate hills; it was not altogether devoid of vegetation, for just beyond the opening the road wound among the stems of stunted and thorny trees, and the deep-lying hollows were swampy and filled with the waving plumes of tall dry canes. Here we often sat, perched high up in a nook among the crags, to watch the trains of pack-horses or laden camels hurrying through the pass so that they might reach the level road and the gates of the city before nightfall, which follows so closely on the afterglow. And if we waited on until twilight, and until the voices of the last belated camel-driver had died away in the distance, we could sometimes make out far down in the gulley below the shadowy forms of jackals moving furtively among the stones and underbrush, and occasionally a hyena would come out into the light and utter a prolonged wail. Once we discovered a vulture's nest placed on a shelf of rock near the city wall, and while meditating upon the feasibility of scaling the cliff, in order to have a look at it, we were approached by a saintly looking personage, probably a priest from the neighboring temple, who directed a stream of voluble oratory at us, sometimes rising to vehement exhortation, and again falling to tones of gentle and persuasive remonstrance. We could not but admire his elocution; but having left our factotum and interpreter behind, as it was our custom when weary of his presence, I have never been able to divine the subject of his discourse — whether it was an impassioned argument in behalf of the vultures, or whether it was merely a summary of his views in regard to the "Ilbert Bill."

III

The society which watches over the welfare of animals might find work in Jodhpore, if one may place faith in a story which we heard shortly after leaving that city. The narrator, a young man who was at the bungalow during our stay, was detained after our departure by some business with the Rajah, and he was invited to be present at some local "sports" peculiar to the country. Two leopards which had been taken alive were brought into the arena, where they were held down to the ground under *charpies* by a number of coolies. Their claws were then drawn out with pincers, their teeth extracted or cut out, and their tails also cut off, after which they were let loose, and the native gentlemen present then turned to and clubbed them to death with sticks. Not having witnessed the spectacle ourselves, we cannot vouch for the accuracy of this history, but merely repeat it as it was told to us a few days later by the gentleman who had seen the performance. On the morning of our departure, and just before going to the station, a long procession passed along the dusty road under the gray walls, escorting the chief of some neighboring province, who was on his way to the durbar. His favorite horse, draped with scarlet cloth, was led at the head of the cavalry escort, a squadron of loosely dressed horsemen armed with swords and lances; behind were camels and horses carrying kettle-drums draped with red cloth: other retainers carried scarlet and gold banners, silver fly-brushes, maces, and other emblems of authority; and then came a motley crowd of foot-soldiers armed with rifles. But the Rajah himself was hidden behind the crimson silk drapery spangled with silver stars, which was thrown over his palanquin; a long line of tented ox-carts (closely curtained) followed behind, which probably contained the ladies of his household. When we reached the railway station the Rajah of Jodhpore and one of his brothers were on the platform. His Highness, we were told, was in the habit of passing much of his royal leisure there when the line was first opened, and had caused a handsomely furnished reception-room to be fitted up, whence he could view the arrival and departure of the trains. On this occasion both he and his brother were costumed in what their tailor considered the latest thing in English "sporting kit," and in which they resembled the travelling Britons as they appear on the stage of a Parisian theatre. Both wore shooting-jackets and knickerbockers of very pronounced plaids, and the brother carried a dagger stuck in one of his high boots; great "solar topees"* with veils twisted around them completed their attire. The Indian, of whatever rank or caste, never looks his best in a white helmet, which usually gives him the air of a half-caste butler. A few months later we saw him again from the estrade near the Haymarket, on the occasion of the Queen's Jubilee. He was seated in a barouche with other princes, following the Queen's carriage, and somewhere between the splendid escort of Indian officers behind her Majesty and the squadron of Lifeguards in the rear. He looked a different man in his own traditional costume, thickly jewelled and blazing with diamonds.

* Sun-hats.

IV

BIKANIR IN 1893

At the Colonial Exhibition in London some years ago there was a collection of large photographs which looked as if they might have been taken in the days of Saladin. One of them represented a group of warriors in shirts of chain-mail and steel bascinets, mounted on camels, and armed with lances, drawn up in line in front of a vast palace standing alone in a plain of sand. They proved upon inquiry to have been taken at Bikanir, a place which no one seemed to know anything about, except that it was the capital of an ancient Rajpoot state, in the midst of a waterless desert, very far from anything else, and difficult of access. Just before my arrival in India last year the Jodhpore State Railway had been extended to Bikanir, and through trains had been put on, running from Marwar Junction to Bikanir in twenty-seven hours, more or less. Having ascertained that the necessary bungalow existed, and could be occupied "by order of the Regency Council," I decided to avail myself of an opportunity which might not come twice.

At night, Marwar Junction, January 15, 1893.—A crowd of squatting figures, most of them in dirty white raiment, are grouped around the flaring torches of sweetmeat-venders and others who sell "chupatties," hot and greasy, or ladle out a thick white paste from iron pots. An occasional sharp cry of anguish escapes from an inquisitive pariah dog who has pushed his investigations too far. Near by there is a covered waiting-place for third-class passengers, where they all squat or recline, closely huddled together, men, women, and babies, behind the stone arches of the open arcade, lighted by two dim lanterns. Just before the arrival of the mail-train a short, portly Babu, with pen behind his ear, stations himself at the gate, ticket-punch in hand. The gate-posts are iron rails stuck in the ground, and the barrier is constructed of two telegraph wires strung from post to post. A fierce rush takes place when the gate is opened. But the entrance is only wide enough for one to pass at a time, and the Babu, like brave Horatius, holds his own against the tide until the arrival of two black-bearded policemen armed with rattans. On comes the struggling horde of third-class passengers, those behind pushing the foremost into the breach where only one may pass, a sea of swarthy faces with glittering eyes which stand out in the circle of light from the lantern in startling relief against the blackness of the night. Many of these faces have an almost tragic intensity of expression—there are momentary gleams of rage, despair, anxiety, fatalistic resignation. All of these people are loaded down with burdens; some carry huge bundles of bedding, guns, and sabres, others brandish umbrellas; rounded arms sheathed to the shoulder in lacquer bracelets protrude here and there from the seething mass; babies are tightly held and shrouded behind embroidered shawls. But the Babu spares neither age, sex, nor caste, neither the orange-clothed fakir with painted face nor the women weighed down with bundles, babies, and brazen pots, and while they fumble for their tickets the policemen rain blows with their canes on the shoulders of the pushing mob behind. Many faces express positive fear, and one patient old man, who has been thrust back again and again, is pushed forward into the opening by the pressure from behind, but is forced to bide his time while the Babu puts on his turban, which had fallen off in the fray. He repre-

FIRST-CLASS COMPARTMENT ON THE ROAD TO BIKANIR

sents the government with official severity, and when once the gate is closed in the faces of those who are unprovided with tickets, or who have lost them, protestations and despairing gestures are vain, no explanations are listened to, and the Babu saunters off serenely to the platform, where the steady jingle of the electric bell announces the approach of the train.

V

The Jodhpore and Bikanir mail left at the usual early hour. I was fortunate enough to find an empty compartment, and, in fact, there was no other European on the train. The life along the road had lost nothing of its primitive character. At "Metra Road" some belated passengers mounted on camels were hurrying to catch the train along the sandy track which led from the distant village. They were perched high upon the double-seated saddles of the country, and each pair of riders clung fraternally to each other as they bobbed up and down, keeping time to the bone-breaking strides of their camels. While the master, wearing the jaunty little Jodhpore turban above his well-oiled locks, sat in front, the servant took the back seat, holding aloft in one hand the family "hookah." At the station the camels knelt down, bubbling and moaning, while their riders descended and hurried in to buy their tickets. Here the guard telegraphed to Jodhpore, that tiffin might be ready on our arrival; for should one neglect to take this precaution he would probably find nothing to eat but oranges and fat "chupatties," and to drink, only coffee-colored water poured from goat-skins. Everywhere in India, and more particularly in these native states, people are in the habit of carrying about with them considerable live-stock of various kinds.

To be more specific, I refer to the mammals and birds trained to assist in the capture of game; and as a natural consequence the railway hand-books abound with curious information and rules interesting to the naturalist. "Sheep, pigs, goats, calves, if sent singly, small tame *deer*, etc., and *tiger*, *panther*, and *cheetah cubs* in cages, and which are so young as to be harmless, if carried by passenger trains, are charged at double the *dog* rates for each animal. . . . Cats, ferrets, mongooses, monkeys, and rabbits, secured with a collar and chain, are chargeable as dogs." *

Prudent natives, when shifting their quarters during the snake season, frequently take along the family mongoose as a precautionary measure. For those unfamiliar with this unprepossessing but harmless little beast it may be here remarked that he belongs to the ichneumon caste, and as his vocation is the killing of snakes, he is everywhere a welcome visitor. He looks something like an undersized otter, is quick and spasmodic in his movements, and is often found under the bed in a long-vacant dâk bungalow, whence he suddenly scuttles away as the door is opened, and disappears with a whisk of his tail in the chimney-place or down the nearest hole.

At one station four coolies passed along the platform carrying aloft a *charpie*, on which reposed a cheetah, chained and blindfolded. When we first caught sight of him he was sitting up like a cat, with his ears lying flat against his head, wearing the sulky and injured look which all felines have under adverse circumstances. A

* "Camels and elephants are not booked except under special arrangements." Another item refers to "cremated sacred relics" (Allahabad *Pioneer*). "Human ashes in dust-tight cases, fifth class, or ditto securely packed in air-tight cases, by passenger train, at full passenger rates; but when accompanying passengers, at luggage rates."

few passengers who got off before we reached Jodhpore were provided with falcons and hawks, some of them so large and bulky as to be rather unwieldy; and while these passengers fumbled for their tickets, the birds sat on their shoulders, or balanced themselves on their voluminous turbans. The train reached Jodhpore at noon, and made a long halt. In the little restaurant tiffin for one was ready on the table, and for the sum of one rupee was uncommonly liberal in quantity. Ham and eggs, chops, and a broiled chicken were the principal items which were inscribed on the unvarying bill of fare framed and hung on the wall. The environs of the station were hardly recognizable, so great had been the change in six years. Where all had been sand before there were now dense gardens, and the dark and glossy green foliage tempered the rawness of the new stone houses which had sprung up on every side. Had it not been for the distant castle and the desert ridge, one might have fancied one's self in some new suburban town of the far West. From this point on, the line is new, and after leaving the station we passed close to the modern palace of the Rajah, built of dark red stone, with numerous white cupolas, and covering a great extent of ground.

While the train waited at Jodhpore a portly and consequential personage entered the compartment, attended as far as the door by a youth in a crimson frock-coat ornamented with black velvet collar and cuffs and brass buttons, and wearing yellow plaid breeches and a scarlet turban. The personage wore gold rings on his toes as well as in his ears, and he was followed by several retainers, who spread out his bedding on the opposite divan, and after making him comfortable they all left for their own compartments.

Either from curiosity, or from a desire to be agreeable

THIRD-CLASS PASSENGERS

—for the Indian who has not travelled much in English-speaking countries still considers it a mark of courtesy to show an interest in his fellow-man—my vis-à-vis proceeded to open a conversation. Motee, who had been installed on the platform, was called in to interpret, and, having explained my object in visiting Bikanir to my fellow-traveller, he announced himself to be a member of the Regency Council of that state. Now there is one thing in which the Indian caste system is more fortunate than ours. He who is born to the purple wears his birthright emblazoned on his forehead in the shape of a caste-mark. He has besides a distinguishing costume, and moreover his face shows the hereditary stamp of his race, so that there is no mistaking any one of baser origin for a member of that limited but august order. Either his dress or his caste-mark are equivalent to the legend sometimes seen on the patent-medicine bottles, "To imitate this is felony," and indeed it would be felony of the deepest dye, unpardonable in this world or the next, to infringe on the Rajpoot patent of nobility. During our journey to Bikanir the councillor frequently partook of food, strange homœopathic little messes of yellow paste, pomegranate seeds, and sliced cucumbers in small glass dishes, while he gossiped with his "bearer," who served them on a tray at his feet. When time hung heavy on his hands he would get up and change some article of clothing, and late in the afternoon his servants brought him an entire outfit, assisting him first to pull off his thin under-vest, showing an expanse of glossy brown skin. They then proceeded to wind him up in a long piece of warm-tinted white muslin of delicate, filmy texture, and bordered with red. This function, like exercise, seemed to renew his appetite, and he had another "go" at the little glass dishes. A sliding-door at one end of the compartment opened on to a narrow platform with a leather seat at each end, which could be opened across the platform or shut down against the rail when not in use. Prior to the advent of my fellow-traveller I had occupied the time either with writing inside, or had found absorbing interest in the pages of the *Tragic Muse** in the intervals of studying the landscape from the platform seat. As there was room enough for both of us outside, we now studied it together; what he thought of it I know not. It certainly was monotonous, and grim enough it would have seemed under any other heaven than the soft winter sky of India; and although far from being a desert at this season, it must look parched and burned up indeed when the hot winds sweep across it in the spring-time, and every spot of green has disappeared. In the long, dry stretches of jungle-grass herds of antelopes or gazelles were browsing, seldom showing any fear at the approach of the train, and lifting up their heads to look, or racing along for a few rods, springing clear of the grass at each bound, and pausing in wonder, with their slender ears at right angles, when they began to lose ground. At sundown the train waited for a time at a small station in what appeared to be open country, for no town or village was visible in any direction. Two women and a little girl got down and sat in the sand near the platform, while their male attendant packed up their voluminous bedding and bundles, together with pots, kettles, and swords. Both ladies were young and richly costumed, judging from the bits of embroidery, jewelry, and innumerable bangles which were revealed when for a moment they drew aside the transparent shawls with which they veiled their faces. Their persistence in keep-

* The railway book-stall at Ajmeer is quite up to date as regards recent literature, and our own popular authors, together with Kipling and Tolstoï, seem to be the favorites.

AT A WAY STATION NEAR BIKANIR

ing their faces covered, and their small hands and feet showed that they belonged to a higher caste than the man. The demure little girl was so laden with ornaments that she looked like a jewelled idol. When everything had been packed, and the bundles of bedding placed on a low two-wheeled cart drawn by milk-white bullocks, they all mounted and drove away into the open country towards the red western sky.

We were to arrive at Bikanir in the small hours of the early morning, and as the January nights are cold at this latitude,* I had told Motee not to let them rout me up before 8 A.M.

But little of the city can be seen from the station—only the massive outer walls and gateways, and the outline of a strangely shaped, almost pyramidal gray tower.

* Bikanir lies on the twenty-eighth parallel north latitude.

At Bikanir.—A foot-path through sand and low scrub led to the bungalow. It was liberally, not to say palatially, furnished in comparison with the average Indian hotel. A number of glass doors opened from the veranda into a large common room, and there were glass doors on the three other sides. The state seemed to have furnished its guest-house as if to attract a class of visitors accustomed to lavish profusion in the matter of tables and chairs, but who expected nothing to eat, for there was neither cook nor khansamah. Drawn up sociably in front of the fire-place were two roomy lounges, and an ornamental *causeuse* occupied the centre of the room. A varied assortment of arm-chairs and tables was scattered about; the tall, gaudily colored cut-glass lamps, the table service, and plated silver all looked as if ordered without regard to expense, while the two sleeping-rooms also contained a superabundance of furniture. I had neglected to provide myself with letters, having decided to make the trip only at the last moment, and if Motee had not unexpectedly proclaimed his skill as a cook, I should have been obliged to wire down to Jodhpore for something to eat, or appeal to the Resident. He, however, kindly offered me a letter to the chief of the Regency Council, actually the head of the state during the minority of the Rajah, who was still a school-boy at Ajmeer. The great fortress and palace of Bikanir bring to mind the Arab proverb concerning "the prince who builds a palace and ruins a city," for, as is frequently the case in Rajpootana, its magnitude is out of all proportion to the size of the city grouped about it. Although placed on the same level as the town, and without the advantages of an elevated position, like the castles of Jodhpore and Gwalior, it is still an imposing and magnificent pile. Surrounded by massive sloping walls, with embrasures for cannon, and entered by a drawbridge crossing a wide moat, and guarded by sentinels, who present arms as the carriage rattles over it into the gate between two round flanking towers, it looks quite fit to sustain a siege. Over the entrance rises a tall clock-tower, and beyond are gates within gates, opening into narrow courts, some of them with whitened walls, and others displaying great frescoes of tiger-hunts or triumphal processions. At the last gate two life-sized elephants carved in stone and gaudily painted, each with his mahout astride of his neck, stood facing each other; they resembled on a larger scale the painted toys sold in Bombay shops. Towering many stories above the court-yard rose the façade of the palace, with endless tiers of latticed galleries shaded by faded red curtains. Hundreds of vultures and crows circled above, or lighted on the pinnacles and domes which broke the regularity of the sky-line. The highest point of all was a sloping pyramidal roof of blue glazed tiles. Passing through still another gate, we found the chief in his office, protected by a sign with the legend "No Admittance." He was a perfect type of the veteran statesman; his English was unimpeachable; but what I remember most vividly at the present moment was a certain charm of manner peculiar to the cultured Oriental. When I asked him about his camel cavalry, he rang a little electric bell and sent off a servant, who presently reappeared with some superb photographs representing the whole regiment drawn up in the desert, but in place of the steel veiled and armored bandits were stalwart troopers uniformed and turbaned like her Majesty's Sikhs. He presented me with a hand-book to Bikanir written by himself in English, and, accompanied by a custodian, we set out on a tour of the palace. It is highly improbable that any European has ever seen the whole of a Rajah's palace, unless it be one that is uninhabited, but the number

PALACE OF THE RAJAH OF BIKANIR

of apartments shown are sufficiently bewildering to leave only the most confused impressions, and of this palace in particular I retain a distinct recollection of only two or three rooms. There were several janitors, each having charge of a series of apartments opening on a court—for the most part venerable old men decorated with huge yellow caste-marks on their foreheads, and each carried, depending from a ring at his girdle, a great bunch of long steel slips curiously notched, with which he opened successive doors quite as if he were performing a religious ceremony of great solemnity. Opening on to the highest terrace of all there were two salons or sleeping-rooms, for there were beds in both, which were curiously interesting on account of the piquant blending of Eastern art with the products of Western taste. Both rooms were lighted from a narrow exterior gallery, which seemed almost to overhang the boundless red desert, and the sunshine which filtered through stained glass, filling the interstices of the lattice-work, fell on the minutely painted walls of the gallery and inlaid ivory doors of the inner room. Flowery but faded European carpets covered the floors within, and the furniture, mahogany and brass and rose-colored damask, had the stamp of the First Empire. In one corner stood a bedstead with silver legs of Indian design; but what gave to the place its peculiar *cachet* was its collection of exotic curiosities grouped on the tables, and carefully protected by glass globes. There was a ship under full sail tossing on a stormy sea of green glass, a swallow embalmed among gilt flowers, and a leathery and hairless stuffed cat playing on a harp. There was also an abundance of clocks, one of the familiar Connecticut brand with pointed apex, but with one of its pinnacles missing, and another clock placed in the broad stomach of a very jovial sailor.

In the new section of the palace the court-yard just above the great outer keep is still unfinished, and the arcades, richly sculptured in relief, although certainly not Indian in design, are strangely original and not unpleasing. We entered from this court the new series of apartments which had been furnished apparently by a London upholsterer. New and smart furniture in unimpeachable London taste filled the great drawing-room, and there were hanging-shelves and étagères which might have come from Maple's. A large photograph of the Queen-Empress was displayed on a table, and the carpets alone had a taint of the East. They were made in the Bikanir jail, woven from ancient Persian designs, following the original models with absolute fidelity both in color and pattern, and were shaped to fit each nook and recessed

MARKET-PLACE, BIKANIR

window. The vast palace-yard, beyond the elephant gate, seemed to be the centre of life, and was never quiet at any hour of the day. Groups of servants, soldiers, and retainers were continually passing in and out, while here and there a little knot of men, liveried in scarlet and yellow or in white, squatted on their heels around the bubbling hookah, and each group formed the nucleus of a changing crowd; for all appeared to have abundance of leisure, and each loiterer stopped to gossip a moment as he passed through the court. At times there was a wild outburst of barking from the swarm of pariah dogs and puppies in all stages of growth which were scattered about the place; countless pigeons, kites, buzzards, crows, and vultures were ceaselessly whirling about, or settling on the projecting cornices of the palace, and filling the air with the noise of their wings, their shrill screams, and never-ending clamor. Just before noon a burst of barbaric music was added by way of interlude to this intermittent concert, preceded by a prolonged and ear-piercing blowing of horns and trumpets; towards sunset a service of some kind was celebrated by the orange-robed priests of the little temple, accompanied by a harmonious and distant chanting of boyish voices. Three great elephants drawn up in line awaited us on our return to the bungalow, and the scarlet of their robes burned like a flame against the green foliage. They had been trained to raise their trunks and bellow forth a most effective salute.

The streets of the town—and particularly the ornate little houses carved in red sandstone—while they have a general resemblance to those of Jodhpore, have yet a distinct local character. It would seem as if the citizens had built their houses of sand, and had caused the desert to bloom, as it were, into this florid efflorescence of delicate arabesques and fanciful sculptured ornaments, for all

STREET IN BIKANIR

is of the same color and texture as the sand of the streets. An equally strange and persistent impression remained that the houses of this remote capital had a certain affinity with our own, as if some appreciative native had recently visited America and had brought back with him the idea of the artistic little homes of Boston or Philadelphia, and had been particularly struck with the deeply recessed front door and the steps leading up to it. Upon this fundamental idea he had engrafted the elaborate surface decoration of Hindoo artisans, and had thrown out his bay-windows on the story above.

Although many of them may be of ancient date, a still greater number have been recently built, and indicate a certain degree of financial prosperity; and yet, as at Oudeypore, there seem to be few if any manufactures, and but little commerce with the world beyond the sands. Vacant wall spaces, as elsewhere, are often stuccoed and made interesting by frescoes representing the usual rampant elephants and tiger-hunts. One frequently recurring theme, which shows, in spite of what the Rajpoot nobility may secretly believe, that we are all of the same Aryan stock, represents a sort of Noah's ark riding on a stormy sea of the deepest indigo; on the hurricane-deck are stiffly seated a company of Bikanir gentlemen, complacently looking down at the unfortunate beings of lower castes who are vainly struggling with the waves. The people have a way of keeping what at first sight appear to be their dining-tables in front of their houses or in the middle of the street when not in use, and congregating thereon for purposes of social intercourse and for playing little games which resemble chess. These tables, or rather lounging places — which also serve as refuges for street dogs in the heat of the day, who shelter themselves in their shadow—are solidly supported on turned legs like pillars, and are capable of holding up a number of people; they are substantial enough to resist the onsets of galloping heifers, which use the street as a play-ground, and are not to be kicked over by every passing stray camel.

The "corrugated iron age" has already dawned upon this city, remote as it is from all centres of culture. One or two little kiosks of this cheap but inconceivably ugly material have already made their appearance in the palace-grounds, and foreshadow in a sadly prophetic way the architectural future of India. But as yet they have not begun to cover the verandas of whole bazaars with corrugated iron roofing, as at Alwar and Delhi. Every cheap reproduction of conventional ornamental forms which can be cast in metal and multiplied to infinity has a baleful fascination for the average native mind, always quick to seize upon any new evidence of progress. These isolated signs of Western influence are rare, however, and as one follows the narrow foot-path along the battlemented walls of the city there is nothing to arrest the eye in all the expanse of sand which surrounds it, and which seems as limitless as the Sahara itself.

VI

Jeypore is, of all others, the city which is shown to strangers as an example of prosperous native rule. It has two hotels, a college, a church (which, according to Murray, is an architectural gem), a hospital, a school of arts, and a "Medical Hall," which, in the vernacular, is the title applied by the ambitious native apothecary to his place of business. The hotel to which we were consigned was so far from the city that, rather than wait for a carriage, we set out on foot to discover it for ourselves.

In the red haze of the winter morning the shrouded figures, closely shawled and wrapped in wadded coverlets, hurrying along the sandy road under the continuous arch of trees, appeared to feel the cold keenly, and so many of them had their jaws bound up in handkerchiefs that we could not but ask if neuralgic toothache had taken an epidemic form in Jeypore; another delusion was dispelled when we were informed that it was only their way of training their beards to branch out horizontally in the Rajpoot manner, for we had, in our ignorance, ascribed this local fashion to some physiological peculiarity of the race.

There was a hut by the road-side where two or three lynxes dwelt in the company of their keeper; these animals were being educated for hunting purposes, and one of them, apparently recovering from an indisposition, was lying, wrapped in a wadded blanket, on a bed in front of the door, and when we returned, in the heat of the day, his keeper was fanning him with tender solicitude.

The main avenues of Jeypore cross each other at right angles, forming at their intersections large and imposing squares, where are fountains or tanks. Around these centres temples and palaces are grouped, and the broad avenues seem to vanish in perspective. Inasmuch as the idea still prevails on the Continent that all this country is quite on a par with the Congo Valley, it is interesting to know that these boulevards, well kept and lighted at night, existed a hundred years before such avenues were dreamed of in Europe. Upon a closer inspection of the regular and continuous façades which line them, houses, temples, and palaces alike look strangely thin and unstable, like the work of a scene-painter, and when a door is opened or shut one almost expects to see the whole fabric shake and quiver, or to see it rolled back to disclose something more

FEEDING THE SACRED PIGEONS, JEYPORE

wonderful behind. This appearance of unreality is due to the fact that the fronts of all these edifices are roughly stuccoed and washed with a pale pink tone, on which are rudely frescoed white lines and uncertain arabesques, and they have, to a degree, the effect of carelessly painted canvas. But they are, notwithstanding, built of stone, and often mask really beautiful doorways and court-yards of white marble. An hour or so before sunset all this quarter is crowded with idlers; with itinerant merchants and hucksters, who display their wares on the ground or in little booths under the great trees; with daintily barbered and immaculate court nobles, and others who pass in carriages followed by mounted dragoons; great elephants robed in scarlet, each with a clanging bell hanging on one side to warn the riders of timid horses, pass slowly through the crowd; and well-groomed white or piebald horses, their necks maintained at the requisite curve by an embroidered scarf in lieu of check-rein, are also walked out for exercise. Here, too, may be seen lynxes and blindfolded cheetahs* taking the air, and held in leash by their keepers; and at times myriads of pigeons, which are daily fed by the fakirs and maintained at the public expense, cover the ground like a blue carpet, or rise up with a deafening whir of wings. One thinks at once of the pigeons of St. Mark's, but their numbers are far greater. One of the most attractive resorts of Jeypore is the great public garden, containing an aviary and a handsome modern palace or two, which, as a piece of artistic landscape-gardening, would be remarkable in any city. When we drove out from the town to visit the ancient capital and palace of Amber, deserted by Jey Singh in 1728 for the more modern town of Jeypore, our way lay through a suburb of ruined and mouldering palaces, tombs, and garden-houses, half hidden among great trees and thickets of rank undergrowth, where colonies of peacocks strutted along the weed-grown and blackened walls, and added their harsh screams to the shrill cries of the countless green parrots.

At a point of the road where it became too steep for the carriage we found an elephant waiting for us, and the

* The hunting-leopard of India.

slow majesty of his progress upward through a wild and rocky landscape seemed to aid and give a touch of reality to the impression that we were leaving the present and going backward into the past. Few landscapes in India are more striking than the spot where one first comes in sight of the palace, rising against a barren ridge, and repeated in every detail in the glassy lake below, which is

CHEETAH AND KEEPER, JEYPORE

bordered by gardens with terraces and kiosks of red stone. The deserted city, lying along the gorge at the foot of the cliffs, does not give one so much the impression of a once populous capital that has been abandoned forever as of a place where the people had fallen asleep, and one would not be at all surprised to see them pour out from the house doors in the "painted streets" and throng the empty bazaars and temple courts, or to hear again the din of metal-workers in the silent shops. But the palace, to which we mount by a narrow and winding path hewn in the rock, is still occupied from time to time as a royal residence, and is guarded by a few retainers, and as we ascend we meet some of them, armed with swords and leather bucklers. The upper or grand court-yard of Amber combines such wealth of artistic decoration, and is placed in such a marvellous setting of landscape, that one instinctively wonders whether such combinations, which occur so often in India, can be due to happy accident, or whether the builders had cunningly taken advantage of every favoring circumstance of nature. To admit the latter hypothesis would be to acknowledge once and forever their artistic supremacy, and it is easier to maintain that they "builded better than they knew." The great gateway of the palace, elaborately painted with conventional designs, relieved by white marble and plaques of alabaster inlaid with symbolic figures in enamel and gold, and lightened by panels and transparent screens of red stone, showing the blue of the sky behind, has the rich tone of a faded cashmere shawl. As we stand in front of it an open, many-pillared hall rises on our left, with heavy sculptured brackets adorning the capitals. This entire edifice is covered with white chunar, which has been scraped away from one column, revealing the highly polished porphyry beneath. When one stands at the parapet near by and looks down, the eye ranges over the lower court-yard just below, over the white walls and crenellated towers of the outer keep, to the little lake sleeping at the bottom of the ravine, and across it to the wooded and rocky range of hills; and through a gap in these hills other ranges appear, and beyond them the cloud-flecked rolling uplands and the summer clouds. Many birds are flitting in and out through the arcades, pigeons are cooing, and the flocks of sleek green parrots keep up a continual screaming and bickering. There was a table in the centre of the pillared hall, where we were accustomed to lunch among these feathered intruders. The most persistently familiar of all was a small songster resembling a nightingale, which sat quietly on the back of a chair, and when encouraged by our tranquillity would walk about the table and help himself to the crumbs. In the innermost court, in the shadow of a white marble pavilion shaded by red curtains, one or two men and boys armed with bows dozed through the

ELEPHANT'S HEAD, JEYPORE

heat of the day, and in their waking moments exercised their calling of firing ineffectual arrows at the screaming parrots on the mango-trees. Down in the lower court just below the parapet was tethered the old elephant who had transported us up here on his capacious back, and who seemed to bore himself in spite of the beauty of his surroundings. His keeper had led him into a small yard enclosed by rough walls, and after taking off his howdah and coverings, had lain down to doze in a shady corner. Before going to sleep he had prudently tied a cord around the elephant's fore-foot, and had attached the other end to a peg between his own feet; the cord was probably intended as a slight moral restraint. The great brute was quiet enough for a time, rocking gently from side to side, and at last, from sheer want of occupation, he began to scrape together with his trunk and one ponderous fore-foot a quantity of loose, dry grass, until he had collected a mouthful; when the supply at hand was exhausted he began to feel in the crevices of the wall with the tip of his trunk to see if perchance anything eatable had been left there; discovering a small earthen pot, he carefully investigated the interior, but smashed it against the wall in disgust at finding it empty. Overcome with ennui at last, he moved slowly and stealthily towards the exit, keeping one eye on his master, and taking great care not to awaken him; but the sleeper was roused by the gradual slipping of the cord over his foot, and his charge, like a great baby, was led back in disgrace and soundly chastised with a broomstick. His last resource was to shoot showers of dust and gravel over his back, so that it took his keeper a full half-hour to sweep him clean.

Amber, with its garden courts, its fountains and rills of clear water rippling through channels of inlaid marble, its secluded chambers and halls adorned with gilding and

COURT OF THE PALACE OF AMBER, JEYPORE

Persian mirror-work, or with panels of white marble on which are sculptured the rose and the lotus, the doors of sandal wood and ivory, the vignettes of lovely mountain landscape seen through the lace-work of the window-lattices, and, above all, the sentiment of repose, and remoteness from the work-a-day world of coal and iron, seems a perfect parallel to the Alhambra, and completely embodies the Arabian idea of a kingly retreat.

VII

Our impressions of the marvels of Rajpootana would be incomplete without at least a brief reference to Gwalior and the fortress of Scindia. Shattered, ruinous, and rapidly falling into decay, it still remains a striking landmark, and a unique monument even in India — unique, for although there is something in the bizarre forms of its architecture akin to the early Persian palaces at Persepolis and elsewhere, as well as to the later edifices in Toorkistan, it bears the stamp of complete originality, as if its builders had been allowed to work out their own conception unhindered. I refer more specifically to the older portion, called the palace of Man Mandi.* Its long line of round sloping towers, capped with broad-rimmed cupolas, overtops the rocky ridge which rises straight from the plain, and the whole façade, within and without, is

*Fergusson says: "Of those buildings which so excited the admiration of the Emperor Baber, probably little now remains. The Moslems added to the palaces of the Hindoos, and spared their temples and the statues of the Jains. We have ruthlessly set to work to destroy whatever interferes with our convenience, and during the few years we have occupied the fort have probably done more to disfigure its beauties and obliterate its memories than was caused by the Moslems during the centuries they possessed or occupied it."

PALACE OF THE MAHARAJAH OF GWALIOR, SCINDIA

decorated with bands and panels of brilliant enamelled bricks, blue and green and vivid yellow, varied with courses of sculptured stone-work. When the Emperor Baba saw it in 1537, the domes were covered with gilded copper, and the whole vast fabric must then have been a blaze of color. One amusing feature is a band or ribbon of rich blue faience extending entirely round the façade, on which is a line of yellow ducks; at one point only, where a monkey is chasing one of them, the movements of these ducks depart a little from the conventionalized stiffness of the others. Within the fortress walls are temples of earlier date, and there are two exquisite little courts in the palace, so original in design that it would puzzle an architect to classify them; and just outside the western gate are colossal statues of gods wrought in the face of the yellow cliff, like those at Abou-Simbel. This fortress has long been the stronghold of the Mahratta rulers of the line of Scindia, and at the time of the Mutiny was occupied by the English, who have recently restored it to its original owners. Each race has left traces of its occupancy, and during the English régime many modern improvements were effected; ruinous palaces were fitted up as mess-rooms and officers' quarters, and as Cunningham says, "a lot of antiquarian rubbish was cleared away to make a parade-ground."

The ancient city of Gwalior lies at the foot of the hill, but the new town, where the modern palace is situated, is some distance away—nearly an hour's drive, in fact, over circuitous roads. Near the palace are several walled and arcaded enclosures of great extent, where hundreds of horses are kept, belonging to the Maharajah, who is still a minor; and in a similar place are the royal carriages. Nothing could give a better idea of the scale on which such establishments are maintained than the number and variety of these equipages, many of them built by noted London or Paris firms. There are broughams or coupés, landaus, dog-carts, traps of all sorts, mail-phaetons and mail-coaches, victorias and double-seated "beach-wagons." and, to complete the catalogue, a regulation Paris omnibus, with "impériale."

A royal household, in order to keep up to the times, must include every article of luxury appertaining to European royalty, as well as the whole antique "kit" and picturesque lumber, palanquins, howdahs, and state chariots, which have come down to it from ancient days.

OUDEYPORE, THE CITY OF THE SUNRISE

I

The little station at Chitor, asleep in the noonday glare, seemed more akin to a caravansary in the desert than to the noisy and bustling railway centres farther up the line. Only the station-master, whom it is correct to address as baboo, whether he may have any right to that title or not, and whose brown, spectacled visage was surmounted by a black velvet cap, the telegraph clerk, clad in a long white cotton garment, and the sepoy on guard at the freight-house, were present at our arrival. Across the railway track, which still rang with the reverberation of the departed train, arose, some distance away, a long wooded and bushy ridge, crowned with the level line of gray walls and towers of Chitor, the ancient capital of Meywar. The slender silhouettes of the two towers of Victory, which alone rose above the level sky-line, were so far off that one could only divine their exquisite sculpture by the irregularity of their outlines.

From the platform of the station only three other buildings were visible in all the vast and undulating half-desert landscape which stretches away westward to the line of purple hills in the direction of Oudeypore, seventy-two miles away. I had expected to find a letter or telegram from that city, with some information as to means of conveyance, not having then learned that telegrams or other messages had to be sent by "dák post," or by special runners, in the absence of either telegraph or railway connecting the Rajpootana-Malwa line with the remote capital.

The baboo in charge of the station said that nothing had been received; and having directed Motee to find some coolies and follow on with the luggage convoy, I wandered off along the sandy track in the direction of the dák bungalow, the last of the three buildings seen from the platform. Although it was the middle of January, the noonday sun, slightly veiled by haze, and with the addition of the reflected glare from the sandy and weedy waste about us, already began to be somewhat oppressive. The question of transport was speedily solved by meeting half-way to the bungalow an old and battered victoria, with a pair of brisk horses, a turbaned driver, and "syce." Upon the arrival of Motee with the coolies they deposited the luggage by the road-side, and we plunged at once into an animated discussion with the driver as to the price and other preliminaries, for, as I had supposed, the conveyance belonged to the Maharana of Oudeypore. Just as we had come to an understanding about the price, the opportune arrival of the postmaster with a telegram (brought by a runner), to the effect that the carriage had been sent for us, and that there was nothing to pay, settled the matter at once. An elaborate "tiffin" is not to be had in a dâk bungalow at short notice, and we were only too glad to find the usual bill of fare, "sudden death" (which title refers to the untimely end of the chicken which had been alive when we reached the house), bread, potatoes, and jam, with whiskey and tepid soda. When the horses had been fed, and the baggage piled into the vehicle and corded together, leaving barely space on the back seat to accommodate the writer and the tiffin basket, we drove briskly off in the teeth of a strong south wind and in the glare of the afternoon sun, over rolling uplands, towards the hazy line of far-off hills. There were spots of rich cultivation at intervals, with clumps of wild date-palms, and dense, wide-spreading banyans, sheltering the rare villages and way-side shrines; either a tank or a pool of water at these oases invariably reflected a patch of amber-tinted western sky beyond the dark trees. At each village we changed horses, which gave one an opportunity of walking on in advance—always a relief after the cramped confinement of the carriage.

MAIL-CARRIER AND GUARD

Groups of camels which were browsing among the sparse undergrowth by the roadside ambled clumsily away at our approach, and we often met whole families of villagers toiling along the dusty track in tented bullock-carts.

Somewhere along the road the mail-carrier, that mediæval ancestor of the modern postman, met us on his way from Oudeypore. He carried his small letter-bag suspended from a lacquered stick, on the end of which hung a little cluster of bells, and he was preceded by his protector, a wiry youth, armed with a drawn scimitar. There is but little danger, however, to be feared on this road, most of the tigers having been slain by the royal sportsmen, and there are no brigands, so that one may travel alone more safely here than in Europe, and the scimitar is only an emblem of authority.

When the burning after-glow had deepened into twilight, it became impossible to resist the feeling of drowsiness engendered by the strong dry wind and the monotonous movement of the carriage, in spite of the increasing chill of the night air.

At midnight I was awakened, either by the cold or by the sudden cessation of motion. Behind the carriage the men, wrapped in their frieze ulsters, such as are worn by the sepoy infantry, were squatting over a blazing fire of dry leaves, which quickly smouldered as the supply was exhausted, and again flashed up fitfully with each armful of the damp, earthy-smelling fuel, suddenly revealing the grotesque sculpture and pillared porticoes of a little group of half-ruined temples. It was quite cold—40° Fahr. at least. We reached at last a gap in a line of hills, which might have been of any height in the darkness, and halted at a towering gateway. The huge doors, which swung open, moved by invisible warders, were studded with long iron spikes and hooks, which have survived from the days when fortress gates were so protected as a defence against the battering power of mailed elephants. On either side of flanking towers high crenellated walls climbed the hills and disappeared in the gloom. There were still nine miles before us, but the thickening trees and temple spires showed that we were nearing the capital, and finally we drew up at the dák bungalow, and with noise and clamor aroused the sleeping khansamah.

II

Oudeypore.—Even the first impression is agreeable, and has a fresh charm after the monotonous levels of the Punjaub, which lie far enough to the north to have the chill, at least, of a Northern November. From the bungalow the ground slopes down on either side into a valley ringed about with bushy hills. Rounded tree-tops cut off the view here and there, and little temples or shrines, some black and weather-stained, others gleaming white, nestle in their shadows. Upon arriving in a native state, one's first proceeding is always to call on the Resident, and it is but a short walk from the bungalow to the Residency. From the entrance, guarded by an armed sentinel, the driveway winds upward among flower beds, and through checkered light and shadow, to a white house which stands on a low hill. The tall columns of the portico give it something of the character of an Italian villa, but the white domes of the little pavilions, or "chatris," which flank the terrace add the local color of India: the verandas, half hidden by striped "dhurries" and awnings, are partly covered, like the hexagonal pavilions, with great masses of violet-purple bougainvilleas. From the long drawing-room, which traverses the house, a matchless vista is seen through the open glass doors at either end: through one the sunshine streams in over the gay parterres of flowers which deck the terrace; and beyond the other door, which opens on to a veranda, answering the purpose of a conservatory, there is a delightful confusion of light and color, of polished white columns, seen through a tangle of trailing vines and broad glistening leaves of fan-palms, of scarlet and violet and orange blooms, of patches of sunlit lawn and great trees, and then the towering white castellated palace of the Maharana, a mile away. On all sides the view is bounded by the circle of lovely wooded hills, steeped in sunshine, which shut in this happy valley from the busy world, and shut out the telegraph, the railway, and the automatic distributor.

Although I had intended to take up my quarters permanently in the bungalow, it seemed like a bit of quite superfluous self-denial to decline the cordial hospitality of the Resident, which was meant to be accepted; and indeed my resolution to lead a life of hermit-like seclusion, a prospect which looked far less seductive from this point of view, was easily broken. At Oudeypore, as at many other capitals of native states, everything seems to be the property of the reigning prince: there is not a carriage for hire, nor a boat on the lake; and if one only desires to stay a day or two in the travellers' bungalow, he must, as a matter of form, ask permission of the state, which will be granted only through the Resident. But as the hospitality of the state is willingly extended to visitors armed with proper credentials, there is usually no difficulty about obtaining conveyances and a place to sleep in. One of the first evidences that the authorities were hospitably inclined was the arrival of a smart victoria, with driver and syce in scarlet liveries, all to be kept at the Residency during the length of my stay.

Oudeypore is a white city. Not only the pavilions, kiosks, and arcades which rise from the shores of the lake, but the lower walls of the great palace, the island palaces, and the town itself, are positively dazzling with whitewash.

A fellow-countryman whom I met on the road, whose name is everywhere known as an authority on Indian art, said that he had been greatly disappointed in Oudeypore, mainly because the whitewasher's brush had given it the semblance of a whited sepulchre. With all deference to his taste and judgment, I found the prevailing color to be rather agreeable than otherwise, and to have an enhanced value from its setting of dark foliage, so often relieved by brilliant masses of flowering vines.

The whitewash is not used in order to hide baseness of material, for most of the architecture is solidly built of the dark red sandstone of the country, purely Hindoo in style, abounding in colonnades with dentilated arches, and with richly sculptured brackets upholding the horizontal eaves: white, with its luminous reflections and cool shadows, is far more restful to the eye than the dull brick color of the stone beneath.

The warmer tone of marble, where it appears in the upper parts of the palace and in the inner courts of the island pleasure-houses, gains in value from its rarity. In going through the town for the first time one cannot fail to be impressed by its bright and generally attractive aspect. A drawbridge across the moat gives access to the great gateway studded with spikes; beyond this is a court-yard surrounded by high walls and guarded by soldiers. Here we enter the broad sandy road which leads us to the main bazaar. The continuous rows of shops are sheltered behind wide verandas and in the shadow of projecting eaves, which are supported by square Hindoo columns, shaped like the more ancient columns in the temple of Chitor, and by sculptured brackets or consoles. Behind these colonnades there is an ever-changing play of reflected light, and the patches of crude or half-effaced painting on the inner walls have an added value from the warm white which prevails. Even the costumes of the men are of the universal tone, varied by the scarlet and gold lace of turbans, and the costumes of the court retainers, while the embroidered shawls and skirts of the women are of every imaginable hue, so that these brilliant flashes of color in the passing crowd, together with the gaudy dyes displayed around the shop doors, toned by the luminous obscurity of the shadow, all unite in producing an impression at once sparkling, joyous, and festal. A long flight of steps leads up to the door of a temple, which is guarded by two elephants with uplifted trunks, carved in stone, and posted one on each side. From this elevated perch they seem to be saluting the living elephants as they pass in the street below, and, like the temple, they too are whitewashed. There is another temple farther on, where the sculptured friezes of fighting elephants, probably reproductions of those at Chitor, retain the natural tawny color of the stone. The busiest corner of the bazaar

STEPS OF THE TEMPLE

is at the intersection of another long street with this main artery, and here stands a modern clock-tower of striking and original design, and quite in harmony with the architecture around it. Instead of keeping straight on to the trifolia gateway and the precincts of the palace, if we turn to the right, where the street ascends a slight rise, we shall enter a quarter of handsome houses, many of which belong to court retainers. There is not much exterior ornament about them, save for the projecting brackets and latticed windows, which are not as delicately wrought as in many other cities of Rajpootana, but the broad spaces of blank white wall are decorated with great mural paintings, wherein elephants, with much vigor of action, and prancing camels, some of which seem to be throwing their heads upward as if to incommode their riders, are depicted as large as life. The Hindoo artist is not quite as happy in rendering the action of the horse; and as to his anatomy, there seems to be a tacit agreement that much of it is to be left to the imagination.

When I first saw these frescoes, or, rather, similar ones in other cities, they seemed grotesque and barbaric, although not lacking in a certain amount of decorative force. Whether these examples were really better, or whether, since it has become the fashion to borrow the ideas of the early Primitives and to express them in a manner more primitive still as to technique, we have learned to accept many things in art which we could not have understood before, it would be somewhat difficult to determine. But of one thing I am certain, that these decorations impressed me as being much less eccentric than at first, the drawing of the prancing elephants and supercilious camels less exaggerated, and the tigers as more seriously fierce: the crude yellow of these tigers

STREET AND PAINTED HOUSES

seemed actually to harmonize with the great washes of raw blue and violet on the elephants. It may be that while these artists have worked steadily on in the same way for ages, we have just begun to appreciate the value of simplicity, and one may easily believe that, with judicious initiation into the mysteries of the artistic "cuisine" of to-day, many of these village Giottos might find themselves quite "in the movement."

III

The great white palace, which is the key-note and the dominant feature of the landscape, and which so fascinates the eye when first seen in the morning light rising above the tree-tops against the background of mountains, gains in interest as we approach it. There is so much of it that the eye cannot grasp it all at once, but is first bewildered by its vast extent, and then confused by the multitude of interesting details, and not until one has seen it from the lake or from one of the island palaces can he form an idea of the mass as a whole. From the landward side and from the city the most imposing approach is through the first gate at the end of the long bazaar, where one enters the outer precincts and stands in front of the "trifolia," or triple-arched gateway, which is in itself a noble structure, placed high upon rising ground, commanding the entrance to the long terrace in front of the castle walls, and crowned by open and delicately fashioned cupolas, connected with each other by a white wall or curtain of transparent stone lattice-work. Above this gateway soars the great white fabric, airy, unreal, and fantastic as a dream, stretching away in a seemingly endless perspective of latticed cupolas, domes, turrets, and jutting oriel-windows, rising tier above tier, at a dizzy height from the ground. A single dark tree spreads its branches above the walls of the topmost court, at the very apex of the pile.*

* Fergusson, in his *History of Indian and Eastern Architecture*, says of this palace: "It has not unfrequently been compared with the castle at Windsor, and not inaptly, for both in outline and extent it is not unlike that palace, though differing wonderfully in detail and in situation.

Seen in the morning light, with the sunshine slanting obliquely across the dazzling white of the lower walls, and accentuating the balconied windows, while it leaves the trifolia gateway and whole masses of the palace in shadow—a shadow full of mellow reflections and the azure of the sky—it has the coloring of a great cumulus cloud, and seems hardly more material.

It was not by this gate, however, that we entered the palace for the first time, but we followed the carriage drive at the very opposite end, passing under the round gray towers of the new wing, not yet finished, and which will probably embody in its interior decoration the choicest examples of South Kensington and Chippendale art.

By this route, which winds past the towers by a sort of ascending ramp, we enter a narrow garden, where the glass globes of electric lamps rise among the flower beds and low shrubbery. Here stands a detached white building, like a modern bungalow of superior architecture, with broad, open doors. The first apartment is a sleeping-room of generous dimensions, which is furnished entirely with glass and crystal; the furniture, tables, arm-chairs, mantel ornaments, even the bed itself and the "punka" frames, as well as the great chandeliers and lustres, are all of glittering cut glass. A long dining-room opens out of this first chamber; one end of it, used as a billiard-room, has a bay-windowed recess overlooking the garden.

In this latter respect the Eastern has the advantage of the Western palace, as it stands on the verge of an extensive lake, surrounded by hills of great beauty of outline, and in the lake are two island palaces, the Jug Navas and Jug Munder, which are more beautiful in their class than any similar objects I know of elsewhere. It would be difficult to find any scene where art and nature are so happily blended together and produce so fairy-like an effect. Certainly nothing I know of so modern a date equals it."

CASTLE OF THE RANAS OF OUDEYPORE

Some full-length portraits hang on the walls, among which is one of the late Maharana, by the English painter Prinsep. On the floor above are suites of sleeping-rooms, furnished according to the latest English ideas of comfort. But the most charming feature of this palace is the little marble belvedere perched on the low garden wall overlooking the lake. From the principal entrance it is hardly more than a step across the gravelled walk and the prim flower beds to the little pavilion with slender and fragile arches of white marble upholding the canopy. Two hundred feet below, at a rough estimate, lies the blue lake, fringed with green, surrounded by gardens, the palm-tufted islands, each with its gleaming white palace, and always the same horizon of lonely hills.

We reached the more distant and ancient part of the palace, which is so impressive when seen from the trifolia gate, after a short drive along the connecting walls and towers, from the great terrace on the landward side. This long expanse of gravel, often used as a parade-ground, with a line of arcaded structures for the stabling of horses and elephants, standing on its extreme verge above the town, is built upon tiers of arches, resting on the rocky ridge below.

Beyond the gateway by which we enter this wing of the palace we reach a small court-yard by a few steps upward, and are confronted by a huge and portentous image of Vishnu, enshrined, in a niche, and daubed with red paint; bedecked with yellow flowers, but stern and aggressive of aspect, he watches over this part of the palace as if to repel the invasion of latter-day Philistines. A strange old figure, which might claim kinship with the image in the niche, comes hobbling out to meet us; his forehead is decorated with a brush-mark of yellow paint, he has a long white mustache, faded yellow garments, and carries a curved "tulwar." His general make-up gave him the aspect of a fakir of some sort, but he proved to be a superannuated captain of the palace guards, and the janitor of this particular quarter. A few steps higher we come to another court, with a dark hall on one side, entered from an open gallery with low eaves upheld by sculptured consoles. In this hall the dead Ranas are laid in state. The steep and narrow stairways, the angular, winding, and dimly lighted passages of solid masonry.

CASTLE AND PALACE FROM ACROSS THE LAKE

faced with polished "chunar," * dingy with age and use, which lead us from one marvel to another, seem strangely out of keeping with the grandeur of a palace, where one would expect to find at least one monumental staircase. But the young Rajpoot who is guiding us through the labyrinth is well up in the history of his country, and explains that this structure, like most others of the same epoch, is so built for defence against possible invasion. For most of these narrow stairs and dark winding passages will admit only one at a time, and the invaders must perforce enter in single file. By one of the passages we came to a balcony overlooking a court-yard where "durbars" are sometimes held. Red awnings roof in the court below, and the dim light which pervades the place filters through a range of latticed windows on the same level as the balcony where we stand. In the centre of this line of windows and latticed arches a marvellous projecting oriel of blue glass overhangs the court; the slender columns supporting the canopy, and the brackets or consoles which uphold the entire structure, and which are shaped like peacocks, are all of glass and crystal, vivid ultramarine blue and pale green in their prevailing tints. Descending to the level of the court-yard we find at each end an arcaded recess, each with a fountain set in the wall. These two fountains are alike: a shell-shaped basin projects from the wall, above which stands in the arched recess a gorgeous blue and green peacock, pre-Raphaelite in fidelity of color and design, and of the same glittering crystal as the balcony above. When we ascend again to the line of the upper balconies we continue on through a long range of small chambers, each commanding by its

* Chunar is a sort of cement or stucco of fine texture, and capable of such a high degree of polish that it is often used as a substitute for marble.

A TILED WINDOW IN THE PALACE

projecting bay-window a view of the terrace below and a vast sweep of landscape, the snow-white domes and flat terraces and temple spires among green tree-tops of the city which sleeps beneath us, and on all sides the far-reaching horizon of faint purple hills. One of these balconies within and without, as well as the little chamber to which it gives light, is covered with old Dutch tiles, in which blue prevails. Seen from the terrace below, this blue window makes a pleasing note of color in the endless expanse of white. Another room is walled with dull glass in long straight slabs, in horizontal, vertical, and zigzag, zebra-like bands; on the walls are little portraits of old monarchs and men of state, painted on rice paper, and resembling in delicacy of design and coloring the work of the older Japanese painters. Beyond this long range of apartments, of which no two are alike, we come to a marble court-yard open to the sky, and not unlike that at Secundra, where the tomb of Akbar is placed. A small garden in the centre is enclosed by a low lattice of white marble, and a solitary cocoanut-palm, which can be seen from all the surrounding country, rears its golden plumes high above the palace walls. The marble here is tawny with age. From this court opens a summer sleeping-room of the Maharana, which is truly original; it is a large square hall, of which the only visible material is marble. A row of columns separates it from the court, and the other three sides, save for the supporting piers or columns, have transparent walls of that delicate stone tracery peculiar to India. In the centre there is a tank of water, and from the tank rises a sort of island platform, with low trellis-work around it, and slender columns supporting a dome. This is the bed where royalty sometimes sleeps on hot summer nights, in the spring-time, or in "monsoon weather," when kept in town by pressure of affairs. The island couch and the bridge connecting it with the mainland or floor, as well as the broad expanse of pavement, are of the same polished white marble. Perched on the very summit of the castle, every chance breeze must draw through it from the outer court, or through the latticed walls. From the balconies one may look directly down on the broad backs of elephants chained to a low wall, and busily engaged in powdering themselves with dust. Here the elephant fights take place, and the great brutes are made to charge at each other from opposite sides of the wall. In one of the preceding courts there is a curious example of glass inlay. On either side of a very small window the wall is decorated with life-sized figures in groups, and trees resembling the weeping-willows worked by our grandmothers in the funereal "samplers" of their day. The figures are clothed in a nondescript fantastic costume, between the Rajpoot costume and the fashion of European dress in the days of the First Empire, and the subjects seem to be episodes of courtship conducted in a highly jovial and eccentric manner.

From the upper windows a series of curious structures is visible, standing in a row along the wall near the trifolia gate. They consist of carved Hindoo arches supported by stone columns, and from the apex of each arch hangs a gigantic pair of scales. They are called "torans," and were built by successive Maharanas, who were in the habit of weighing themselves on the day of their accession to the throne, or upon other festal occasions, against their weight in gold, in rupees, or in other valuables, and the plunder was afterwards distributed among the priests and the inferior castes.

As one seldom has the opportunity of seeing this ceremony performed, we cannot do better than to give the account in the Journal of Sir Thomas Roe, the first English ambassador to the court of the "Great Mogul," early in the seventeenth century. He saw the Emperor Jehanghir "weighed in the balance," and seems to have found the spectacle amusing:

"The first of September was the King's birth-day and the solemnity of his weighing to which I went, and was carryed into a very large and beautiful garden, the square within all water, on the sides flowers and trees, in the midst a Pinacle, where was prepared the scales, being hung in large tresseles, and a crosse beame plated on with gold thinne: the scales of masse gold, the borders set with small stones, Rubies and Turkey,* the scales of gold large and masse but strengthened with silke cords."

Then follows a detailed description of the gorgeous raiment and jewelry of his Mogul Majesty, and then: "Suddenly hee entered into the scales, sate like a woman on his legges and there was put in against him, many bagges to fit his weight which were changed six times, and they say was silver, and that I understood his weight to be nine thousand Rupias, which are almost one thousand pound sterling: after with gold and jewels and precious stones, but I saw none, it being in bagges might be Pibbles."

This was doubtless all very fine indeed; but after contemplating the Rajpoots and their indisputable "claims of long descent," one cannot but look upon those Mogul emperors as a set of upstarts and parvenus who would have found it difficult to trace their descent even to the days of the Crusades, and upon their gaudy splendor as mere vulgar ostentation.

. . . The goal of one of our pilgrimages to the town was the state school situated in this quarter. It seemed to be an event for both masters and pupils, for one of the company was a statesman whose temporary retirement was just then the chief topic of the London press; but of this I was not aware at the moment. An amusing episode for this impromptu school committee was a dialogue in English between two Hindoo youngsters of eleven or twelve, in which one represented Alexander the Great and the other personified Socrates. They were watched with breathless solicitude, and egged on, when their en-

* Turquoise.

THE MARBLE STEPS—PICHOLA LAKE

thusiasm seemed to flag, by the English teacher, a turbaned Mussulman, to whom we were afterwards introduced by Mr. Fateh Lal, who had been his pupil. A class of young men from fifteen to twenty were well up in the higher mathematics, and the visiting committee wisely abstained from any very searching examination. In the primary section below, a class of little Hindoo girls had already commenced their English grammar. I may here note, what I have remarked elsewhere in India, the unexpected and sometimes startling precocity of the young in matters intellectual.

As we leave this quarter the street descends a steep hill between tall houses, and at the bottom we come to another three-arched gateway, which is an extension of a palace belonging to some branch of the reigning family. Above the arches a long latticed gallery connects the structure with the main body of the palace. All this upper portion is ornamented with frescoed designs, and in places with an inlay of blue glass, having the effect of tiles. Passing under the arches, we emerge from the shadow into a dazzle of light; from the broad platform of old and yellow marble, well polished by the constant friction of bare feet, a few low steps lead down to the blue waters of the Pinchola Lake. On one side a white wall ending in a little temple cuts off the view; the dancing reflection of the sun in the water is thrown up in long rippling waves of light into the shadow of the eaves. The view down the lake on the other side is unsurpassed in India. A long perspective of white palaces, with many domes and oriel-windows, with solid masses of dark foliage rising from the water here and there, reaches to the great supporting walls of the Rana's castle, and at this point the lake opens out into greater width; its horizon of gardens and hills beyond is interrupted only by the fantastic silhouettes of the island palaces, which seem to float between water and sky; it is as if the elusive mirages which we had so often seen on our way across the white salt deserts of Persia, and which had always melted into thin air, had at last become materialized here. As we stand on the steps and look across the water in front of us, which is like a narrow river at this point, we see other temples among dark trees, all in the shadow, and there are also little garden pavilions, with steps descending to the water, and sometimes with graceful arcaded galleries overhanging it. Just now the platform behind us and the steps are crowded with women and young girls, babies and children, all either bathing or washing their brazen water-jars, chattering, gossiping, laughing, or lying about in the genial afternoon sunshine of January, and not at all in a hurry to finish their work or to go home. Under and through the white arches an endless throng of these gracefully draped, swaying figures, in scarlet, in crimson and dull gold, in faded reds and warm blues, carrying on their heads the great vases of glittering metal, is continually passing to and from the wet and glistening steps. The golden afternoon haze is beginning to soften the white of the walls, but to-morrow morning, when this side is in shadow, we shall see exactly the same mellow glow on the opposite side, and the difference between morning and afternoon is quite too intangible to express with any painter's medium. A boat with a numerous crew is waiting at the landing, and, having settled ourselves comfortably among the cushions, we are pushed off from the shore, and steer for the island of "Jug Navas," which is the nearest of the larger islands, and seems to be the more material. Just as we leave the steps an elephant emerges slowly from the gloom of the arch and comes down to the water; his "mahout" has no need to guide him with heel or prong; he knows well where the water is, and when he reaches the steps, he first puts one foot cautiously down and tries the lower step, and then solidly plants the other fore-foot with equal deliberation. He has taken the same precaution many times before, and will not fail to do so the next time. Having assured himself of his present safety, he proceeds to suck up the water through his long, flexible filter. As the boat moves down the lake towards the islands, the glow and power of the white light thrown back from the vast and towering expanse of blank wall from which the Rana's palace soars upward against the deep blue of the sky, and from the white city at its side, is almost too much for the eyes. All this white, streaked in places with the golden green of the hanging terraced gardens, and the scarlet and multicolored figures on the steps, and the drinking elephants, are mirrored below, and

ISLAND OF JUG NAVAS

until the prow cuts the glassy surface it seems at times like passing over a white cloud.

IV

The low wall of an island kiosk hides a garden court. and as the boat glides past the open door we see for a moment the glossy foliage of the orange-trees and the tessellated pavement, strewn with little glass lamps which are used to illuminate the islands during the great festival of the "Holi." A few more strokes of the oars and we pass into the shadow of the island palace of "Jug Navas," a shadow broken by long shafts of sunlight which slant through the low arches of the arcade, and through open balconied windows overhanging the water.* Through these openings, and between the interstices of the intricate vine-like lattices, there are glimpses of tangled foliage touched with golden light, where the sun pierces the green transparency of banana leaves or the drooping fronds of cocoanut-trees, and high above all rises a slender-stemmed fan-palm. A few of the window lattices are filled in with stained glass. and across them are etched the flickering shadows of long leaves, which sway and shiver with every breath of wind. The domes which rise above the outer walls are tipped with great pear-shaped knobs of crystal or of emerald-green glass which flash like jewels against the dark foliage. Even should one succeed in describing, like a guide-book, and in the natural order and sequence, the different nooks and corners of this miniature labyrinth, he would fail in giving the truest impression of a place

* The Pichola Lake is artificial. like the three other lakes in the neighborhood. The "Jassamund" or Dehbor Lake, some miles away. is the largest artificial lake in the world. being twelve miles in length by nine in breadth.

which seems designed intentionally to confuse and bewilder the visitor, and which owes one of its chief charms to the element of the unexpected. It was evidently not intended to be imposing or grandiose in its architectural effect, but it certainly impresses one as a delightful medley of cool and dimly lighted retreats, opening suddenly on to terraces or into bright gardens, watered by tortuous channels confined by low parapets of chunar, with great central tanks choked with lotus leaves; and of dark winding passages and steep and narrow stairways, whence one emerges out of the gloom, after knocking his knees on the steps or his head against the roof, into the blinding outer light with some new vista before him. As a hot-weather retreat, no more perfect spot could be imagined, and the exquisite little vignettes of calm lake and mountain seen through the arched windows, framed by long, swaying palm leaves, together with the subdued, monotonous lapping of the water against the walls, and the dry rustling of the great leaves, all combine to create an atmosphere of repose, of tranquil and indolent forgetfulness. One of the most inviting little nooks is an oblong bathing-tank, surrounded by white chunar walls with marble arcades, and quite open to the sky. We enter at one end upon a narrow platform, and in the centre of it rises a steep inclined plane of highly polished white marble, edged by a narrow border of inlaid blue glass; the top of this slope is reached by a narrow stairway, and from this elevated station the amber-hued fair bathers were wont to slide down into the water, doubtless with the same chorus of shrieks which is heard from the "montagnes russes," or Switchback Railway, when the fête at Neuilly is in progress. At the opposite end of the tank a low open-work parapet of marble fences off a portion of the platform, probably reserved for royalty. Upon either side a

ELEPHANTS DRINKING, PICHOLA LAKE

series of arches opens into the cool halls, with various little cushioned retreats beyond. Here again arabesque borders of dull blue or green glass, inlaid in the marble, accentuate the outlines of the arches and relieve the squareness of the supporting columns. I have never seen elsewhere in India glass used in this way, and it is quite as effective as the inlay of more costly materials in the northern palaces. From the wall of one of the rooms projects a curved shallow basin, which forms the base of a niche, ornamented with glass mosaic, and it is so contrived that it may perform the office of a bath, or at least provide a cool place to sit in of a hot afternoon. There is little other furniture but a few brocaded arm-chairs and sofas ranged against the wall, and heavy portières shut out the light of the court. Another little detail seemed quite peculiar to this palace: the high white walls which shut in the tank from the other buildings have spear-head battlements along the top, and the interstices between them are filled with stained glass. A small room, which is entered from a higher level, is unique and decidedly artistic in its decoration. Two narrow spaces on each side of a door are filled by portraits frescoed on the walls—one of them is a seated life-size portrait of the late Maharana, and the other may have represented the queen or some favorite of the day. These royalties are depicted with the fairest of English complexions, but they would have been far more decorative with their own golden-brown skins, no darker in reality than the tint of a sun-burnt European.

This delicate bit of flattery shows that the concessions which insure the prosperity of the fashionable portrait-painter elsewhere are expected here as well. Both of these pictures are drawn with much skill and delicacy of handling, and are quite in the spirit of Japanese art. Upon another high and narrow panel there is a hunting scene, or, rather, what seems to be at first several different hunting scenes, but which, after careful study, resolve themselves into different phases of one. All these incidents are represented as taking place upon a common background—a perpendicular rocky cliff or face of a mountain, with thin trees or low scrub growing in places. In the uppermost scene the prince, standing in front of his retainers, is taking aim at a tiger; in the second, just below, the tiger is wounded, and gets his final *coup de grâce;* in the third he has rolled down into a gully; and in the final scene he is being carried off on a sort of improvised stretcher by the "shikarries," and the whole cavalcade follows behind. The landscape is all very vast, and the figures are very small and delicate in execution; and as a work of art it is exceedingly naïve, and is quite serious in intention. Another companion panel is quite in the same vain, and the background is a similar vertical and rocky landscape. In this series his Highness is firing at glass balls thrown up by his attendants, after the fashion of Buffalo Bill. I do not remember the date of the fresco, and it may be that the late Maharana invented this pastime. Even the shattering and bursting of the glass bulbs, filled with red powder, is successfully achieved by the artist. But there is one note which is slightly out of harmony with the rest of the decoration. The door by which we entered being closed, we see that on each side there is a vertical range of square panels, and that each of these panels frames a colored chromo taken from the Christmas *Graphic*, or from some German periodical, representing beautiful damsels, blonde and brunette; and they have been varnished, so that they are like the pictures produced by that once fashionable but now defunct art called "Grecian painting."

The European note which we find here and there in

Eastern palaces is usually discordant, but it is quite possible that the intelligent traveller from Japan may be occasionally shocked by crudities which are thought to represent the art of his country in Western homes. The small boudoir decorated with these paintings opens from a larger sleeping-room sometimes used by the Maharana; the light from the water below the windows is thrown up through the closed Venetian blinds, and reflected on the walls and ceiling. The furniture is evidently designed and carved by native artisans after European models, and the most striking feature of the room is an enormous mirror, with a frame of carved black wood, reaching from the ceiling nearly to the floor; it is, in reality, a door which when opened discloses a small room two feet higher than the sleeping-room, and in its marble floor there are rows of little star-shaped orifices which send up jets of water upon the pressure of a spring. This is another device against the hot spring-time, when a wet marble is more inviting than the dry, hot linen or silk of a couch. This island of Jug Navas has its modern palace, with rooms which recall the Trianon at Versailles, with Empire furniture, maps, and pictures on the walls, and a well-lighted drawing-room overlooking the lake and the gardens. With this exception most of the little palaces in this island were built during the reign of the Maharana Jugat Singh II. in the last century, and the whole island, according to Rousselet, covers a surface of one hundred and sixty "ares anglais."*

The larger island of Jug Munder presents the most fascinating silhouette when seen either from the public gardens, along the shore beyond the new wing of the great palace, or from the lake at sunset. It is not easy to

* An are is about 11.96 square yards.

find words in which to express either its beauty of color or its grace of outline, for it embodies more completely than any landscape I have yet seen that intangible charm of the tropics. Modern art has done much to show that things ugly in themselves and phases of nature which are sombre and almost colorless can be

ON THE ISLAND OF JUG MUNDER

made beautiful and appealing through art, but it is still questionable whether the means which are sufficient to express the one can also interpret the other. Meanwhile it is enough to be in it and of it, and to enjoy without striving hopelessly to render the unattainable.

At sunset when the water, unbroken by a single ripple, repeats the glow of the sky, the island is the one dark note in all the expanse of pale rose, save for the purple range of hills on the mainland beyond. Over the low line of arches and domes and white garden walls, which repeat the cool azure tint of the sky above, rise the dusky and massive crowns of ancient mango and banyan trees, and high above them towers a fringe of graceful fan-palms and cocoanuts. But few of the slender stems are straight, and the others lean across them at various angles. From the landing-place they rise up in a compact bouquet, and from any point of view they are picturesque and altogether satisfactory. On one side of the landing-place there is a long row of stone elephants with upraised trunks which stand with the feet in the water. When we enter the open gate we find ourselves in a long court, and the palace, which with its dependencies occupies the greater part of the island, rises on our right. It is architecturally more imposing than any structure on the other island, and the tawny yellow hue of its domes and upper stories contrasts pleasantly with the white below.

The great oblong court above which rises this simple and stately façade would make an ideal *mise en scène* for some Eastern drama by Sardou. To qualify it as theatrical might seem disparaging, and yet one cannot see it without thinking of the theatre, or, rather, of the opera, and longing to see it peopled with a crowd of courtiers and attendants, and a glittering ballet of Nautch girls. Close to the water-gate there is a low platform, a

JUG MUNDER—THE LANDING

throne, and a domed canopy above it, all of white marble. A long checkered expanse of pavement extends in front of us as we stand there, flanked on the right by the palace, on the left by huge old trees, and the lofty palms which we saw from the water. They rise from thickets of banana leaves which hide the lake. At the opposite end, near the entrance of the palace, there is a broad tank near which stand several kiosks, one of which is of delicately sculptured black marble. The legend runs that this palace was built by the Rana Koroun as a refuge for Shah Jehan, who had mutinied against his father, the Mogul Emperor Jehanghir, and had sought shelter at the Rajpoot court of Oudeypore. To use the words of Rousselet, "the interior is decorated with mosaics of jasper, agate, and onyx," and in one of the halls there is a low throne or platform, supported by caryatides, and hewn from a single block of green serpentine. Mr. Fateh

Lal, who was one of the party when I first saw this palace, said that there is good authority for the belief that here Shah Jehan first conceived the idea of the precious mosaic with which his architects decorated the matchless Taj-Mahal and many of the imperial palaces erected during his reign. Here also were sheltered the English refugees from the garrisons of Neemuch and Indore during the mutiny of 1857. When I made my last visit to the island in order to finish a sketch, my wish to see it as a spectacular background was realized, although the performance did not take place in the great inner court. On one side of the landing there is an extensive area of pavement, one corner of which is filled by a group of great trees and a tangled thicket of bananas, separated from the platform by a low stone lattice; a temple-like edifice, with sculptured columns supporting a low flat roof, stands on the extreme verge, and between the columns there is a view of the shining water and the wooded hills beyond. One of the great state barges, with high bow and poop, like the old Greek galleys, was anchored at the steps, surrounded by a fleet of small craft, and the passengers—a crowd of holiday-making women and children from the great palace across the water, accompanied by their male attendants and servants—were all seated on the pavement. A long shaft of sunlight streamed through the open gateway of a garden behind, falling upon the sitting groups, kindling into vivid scarlet the prevailing reds of their costumes, touching the flashing ornaments and the rare spots of white, until it resembled nothing so much as a glowing parterre of geraniums. When, by a common impulse, they all rose and moved towards the boats, there was an indescribable tumult of color, which seemed to culminate when the great barges floated slowly out, crowded with their scarlet and crimson freight, all in the shadow of the tall trees, into the long white reflections, shot across with azure and violet from the sky, and beyond rose the palace walls and hanging gardens of the white city. Something like this combination was attempted at the opera in Paris, when *Zamora* was given nine years ago, and it all seemed fairy-like, ideal, and altogether very superior to anything in this matter-of-fact world, so near the grimy suburbs of Levallois-Perret and Asnières—but I had not then seen the island of Jug Munder. A prolonged sojourn at Oudeypore, where the emotional element seems to survive only in the world of color, might become monotonous in the course of time, merely from the absence of anything ugly and "philistine" by way of contrast.

BOY DECORATING IDOL WITH FLOWERS

As yet no "hustlers" have disturbed the peace of the white city, sleeping in the hollow of its hills; no tall chimneys arise from the shore of the lake, and there is a total dearth of saw-mills, lumber-yards, and other evidences of commercial activity; no one seems to manufacture anything, and these placid heathen are still painfully ignorant in regard to socialism, dynamite bombs, and epidemics.

It might, then, become tedious to follow always the same routine: to leave the island, as we did, at sunset; to look back at the fringe of tufted palms fading into the dull red of the sky; to glide along under the palace walls; to land always at the same water-worn marble steps, and drive back in the twilight through the crowded bazaar and the bowers of tropical foliage in the park. But when one wearies of so much repetition a telegram to Bombay will insure a cabin on one of the new fast boats, and within eighteen days one may enjoy the wet winter twilight on the boulevards, under the gas-jets and a dripping umbrella; find the same men in their accustomed corners at the Salle d'Armes, the same crowd of idlers passing in and out of the Café de la Paix, and hear again, as of old, the hoarse cries of the news venders: "Résultats complèts des courses!" Possibly his surroundings may gain in value with the souvenir of Oudeypore as a foil.

V

No better spot could be found than this city in which to observe the ways of high-caste native life. As I remember the resplendent personages who came to make brief visits of ceremony or to pay their respects to some passing notability of official or diplomatic rank, the glittering bravery of their attire and the elaborate trappings of their horses, the inimitable twist of their blue-back beards, and the deferential grace of their "salaams," carefully graded to the correct degree, the melancholy truth is borne in upon me that the "dude" of Western descent is, after all, but a crude and unfinished production—in fact, he is "not in it at all." The term Western, used in this connection, and from the standpoint of Rajpootana, is sweepingly comprehensive. When arrayed in his court dress, and mounted on his horse caparisoned with corresponding splendor, the Rajpoot noble is at his best, and in the full glare of sunlight he is decorative to a dazzling degree. One toilet which I had the opportunity of studying in detail might have furnished sufficient inspiration to Worth for an entire series of fresh "creations." The scheme of color, as a whole, might be termed a "symphony" in white, relieved by color sparingly used, and by the sparkle of gems. The wearer of this costume, who appeared thus attired on state occasions only, was a

IN THE BAZAR, OUDEYPORE

young man of twenty, and sat his horse like a white statue. A long-skirted tunic or frock of white muslin, close-fitting white trousers, and a rose-colored turban with a broad band of gold lace and tall flashing plume of dark heron feathers and gold filagree were the salient points. Other accessories were the sword-belt, crossing his breast and encircling his waist, of dark green velvet, richly worked with unalloyed gold, and thickly studded with emeralds, rubies, and brilliants; a transparent yellow shield of rhinoceros hide, with knobs of black and gold enamel; a sash of stiff gold lace, with a crimson thread running through the gold; bracelets of the dainty workmanship known as Jeypore enamel thickly jewelled, which he wore on his wrists and arms; and there were strings of dull, uncut stones about his neck. The skirts of his tunic were pleated with many folds, and stood stiffly out, like the skirts of a "première danseuse" in the ballet; and when he mounted his horse a servant on each side held them so that they might not be crushed. Four valets had charge of this costume, and it took them some little time to array their master. The trappings of the horse were scarcely less elaborate; his neck was covered on one side with silver plates, and his mane, which hung on the other side, was braided, and lengthened by black fringes relieved by silver ornaments. White yaks' tails hung from beneath the embroidered saddle cover on both sides; and his head, encased in a headstall of white enamelled leather and silver, topped with tall aigrettes, was tied down by an embroidered scarf in order to give his neck the requisite curve. The idea of the pendant yaks' tails is an old one, and they probably served in the first instance as fly-brushes, being always in motion with the movements of the horse; but increased in number, they serve the double purpose of helping the decorative effect and keeping the rider's skirts from being soiled. The every-day dress of this gentleman was far more quiet in tone; but he seldom appeared twice in the same turban, which was of quite a different shape from that worn with the state costume, being small and closely folded, and it constantly varied in color.

RAI META PANNA LAL, PRIME-MINISTER

One of the most striking and characteristic faces belonged to an officer of high rank who called at the Residency in the company of the Maharana's brother, and it may be described as typifying, like a composite photograph, the higher Rajpoot race. This face, when seen in profile, closely resembled the type of the Assyrian warriors and courtiers on the bass-reliefs of Nineveh: there was the same straight line of the forehead and nose, and the long, narrow eye, with full projecting eyeball, which appears in the bass-reliefs to be either out of drawing, or to be greatly conventionalized, but which probably rendered the leading race characteristics with a certain degree of accuracy. This modern prototype of the Assyrian wore his jet-black beard horizontally trained to follow the upward twist of his curled mustaches, and his tunic or caftan, of purple silk embroidered with a palm-leaf design in dull gold, fitted him so tightly as to accentuate the rotundity of his person, as he was, to draw it mildly, inclined to fulness of habit.

Another representative of the same exclusive order, whom I chanced to meet just as he was taking his leave, being on his way to join the Maharana's hunting-party, had quite the same profile, and a still more pronounced upward curl of beard and mustache. He was the ruler of a neighboring state, and a dark jewelled turban was his only mark of rank. His elephant was waiting on the gravelled walk, and as his master descended the steps the great beast knelt for him to mount. These "mashers" of ancient lineage do not shine with the same splendor in European dress. In this respect they are not as apt as the Japanese—which, however, is not much to their discredit—and two centuries of contact with the best English models have not taught them to wear their costume successfully. There is a sort of "compromise," a sporting costume, in which the English element is limited to a tweed jacket or blouse, and which is rather effective. Could we look back a few centuries, not to go further than the Norman conquest, to a time when but few families of the governing race had emerged from obscurity, and when the Plantagenets were still parvenus, we should undoubtedly find this long-eyed, black-bearded gentry living in much the same fashion as to-day, and wearing the same elaborate and glittering costumes, which, if we may judge by the old paintings and portraits which have come down to us, have not changed in any essential particular since the days of Tamerlane. The Mogul emperors, who were descended from that conqueror of kings, much as they would have liked to exterminate the whole Rajpoot race, seem to have adopted their costume with but slight modifications. Sir Thomas Roe describes at great length the costume of his Majesty on the occasion of a "durbar:" "On his head he wore a rich Turbant, with a plume of horne (heron) tops, not many but long; . . . his coat of cloath of Gold, without sleeves, upon a fine semian as thin as Laune."

We find them to-day living in much the same fashion as in the days of Sir Thomas Roe; going out to hunt with trains of vassals—"shikar coolies" is the correct term now—or sleeping away the long, hot hours of the day in the wind-swept upper retreats of their lofty palaces; but with this difference: that in those days their periods of luxurious idleness were relieved by periods of fierce warfare, of hard riding, and cattle-lifting border forays. Now that these dissipations are no longer to be had, and a paternal government relieves them of the necessity of staying at home to guard their territories from the encroachments of jealous neighbors, they may, by way of contrast and compensation, pack their trunks with English outfits and sail for Brindisi. Laying aside the dress and the ways of their caste for a time, they may astonish the idlers at Vichy or Homburg with fêtes which will be described at length in the *Gil Blas*, become the lions of a London season, or, if their appetite for social distinction craves newer fields, even Newport will not close its doors to them. Notwithstanding the bejewelled daintiness of their attire, which might seem to imply a certain degree of effeminacy, many of them are experts with a boar spear or an express rifle. The present Maharana is said to be an adept in the slaying of tigers. Throughout his dominions they are preserved for his own sport, and he frequently exposes himself to considerable personal risk, having determined apparently to leave very few for his successor. The royal emblem of Oudeypore is the Rising Sun, and its rulers have always styled themselves "children of the sun," as they claim descent from the great luminary himself. Says Rousselet in his *Inde des Rajahs:* "If we compare the antiquity and the illustrious origin of the dynasties which have reigned or which still have sway over the different states of Rajasthan with the most celebrated dynasties of Europe, it is easy to see that the superiority remains incontestably with the Rajpoots. Already the masters of a great empire in the first centuries of our era, we see them still reigning over vast and rich provinces, in the midst of cities embellished with superb monuments, even in the time when a few half-civilized tribes in the West elected their first chiefs. The powerful Jehanghir, the Mogul Emperor, was, like Cæsar, a commentator, but upon the history of the Sesodias. The supreme arbiter over twenty-two satrapies of India enlarges with pride upon the treaty which he made with the Rana. He thanked Heaven for having reserved for him the success which neither his immortal ancestor Baber, the founder of the Mogul dynasty, nor Houmayun could obtain, and which his father, the illustrious Akbar himself, had only partially achieved. The poorest Rajpoot of our day, thanks to the genealogy of his clan, may trace his origin back to the point from which it separates from the principal trunk, and beyond that to the common beginning, which, according to the most authentic traditions, goes back at least fifteen centuries. And with what pride he points out that his order is unstained by any misalliance with the Moguls!" Mr. Fateh Lal Mehta, the young son of the Prime Minister or "Dewan," who has written a guide-book in English to Oudeypore,* says: "The ruling chief is considered to be the direct representative of Rahma, from whom was descended Kanaksen, who was the founder of the Oudeypore family, about 144 A.D. . . .

* *Hand-book of Meywar, and Guide to Its Principal Objects of Interest.* By Fateh Lal Mehta. Bombay: *Times of India* Press.

No state in India made a more courageous or more prolonged resistance to the Mahommedans than Oudeypore. It is the boast of the family that they never gave a daughter in marriage to any of the Mahommedan emperors. They belong to the Sesodia sect of the great Gehlot clan, often called the nobles of the Rajpoots."

The present Maharana is entitled Maharana Dhiraz, Maharana Sahib Shree—Fateh Sing ji Bahadur, G.C.S.I. He is given a salute of nineteen guns, "but the late

FATEH LAL MEHTA, OF OUDEYPORE, IN COURT DRESS

ruler," says Mr. Fateh Lal, "was entitled to a personal salute of twenty-one guns." Like other Indian princes, he has a standing army, but it is not at present on a war footing, and does not therefore represent the available strength of his province. It is divided into four parts: one Regular, one Irregular, an Orderly (or personal) Guard, and the City Police. The regulars only number about seven hundred men at present, and are uniformed, drilled, and equipped like the English troops. The irregulars are nearly three thousand in number, including six hundred cavalry. The guard has about five hundred men, and the police four hundred and forty, which seems amply sufficient for a city of 50,000 inhabitants.*

The lesser chiefs and rajahs perform feudal service, quite as it was done in Europe during the Middle Ages, sending in their horsemen and soldiers to the district headquarters. Should any sceptic have private doubts as to the authenticity of their descent from the sun, or even from the god Rahma, to come down to later days, the "hoary antiquity" of the race, in comparison with anything west of Suez, is beyond dispute, and one would have to go a long way back at least in order to find the "ancestor in shirt sleeves," or the grandfather who was forced by stress of circumstances to found his line in a penal colony. If in this age of social scepticism it be conceded that a privileged and gilt-edged order has any *raison d'être*, where could we find another as genuine, and, withal, as picturesque? According to our own standards, the Rajpoot caste may well lay claim to the supremacy. It is not only in the matter of clothes that the

* The most reliable authority states that the Maharana's troops number about 5000 infantry and 1200 cavalry, with six pieces of artillery.

gommeux of this order is pre-eminent, for he excels all other rivals in the art of doing nothing gracefully, an art which is a part of his rightful inheritance; and there is no trace in him of the nervous unrest and hurry, which have been handed down, together with the wealth, of the more energetic ancestor to his descendants. It will be a matter of regret from more than one point of view when these last representatives of feudality shall have become utterly and hopelessly modernized: when, in their ambition to be abreast of the times, in this latter end of the century, they shall have put aside their hereditary manner of life, with the pomp and state which can nowhere be studied to better advantage than here in Oudeypore.

THE MAHARANA

Under a more despotic tutelage than that of the viceregal government, all these things, their prerogatives, as well as their outward emblems of rank, would probably have been long since swept away. While the present régime lasts they will continue to be in a measure the arbiters of their own destinies, but abundant evidence is not wanting to show that their conservatism in these matters of externals is being slowly and insidiously undermined; that many of them now prefer the modern luxury of their renaissance or rococo villas, furnished and upholstered by some firm on the Boulevard des Capucines, to the steep winding passages and latticed "miradors" of the moated palace, and the dashing tandem to the lacquered palanquin or gilded howdah of the traditional elephant. Nowhere in the world does there exist a more progressive country than the "New India," or one where existing conditions change more rapidly. Already these little feudal states are being hemmed in and surrounded on all sides by its advancing lines; some of them are already kindled into action, and it is but a question of time with the others.*

VI

Dr. John Fryer, who visited India in the year 1672, described the wonderful things which he saw in a manner often inflated and verbose, but sometimes graphic and quite to the point, as in the description of an elephant:

". . . Alighting from our Palenkeens, they loosed one which was Fourteen Feet high, and the Black, clawing his Poll with an Iron Engine, he stooped down for him to get up, and being upon his back, guided him as he lifted. His Body is a symetrical Deformity (if I may so say); the Hanches and Quarters clapt together seem so many heaps; his neck short, slapping ears like Scates, little Eyed, a broad Face, from which drops his Proboscis or

* Oudeypore, as well as other states of Rajpootana, after having long suffered from the tyranny of the Mogul Empire, fell a prey to the Mahrattas, and was only saved from utter ruin and extinction by the protection of the British Government, which was extended to it in the early part of this century.

Trunk, thrusting it out, or shriveling it in as he choses; through its hollow he sucks his Liquor, and with two Fingers, as it were, reaches his Fodder, shaking off the dirt against his Thigh, or Vermin, such as mice, which he abhors, he brings it under to his mouth, from whence proceed two huge Tusks of Ivory for Defence, not mastication, for which he is supplied within with others; his Tail is curt; he shuffles an end a great Pace, moving all the Joints of his Legs, though the Motion of his Hinder-Legs imitate Human Progression, having a Patella or Knee-Pan afore, not articulated behind as other four-footed Beasts are. When he stands, his legs appear so many columns, scolloped at bottom, being flat-hoof'd." The learned doctor's description of the elephant's gait is inimitable.

Early one morning the servants at the Residency were all excited by the arrival of one of the Maharana's elephants arrayed in his gala dress; he was rolling along at a "Great Pace, moving all the Joints of his Legs," and looking, as he proceeded, very much foreshortened, up the gravel walk, like a great golden idol. He was followed by his footmen and valets to the number of a dozen, who were likewise resplendent in immaculate white muslin, and they all carried flags of gold tissue. There was a momentary hitch in his stately progress, as the horizontal branches of a tree interfered with his top hamper, and presently he came to a standstill at the foot of the steps, holding out his hand, like a mere circus elephant, for saccharine backsheesh of some kind. This was the elephant which had been promised as a model, and he was conducted to a grass plot behind the house, where the white wall of the terrace made a good background.

I have never yet met with an elephant who posed well or willingly; he is forever turning, twisting, and shifting his weight, first on one foot, then on the other.

Then he spreads his legs apart or sways from side to side, industriously foraging meanwhile in the dirt with his trunk, sidling up a little nearer to watch one's proceedings out of the corner of his little eye, and at this moment it is wise to move farther off. Then he turns his back entirely, and is only to be brought into position again by repeated digs with the "Iron Engine," which, I take it, means the mahout's steel prod. This elephant wore a magnificent robe of dark velvet, thickly incrusted with embroidery of gold bullion, and fringed with silk tassels; a small carpet more delicately embroidered with the same material hung from each side of the howdah; he wore a head-cover or frontispiece of dark green silk nearly black, starred with gold, and on the very top of his head sat two little burnished lions crested with glittering plumes; two long pendants of black and gold tinsel hung from the brazen tips of his tusks, and two others hung behind his ears. The double-seated howdah or chariot on his back was carved and sculptured with arabesques framing bass-reliefs of mythological divinities, all burnished, gilded, and glittering, like the chains which crossed his forehead, or ornaments which hung about his neck, and the bracelets of bells around his ankles kept up a continual jingle with his restless movements. Even the mahout who sat on his head was sumptuously attired, and as a last touch of *coquetterie* a shawl of green and gold silk tissue was thrown negligently over the railing of the howdah.

But however lavishly the elephant's overcoat may be adorned with tinsel and gold and jewels, his tailors have never thought it worth while to cover up the unseemly, disreputable, and ill-fitting pair of trousers which nature has given him. When he shuffles away and shows the nether side of his continuations of greasy leather, they are seen to be worn, creased, and baggy at the knees, and altogether out of keeping with the splendor above and in front. On the second morning, when my model came for a final séance, he was accompanied by the chief of the elephant stables, a man of authoritative and hirsute aspect, and I was not surprised to hear, knowing a little of the intricate workings of the Hindoo mind, that the elephant had shown symptoms of lameness, and was quite unable to stand. One of his ponderous fore-feet, in fact, was carefully tied up in a piece of canvas, and I could not for a moment doubt that this driver had become heartily tired of sitting up there in the sun and trying to keep his charge in the same position.

The Oriental mind seems to consider the function of painting as a highly concentrated and summary means of producing photographs, and when the sitter, whether man or beast, has posed for full ten minutes, he begins to fidget at the protracted delay. It was the custom in old days for these royal elephants to wear armor, and to carry their masters into battle. One of these caparisons, which is still preserved, consists of a head-piece and quilted robe, thickly covered with steel scales overlapping each other like the scales of a fish. Dr. John Fryer saw a regiment of war elephants equipped in this manner. Another way in which the court elephant was utilized, now happily done away with, was to make him the executioner of criminals. The unlucky wight condemned to the "punishment of the elephant," having first been bound hand and foot, was attached by a long chain to his hind leg, and the elephant was then driven through the streets of the town; when the culprit survived this ordeal his head was laid on a block, and the elephant put his fore-foot gently down on it. It must have been this performance to which Sir Thomas Roe refers when describing the emperor's method of administering justice: "On Tuesday at the Jarrneo [which was a window at which he showed himself to the people] he sits in judgment, never refusing the poorest man's complaint, when he hears with patience both parts, and sometimes sees, with too much delight in blood, the execution done by his elephants. *Illi mernere, sed quid tu ut adesses?*"

VII

In order to visit Chitor it is customary to petition for an elephant to cover the short distance between the dâk bungalow near the railway station and the great hill fort. But as the elephant is exasperatingly slow, and the distance is short, the writer preferred to walk. In the perfect weather physical exertion of any sort was a luxury, and particularly after the lazy life of Oudeypore. The only drawback to one's perfect peace of mind was the reflection that many people in India have a belief that this exercise derogates from the dignity of a European, and natives cannot yet understand why one should walk when he can by any possibility ride.

As we set out in the morning an elephant passes us, ploughing majestically through the low bushes, but we do not want him, and we shall arrive at the summit of the ridge by a short-cut much sooner, although Motee casts longing glances at his comfortable back. There is one wide river to cross, spanned by a stately but dilapidated bridge, which begins far inland, and there is also a shorter way by which we cross the shallow river-bed on stepping-stones. On the road beyond we pass an itinerant juggler with a couple of trained monkeys; he had halted by the stone parapet, and was endeavoring to teach his unwilling pupils some new trick. Near the road-side there is a collection of black tents, which are peopled with other vagabond gypsies with other trained monkeys.

And then we straggle up through the main bazaar of a little town at the very foot of the steep wooded bluff; and here begins the rocky path, which we follow, to the great discomfort of Motee, until it intercepts the paved causeway leading up to the gates of Chitor. There are several gateways before we reach, after many angular turns, the great portal at the summit, called the "Ram Pol": it is enriched with sculpture, and long processional friezes of horses and elephants are wrought along the base of the round towers and the stone platforms on either side. Here there is a guard of the Maharana's soldiers uniformed in yellow "karkie drill." Beyond this gate there is a little village among the trees and débris of temples, and then we enter at once, by paths overgrown with jungle and briers, the precinct of the deserted capital.

JUGGLER WITH TRAINED MONKEYS

By a route which ascends sharply on the right we reach the ruins of the Rana's palace: although only the roofless walls have been left standing, and nothing remains of the original pile but a hollow shell, one may still form a fairly just idea of its former extent. Several tiers of square projecting bay-windows rise one above the other, each window having two columns supporting its roof; and they are almost the exact counterparts of the windows in the mosques of Ahmedabed, built of the same tawny stone, and having similar designs in the narrow courses or bands of ornamental stone-work which relieve the plain wall surfaces. There are no curves in this early (or late) Hindoo architecture; everything is square and angular, but at the same time it is far from being heavy in its general effect. The great horizontal limbs of ancient trees protrude through the windows and reach over the upper battlements. Although this edifice is known as the palace of the Rana Khoumbou, he is now believed to have added only a few portions.*

One of the most interesting groups of temples stands almost on the extreme verge of the high ridge, whence one may look far away over the cloud-flecked plains towards the distant hills of Oudeypore. One feels that the storms of many monsoons have beaten directly upon them, for the trees on the bluff are low and twisted by the wind, and the walls which face the west, with the interstices of the sculpture, are inky black, while the friezes of statuettes in high relief gleam like yellow ivory against black velvet. In some places one has to force his way through a tangle of briers and undergrowth to get a nearer view of them. As in all Hindoo work of that epoch, the human figure is more or less conventionalized, but in one temple, the finest of this group, nature is interpreted with less formality and with greater realism of detail. These long friezes of statuettes which girdle the exterior walls for the most part represent dancing "bayaderes" or "Nautch girls," turning and twisting, and gracefully writhing in

* The date of its erection, according to Fergusson, is 1468–78 A.D.

postures which could hardly be rivalled by the professional contortionists of to-day, and they triumphantly show that not a phase of the "serpentine dance," that latest revival of the choregraphic art, was unknown to them. Some of these ladies, costumed like the Nautch girls of to-day, when they beguile the native amateur with dance and song, seem to be making merry at the expense of the spectator, and might well have exasperated the sombre "moollahs" of Akbar's day. At all events, they convey in a subtle way the vivid impression that the faith of the Hindoos was not morbidly ascetic.

Although the Mussulman iconoclasts labored conscientiously with hammer and chisel, and left not a single figure undefaced, the joyous dancers would not have fared much better had the conquerors been Puritans of Cromwell's time; indeed they might yet fare still worse should the government of India, like the artistic centres of some modern states, see fit to maintain a salaried fanatic, licensed to make war on all art in which nature is represented "undraped."

The great Tower of Victory, which is the principal landmark of Chitor, stands near these temples, but farther back from the bluff. It appears to have suffered but little from time and fanaticism, and it is still beautiful and complete as a work of art. The nine stories which make up its height are covered within, as well as on the outside, with sculptured figures, and square bay-windows project just enough from each story to diversify the outline; an open gallery with colonnade supports the modern dome at the summit. This tower was erected to commemorate the victory of the Rana Khoumbou over Mahmud, Sultan of Malwa, in 1439, and according to Ferguson "it is a pillar of victory, like that of Trajan at Rome, but in infinitely better taste as an architectural object than the

Roman example." If I remember rightly, Fergusson says somewhere that "the high-caste Hindoo is almost incapable of bad taste." The lesser tower is of greater antiquity, having been erected in the ninth century, and is more picturesque and irregular in outline, while its black and weather-worn exterior, stained with the rich tones of old iron, offers a striking contrast to the ruddy color of its neighbor. Near the great tower there are steps, broken, irregular, and in places overgrown with weeds, leading down to the deep and sunless pool called the "Cow's Mouth," where the few remaining sculptures hewn in its rocky walls are half concealed by rank and dripping vegetation. Somewhere down in its weird depths, in darkness and slime, there once existed an entrance to great subterranean galleries now walled up. It was here in these hidden chambers, according to tradition, that the women escaped bondage by voluntary cremation at the first capture and sack of the city.*

The annals of Chitor teem with picturesque and dramatic incidents, with heroic resistance and useless sacrifice, with savage barbarity and slaughter.

According to authentic records, it has been taken and sacked "three and a half times"; the half refers to the first siege by the Emperor Alah-ou-din in the thirteenth century; and this siege resembles in some features the Trojan war, as the pretext for the war was the beauty of the Regent's wife, a Cinghalese princess. By stratagem and treachery the Regent himself was captured and held as a hostage, to be exchanged only for the person of his princess. In order to save the princess and rescue the Regent at the same time, the Rajpoots resorted to a trick

* According to the most authentic historians, the founder of Meywar state was Bappa Rawal, who settled at Chitor in 728 A.D.

which quite paralleled the episode of the wooden horse. The princess consented to sacrifice her liberty in exchange for that of her husband, but on condition that she might bring with her as far as the Tartar lines her companions of the zenana and the household servants. This condition being granted, on the following morning seven hundred litters and palanquins came down the hill in the train of the princess, but their closely drawn curtains concealed not the ladies of the zenana, but the élite of the Rajpoot chivalry. In the confusion of the battle which

FRIEZE OF ELEPHANTS AT CHITOR

followed, the Regent escaped, but his followers were killed to a man, and Alah-ou-din was so discouraged by his own losses that he raised the siege and retired. He returned again some years later, and this time, after a siege of more than twelve years, he captured the city, which he proceeded to pillage and destroy after slaughtering the inhabitants.

In 1537 it was again taken by the Sultan of Guzerat, who destroyed the fortifications with cannon, and blew up the walls and bastions with mines, the defenders having remained true to their conservative principles, which led them to despise such modern inventions. No sooner had the city been rebuilt than it was again invested by Akbar, and destroyed for the last time. It was then that Udey Sing, the Maharana of Meywar, took refuge among the distant hills and founded the living capital, Oudeypore. Since that day Chitor has remained, and probably will remain forever, deserted. Its titular goddess has withdrawn her protection; no Rana has since set foot within its walls, and the ruined city is still believed to be under a spell. It is not, however, entirely devoid of life; women and children pass from time to time along the paths which lead past the temples and through the scrub to the little village near the principal gate. Some of these paths still preserve something of their original character, and show that they were once important thoroughfares, so that it is easy in imagination to reconstruct and people the bazaars as they once existed. On the side of the hill opposite the Ram Pol gate and the village there is another great gateway, from which an exceedingly steep and slippery paved causeway descends into a wild valley overgrown with jungle, and here one may always meet groups of women laboring up the hill with great loads of brushwood and fagots. Among the temples which surround the Cow's Mouth there are still priests, reputed of great sanctity, who perform the customary rites in their temples, and issue forth at the appearance of a stranger, as avid of backsheesh as any of their brotherhood elsewhere.*

* One of the strangest and most tragic incidents in the history of this state occurred about the beginning of the present century, when the beautiful daughter of the Rana was sought in marriage by the princes of Jodhpore and Jeypore. In order to put an end to the ruinous wars which ensued in consequence of their rivalry, the girl was poisoned by

During the two or three days which I spent at Chitor a strong dry wind blew from the cloudless west, stirring the long tufts of yellow grass, which waved on the high ledges of the temples and on their shattered pyramids, and made working difficult in any exposed situation. Notwithstanding the ruined and desert character of this open hill-top, its solitude is far from being depressing; open on all sides to the sky, flooded with light and swept by the wind, there is a charm about the place which may be due in part to the festal spirit of its decoration, but much of it is owing to the feeling that one has of being high up, and to the glorious panorama of hill and plain which lies spread out below us on all sides.*

At sunset we left the deserted city, where only the mutilated bayaderes seem still to live and perpetuate the spirit of past revelry, and descended the hill towards the railway, where the mail-train was to take us to Bombay, and so back to the nineteenth century, and the city which best represents the *fin de siècle.* We crossed the old bridge, meeting a long procession of laborers returning through the fading after-glow to the village at the foot of the hill; and as we looked back the long gray walls of Chitor stood grandly up against the sky.

her father, and the curses which were uttered by the fakirs against the reigning family have since been fulfilled to the letter.

* It should be mentioned that these hills are inhabited by three aboriginal tribes having no affinity whatever with either Rajpoots or Mussulmans. Of these, Bheels are the most numerous. They were formerly brigands and cattle lifters, and still carry bows and arrows.

NOTES ON INDIAN ART

I

It is only within the last few decades that the government of India has realized the importance of preserving the national monuments from decay, and of restoring those which have suffered from neglect and vandalism.

Although it will always remain a matter for regret that so many have been swept away, much of this apparently wilful destruction was caused by what at the time were considered military necessities, as in the fortresses of Agra, Delhi, Lahore, and Gwalior, and a great deal of it may be pardoned when the peculiarly difficult circumstances with which the conquerors had to contend in early days are taken into account. It should be remembered, also, that the present widely extended state of artistic culture among English-speaking races is of comparatively recent growth, and it would be somewhat difficult to prove that prior to this new awakening they had reached as high a level in æsthetic matters as the conquered races of India. Some future chronicler may assert, and not without reason, that the present rulers of India have contributed but few monuments equal in artistic value to those which they destroyed. It is useless to dwell now on the havoc wrought by the rude conquerors who came in the service of "John Company," who subdued the warlike races of India one by one by superior organization and by sterner qualities, and who made the *amende honorable* by substituting a responsible government for the despotic and capricious sway of the Moguls and their successors—a government which seems to have taken upon itself the heroic task of preparing these widely differing races for self-government. In those early days of conquest and plunder, when horses were stabled in memorial tombs and in palaces, audience-halls converted into powder-magazines, barracks, or offices of district magnates, sculptured colonnades roughly boarded up and pierced by windows, panels and screens of exquisite fret-work in sandstone or marble plastered with thick layers of stucco and whitewashed, whatever could be altered and adapted to the temporary use of the conquerors was spared, and whatever stood in the way of improvements was ruthlessly torn down. In many cases articles of intrinsic value, such as the linings of marble baths, were dug up and carried away, just as Nadir Shah carried off the Peacock throne of the emperors to Teheran. The grand gateway of one of the most imposing monuments of Shah Jehan's reign, the Jumma Musjid of Agra, was pulled down during the mutiny, and a wide expanse of railway tracks, the approach to the station, now extends up to the walls.

But a volume might be filled with these evidences of early vandalism, which English architects and archæologists have deplored in unsparing terms. It now remains to consider what has been left and to make the most of it. Ample reparation is being made to-day for the ruin and mutilation wrought during the iron age of English rule. Vast sums—relatively vast when we consider the financial difficulties with which the government of India has had to struggle—are being spent by this government, aided by the native rulers, to prop up and restore the decaying monuments which have been considered worthy

UPPER GALLERIES OF HINDOO HOUSE OF CARVED AND PAINTED WOOD

of restoration. How costly and laborious these restorations are, as in the case of the Taj-Mahal, no one can judge without some knowledge of the materials employed and the processes involved. While in Persia we find that the splendid monuments of its former glory have been abandoned to picturesque but lamentable decay, and the public buildings now erected have little if anything of the ancient spirit, in India, on the contrary, the native architects and artisans are still doing admirable work, not inferior in respect to artistic detail and finish to the work of past centuries. The repairs and restorations carried out by them, under intelligent supervision, have the advantage of being done by artisans of the same race as the original builders, who inherit the same traditional methods, and are not, as in the case of the restorations of the Alhambra and other Moorish remains in Spain, wrought by men of an alien race having little sympathy with those who designed them. Some years ago, while repairs were in progress on certain portions of the palace within the "Fort" at Agra, the workmen engaged in cutting out the little stars, hexagons, or flowers of stone, for the precious inlay of the marble walls, sat or squatted on the pavement, each with a tool like a little bow, but with a fine wire in lieu of bowstring, which he moistened continually in an earthen chatty of water placed by his side. These primitive craftsmen, nude to the waist, bending over their work as they patiently sawed out, polished, and fitted each stone in its place with the care and precision of jewellers, must have resembled their ancestors who built the palaces centuries ago, and who, doubtless, worked with the same tools; for each trade or craft is hereditary, and certain families perpetuate from generation to generation the mysteries and science of their calling. Among the groups of artisans who seem to be living over again a scene from the golden age of Mogul art, there were some engaged in chiselling thin slabs of white marble into the lacelike screens which fill the windows; the pattern, accurately drawn on paper, was pasted on one side of the slab, and the interstices cut through, after which they were smoothed over and polished.

These laborers appear to have inherited the deftness and skill of their ancestors, and if they are no longer employed in rearing great fabrics like those of the Mogul age, it is only because such structures have no longer any *raison d'être*, and also because they expect to be paid nowadays in current coin, and not with promises.

In the various departments of decorative art, such as the ornamentation of flat wall surfaces with painted designs or mosaic tiles, or with sculptured reliefs often having original and fanciful "motifs," we shall find no less latent vitality than in the province of purely constructive art, as the many public buildings, gateways, and other memorials, recently erected, bear eloquent testimony. The wood-carvers particularly have lost none of their traditional skill, the many industries in metal work, enamelling, lacquer work, jewelry, and embroidery still flourish, and there seems no reason for supposing that these artisans are less capable than those of past ages. And, indeed, if one may include other departments of a more utilitarian nature, in which the natural imitative genius of the people has found an outlet, they are the worthy successors of the clever Hindoos described by Terry in 1665, who says, "They are also excellent at limning, and will copy out any picture they see, to the life. . . . The truth is, that the natives of that monarchy are the best apes for imitation in the world, so full of ingenuity, that they will make any new thing by pattern, how hard soever it seems to be done; and therefore it is no marvel if the natives there make shoes, boots, clothes, linen, bands and cuffs of our English fashion, which are all of them very much different from their fashions and habits, and yet make them all exceedingly neat." It is amusing to find that to-day the native is competing successfully with the Englishman in the manufacture of artistic furniture of the Chippendale order, but made from indigenous woods, and even underselling him, as one may realize by walking through the show-rooms of the Parsee and Mussulman furniture dealers of Bombay inhabiting the crowded streets near the Crawford market; he will also find that this competition extends to boots and shoes and other articles of wearing apparel, as in Terry's time, when it must have had far less encouragement. Birdwood, in his *Manual of the Industrial Arts of India*, laments the deterioration of the hand-made art of India, by forced competition with the machine-made imitations of Europe, which compels the native artisan to produce an inferior class of work, and which restricts him at the same time in his choice of models. But already the tide has begun to turn the other way, and the increasing interest in decorative art has led to the protection and encouragement of these

WINDOW IN THE PALACE OF AMBER, SHOWING MARBLE LATTICE AND INLAID GLASS DECORATION

various local industries by the new art schools of the empire. It may be that this view of the matter is too sanguine, and it may not as yet be supported by sufficient data. But certainly the influence of these schools, some of which are admirably officered and equipped, is far-reaching, and cannot fail in time to produce the hoped-for results.

II

Setting aside the few scattered remains of the Buddhist period, which have more archæological than æsthetic interest, the existing monuments may be roughly divided into those which are entirely Hindoo in spirit, and which have been sub-divided into the Dravidian, Jaina, and other styles, those which were erected during the early period of the Mussulman conquest, showing a mixture of Mohammedan and Hindoo art, and those of the Mogul period, in which the Persian taste is everywhere apparent, with scarcely a trace of Hindoo influence. Still another class might be made of the more modern palaces and other edifices, decorated exteriorly with ornate windows, which were ever sparingly used by Persian builders; there are also traces of Arabic descent in many of these buildings, so that they constitute a style purely local. In a brief reference to so vast a field, it can only be stated that the most noteworthy monuments of exclusively Hindoo taste are to be found among the temples of southern and central India, as at Vellore, Peroor, and Madura, not to mention the sculptured caves and rock-cut temples of Ajunta, Ellore, and Elephanta, all of an earlier epoch. Some reference has been made in a former article to the sculptures of Chitor, and those at Mount Abu might be cited as representing the high-water mark of Hindoo artists in marble. These temples, erected between the eleventh and the fourteenth centuries, most picturesquely placed in a landscape of surpassing beauty, give little idea, when seen from without, of the marvels of sculpture within their gray and mossy walls. The series of cells on either side of the long enclosure of one of these temples, each preceded by a little portico consisting of a dome supported by columns, contain the choicest and most marvellous work of Hindoo sculptors. The skilled and patient labor which lined these domes with figures of gods, with flowers and leaves and wonderful pendants, hanging, as it were, from their centres, is little short of miraculous, and suggests the ingenious use of ivory by Chinese artisans.

No less marvellously wrought are the columns with sculptured "struts," in lieu of arches, which support the domes.

III

In beginning what can only be a desultory and incomplete notice of the principal monuments of Mussulman art, which are scattered through the north of India, with occasional centres farther south, as at Jawanpore or Bijapore, one naturally reverts to the early period of Mohammedan domination. Here we find traces of Moorish as well as of Persian influence, and the occasional curious and interesting blending of these northern styles with Hindoo elements, as in the province of Guzerat. This ground has been thoroughly studied by such experts and specialists as Cunningham and Fergusson, and the latest treatises show an increasing respect and admiration for works which combine such wonderfully decorative qualities with dignity and often with sound taste. A remarkable and rare use of the Moorish horseshoe arch occurs in the building known as the gateway of

Alah-ou-din at old Delhi, erected about 1310. This is regarded as the most ornate example of Pathan work, and is particularly interesting from the fact that, although the general arrangement of the decorated surfaces surrounding each of the arches (all four sides of the edifice being alike, and each having a door in the middle, with two windows on each side) is similar to that of many other Mussulman buildings, resembling in some respects the entrances of the mosque at Cordova, many of the ornamental details and patterns are purely Hindoo, and of course peculiar to India. The mosque at Purana Kela, near Delhi, is cited as one of the finest examples of the Pathan period. The dark red stone, nearly crimson in places, which is the prevailing material, is relieved by bands of marble surrounding the great central arch, and the interior of the niche or recessed doorway is curiously decorated with mosaic, which in the marble panels is inlaid with geometrical patterns of black and red stone, leaving only lines of white between the figures. The ad-

DOORWAY OF THE MOSQUE OF PURANA KELA, NEAR DELHI

joining arches on each side are of red stone without inlay, thus contrasting by their simplicity with the central arch, while the two exterior openings on each side are of plain gray granite. The whole edifice, while grand and somewhat severe in effect, shows a harmonious diversity of color. The noble group of monuments, some of them strangely original, including the remains at the deserted capital of Futtehpore-Sikri, which were built during the reign of Akbar, are among the most interesting in all India.

GATEWAY OF MOSQUE, FUTTEHPORE-SIKRI

The Mogul emperors were wise enough to realize that if they did not build their own mausoleums they stood but little chance of being buried with fitting magnificence, and took a serious pleasure in rearing these stately sepulchres. That at Secundra is like a city in itself, placed at the end of a vast parklike garden; and there is nothing funereal in its character or surroundings, for these monarchs had the pleasant Eastern fashion of looking cheerfully forward to the inevitable, and made use of their mausoleums while they lived as pleasure-houses, and the surrounding gardens as appropriate places for al fresco entertainments. It was a poetic inspiration on the part of Akbar to have placed his tomb out in the sunshine and in the middle of the wide marble court, with only the blue vault of heaven over it, and the Koh-i-noor flashing like a star from the top of the little marble column at the head. Fergusson does not mention the Koh-i-noor, nor the little column four feet high, said to have been covered with gold; but it still stands there, with the empty socket on the top, and it was, at all events, a unique and pleasing idea. Few deserted cities are more impressive than Futtehpore-Sikri, and the splendid gateway of the mosque which towers to the height of one hundred and fifty feet above the ground, dwarfing every structure within the walls, is a landmark for all the neighboring country. Every building which has in any measure escaped the ravages of time is of the same red sandstone, and the only exception is the white marble tomb of Selim Chisti which stands in the court-yard of the mosque. Such miracles of delicate tracery and such fantastically twisted brackets were surely never before wrought from unyielding marble; and as the sculptured cells in the temples of Mount Abu represent the highest attainment of Hindoo art in this direction, so the tomb of Selim Chisti may stand as an example of what ingenious Mussulman architects may accomplish within the range of purely geometrical design, circumscribed as they are by the limitations of their creed.

The most unique of all the little structures standing in the neighborhood, or on the near margin of the tank in the vast court enclosed by the palace walls, is the one commonly called the sultana's kiosk, and lovingly designed as the boudoir of an imperial favorite. We know little to-day of the jewel which it sheltered, but one may at least hope that it was worthy of such a casket. The red stone is peculiarly deep and rich in quality of color, and as every inch of it is carved and fretted it resembles closely a Japanese bibelot of vermilion lacquer.

The "House of Beerbul's daughter" and all the others, of which no two are alike, show a similar exuberance of fancy so that no one of these fortunate sultanas had reason to be jealous of a rival's installation, since all were equally well lodged. Nothing at Futtehpore-Sikri is more impressive than the view of the walls and the strange outlines of the structures towering above them, when one leaves, at sunset, the gateway on the north where stand the two great elephants of stone with interlinked trunks, and descending the steep pathway encumbered with fallen fragments, reaches the isolated tower bristling with elephants' tusks. Here he may look back to the deserted capital, or forward to the western glow, beyond the crumbling ruins of the last and outermost wall where the great vultures and adjutant storks balance themselves on the broken battlements.

SHAH JEHAN
From an old portrait

IV

In the portraits and miniatures of Shah Jehan which have survived, he is usually represented in the act of inhaling the fragrance of a moss rose, or toying with a buttonhole bouquet, and he has quite the air of an æsthetic *poseur*. He showed great interest in the portraits brought over by the English Ambassador, but preferred the work of his own painters, and boasted that some of them could so copy these pictures, probably miniatures, that it would be impossible to distinguish the copy from the original. Those which found favor in his eyes were doubtless painted with water-colors on ivory, and this art has survived to the present day: "for indeed in that art of limning his painters worke miracles; the other being in oyle, he liked not." Here and there, in India, one chances unexpectedly upon a bit of old work, which has qualities sufficient to show that the artist had something in common with the early Dutch and Flemish painters, not only in technique, but in subject and other attributes of *genre* painting. Somewhere in the labyrinth of winding lanes, cul-de-sacs, and tall old houses between Vazir Khan's mosque, at Lahore, and what might be called the exterior boulevard on the north, there is a forsaken, ruinous, and dusty old palace tenanted by the retainers of some exiled Rajah; at all events there is some half-forgotten history attached to it. On the upper terrace of this palace, whence one has a fine view of the richly colored minars of Vazir Khan, which rose, as we saw them, against a stormy sky, there was a little square room or "mirador," decorated with mural paintings, occupying the panels between doors and windows; there was a hunting-scene, with a prince riding out from the palace, holding a falcon on his wrist. The details of costume, embroideries, and weapons were executed with quaint precision and fidelity. Another represented the prince having an interview with a fair lady in a prim old garden. The lady was certainly meant to be beautiful, and the garden, with its shrubbery and the details of pavement or kiosk, was treated with a certain formal realism, as if painted on the spot, reminding one not a little of Jan

THE TAJ MAHAL

Van Eyck, and the analysis of an English critic, of his early method of beginning on a whitened panel, always preserving the original outline, and gradually glazing the shadows, and leaving the high lights. During my last visit we tried again to find the house, but only succeeded in finding another which recalled it in many features, with nearly the same view of the minars from the roof, but there was no mirador and no trace of paintings. But painting, after all, in this country has only a subordinate place relatively to architecture, in which the genius of Indian artists found its most fitting expression and achieved its highest triumphs. If Shah Jehan had left no other memorial of his reign than the "Taj," he would still be entitled to the gratitude of posterity, and to an exalted rank among kingly builders. In the chorus of praise, of poetry, and sentiment, which the first sight of Taj Mahal never fails to inspire, I remember but one dissentient voice, and that was a written comment in the visitors' book to the effect that the writer, a patriotic citizen of Allahabad, considered it inferior to certain monuments in his own city, and "not worth the journey from Allahabad in order to see it." The force of one's first impression of any world-renowned chef-d'œuvre is often weakened by unfavorable circumstances or by its environment, and, in the case of a painting or statue often placed in a badly lighted gallery, some effort is necessary at times in order to adjust one's mind to the conditions. But in the case of the Taj the builders have cunningly done all that beforehand, nothing unsightly is left to mar the impression, and when one has emerged from the gloom of the great portal which gives access to the garden, two lines of black cypress spires lead the eye straight to the majestic dome which rises white and dazzling at the end of the vista, and which is repeated in the still water of the long canal.

THE TAJ MAHAL, FROM ACROSS THE JUMNA

The setting is worthy of the gem, and on either hand, beyond the dark cypresses, the garden, of matchless luxuriance, is a very carnival of color. From the stately entrance gate of red stone and white marble, and the garden walls, ornamented with kiosks and domes in which every battlement is inlaid with a marble fleur-de-lis, to the beautiful pendent mosques enhancing the brilliancy of the Taj by their variegated color, the same perfection of finish reigns throughout, and one longs almost unconsciously for some blemish, some harsher note to connect it with the outer world, and stamp it with reality. As one enters the little alcove among piles of pointed shoes of strange and varied make, left by native pilgrims at the threshold, and turns to mount the steps leading to the upper terrace through the recessed marble, as transparently luminous as a crevasse in the ice of a glacier, he is met by ragged little pages, who proceed to whisk the dust from his shoes, so that he may not leave it on the immaculate pavement above.

Seen from across the Jumna it rises like a summer cloud against the clear sky, and its inverted image trembles in the deep blue of the water. There is no blackness in the shadows on the sunlit faces, and even under the deeply recessed arches the color is luminous and opalescent, while on the shadowed side it borrows the cool reflected tones of the sky, and is as full of transparent tints and hues of mother-of-pearl as the lining of a shell. Fergusson is the recognized authority on Indian architecture, and in his comments on the Taj his too evident admiration is tempered, and his reputation as a classical critic saved, by placing it on a lower level than the masterpieces of Greek art, while he pronounces it to be unequalled in its class.* When one attempts to paint or draw even a small portion of it he will grow to understand that beneath its apparent simplicity, which is so managed that no detail interferes with the unity and

* "The Parthenon belongs, it is true, to a higher class of art, its sculptures raising it into the region of the most intellectual branch of phonetic art; but, on the other hand, the exquisite inlay of precious stones at the Taj is so æsthetically beautiful as in a merely architectural estimate almost to bring it on a level with the Grecian masterpiece;" and again he writes, "Though their value consequently may be nearly the same, their forms are so essentially different that they hardly look like productions of the same art. . . . Its beauty may not be of the highest class, but in its class it is unsurpassed."—Fergusson, *History of Architecture.*

force of the impression, there is yet a vast deal of complexity and thorough constructive science. But all these unpleasant but necessary elements are so artfully subordinated, that one carries away only the memory of its sensuous charm of color and outline, and is not disturbed by the underlying basis of mathematics. From the terrace behind the Taj, overlooking the Jumna, the view extends beyond a bend of the river to the fortress walls of Agra, topped by the white domes and gilded roof of the palace and the adjacent mosques. Beautiful at a distance, they lose little by a closer inspection. The fortress is entered by the usual mediæval drawbridge and dark vaulted entrance guarded by tall, red-coated Sikhs. Beyond these outer defences, an ascending ramp, flanked by high walls commanding the road on every side, is admirably planned to resist a sudden attack, and this causeway curves upward to the arched gate between two majestic towers. It must have been nearly or quite impregnable against the cannon of Akbar's time, and should a storming column have succeeded in forcing the outer gate, and mounting the steep ascent, with two turns at right angles, swept on all sides by a concentrated fire from above, it would have suffered at least an unpleasant moment of suspense when forced to halt at the foot of this titanic portal as at the base of a precipice. Notwithstanding its formidable appearance, it deserves to be considered as a work of art from the noble proportions of the two octagonal towers and their ornamentation of inlaid marble. While there is always an element of the quaintly exotic, and, to our eyes, barbaric, in most Hindoo work, which necessitates some familiarity with it before we can fully enjoy its æsthetic qualities, in the great monuments of the Mogul epoch so grand and simple in proportion, and at the same time so wonderfully elaborate, we recognize certain architectural principles already familiar to us. This is particularly evident in the great citadels which enclose the imperial palaces, and which, while planned like the feudal strongholds of Europe, and with quite as much military science, have been made more interesting by their external decoration. The walls and gateways of the Agra fortress were built by Akbar, the red stone palace within resembling in style some of the palaces in his deserted capital at Futtehpore. Sikri was built by his son Jehanghdr, and the beautiful marble palaces, kiosks, pavilions, and mosques were the work of Shah Jehan. Throughout the entire series of stately palaces constructed during the reign of this monarch runs a vein of ultra-æsthetic refinement, showing an evident desire to make the most of natural advantages, and a poetic sense of what is beautiful and fitting, and which could only be content with the best. What could be more satisfactory and complete than the lovely open pavilion crowning one of the red stone towers of the fortress at a great height from the ground, with bracketed marble columns supporting the eaves, inlaid like the Taj, and opening directly into an open marble court with fountains. There is a charming view of the Taj rising beyond a bend of the river from the pavilion, and the little court behind communicates by a latticed passage with the gallery reserved for the ladies of the Zenāna, overlooking the great entrance court where the emperor was accustomed to receive foreign embassies.

But in order to arrive at a fair understanding of what was accomplished in decorative architecture during the reign of Shah Jehan one must take into consideration the other monuments of Agra, having begun with the Taj and the palace. The "Moti Musjid," or Pearl Mosque, which is seemingly restful from its appearance of extreme simplicity, artfully conceals beneath this exterior a great deal of studied proportion and elaborate detail. The broad court, when one enters it on a bright day, has the blinding dazzle of a snow-field, for nothing meets the eye but marble and the deep blue sky. Nothing could exceed the delicacy of color and subtle gradations of tint when the eye penetrates from the outer glare into the depths of shadow behind the arches. But, as in the Taj, there is no darkness in this shadow, and the details of the innermost wall are clearly visible from across the court. A short distance from the fortress rise the three great domes of the Jumna Musjid or chief Mosque of Agra, decorated with zigzag bands of white and red stone. This also is of Shah Jehan's reign. When we pass on to Delhi, his chief capital, we are confronted by another series of imposing buildings, the great fortress, and the remains of the palaces within its enclosures, the great mosque, the largest and most stately pile, as a whole, among Mohammedan religious edifices. And farther on, at Lahore, we find still another capital and another series

THE JUMNA MUSJID, DELHI

of palaces and mosques. In the hill fortress of Gwalior there is yet another palace of Shah Jehan, but a small one, only three hundred and twenty feet in length, perched, as usual, on the very verge of an "embattled steep." Many other pleasure-houses might be added to the list, for this monarch seems to have taken pleasure in distributing himself over a vast extent of territory. An approximate idea of the prodigious number of artistic monuments for which northern India is indebted to his splendid extravagance may be gained by supposing that Louis XIV., for instance, after constructing Versailles and its dependencies, had built the Louvre, Luxembourg, and other edifices of Paris, the work of different architectural epochs, had then built himself another capital at London, with citadels, palaces, cathedrals, and still another at Brussels, and linked them all together by a chain of smaller palaces and occasional retreats. Had not death interrupted his ambition, he would have built a pendant to the Taj across the Jumna, and thrown a marble bridge over the river between them.

The most perfect surviving example of this epoch, which ranks with the Taj as a piece of unparalleled but charming extravagance, is the part of the Palace at Delhi called the Dewan-i-Khas, and the adjoining apartments, all that remains, in fact, of what was once the most extensive and sumptuous palace in the world. According to the only existing plan it was more than double the size of the Escurial, or, indeed, of any other palace in Europe.* It would be useless to refer again to the vandalism which destroyed it, as this has already been the cause of sufficient repentance. The verses in Persian characters, extolling its charms with the customary extravagance of

* *Mogul Art*, Fergusson.

Oriental poets, do not exceed the truth. There is not a square yard, either of column, arch, or ceiling, which is left unadorned with precious mosaics and gilding. In some instances one has a feeling of disappointment at first seeing this far-famed jeweller's decoration applied on such extensive scale. When viewed from a distance these delicate arabesques and flowerlike petals seem to soften and temper the blankness of the marble, and when closely examined with a hand-glass they become interesting again from their wonderful delicacy; but when seen from a short distance they appear formal in design and crude in color, like the stamped patterns on chintz. In the Delhi palace the incrustation of gilding, which relieves in places the bluish or opal-tinted tones of the marble, seems to harmonize and enhance the brighter colors of the mosaic, with its frequently recurring flowers of agate and red carnelian. The sun-steeped landscape seen from the windows, with the distant Jumna, here a narrower stream than at Agra, in its repose and vast breadth, is a perfect foil to the lavish magnificence within. The charm of these Indian palaces may be partly due to the fact that nowhere is nature shut out, and one has no feeling of confinement, as in the palaces of Europe; wherever the eye wanders, across the cool marble of the pavement, to the light between the columns, or through the lace-work of the windows, there is always a prospect of flowers and tree-tops, of blue water, or a hazy rim of encircling hills.

The ceiling of the Dewan-i-Khas, said to have been originally of silver, has been recently restored, though not of course to its former magnificence; but at present it seems somewhat garish in color when contrasted with the time-chastened decorations below. The walls and gateways of the citadel enclosing this group of palaces are built in a style of corresponding magnificence, but somewhat more

WINDOWS IN OLD DELHI

severe in character, and are still in good repair, with the exception of the Cashmere Gate and bastion, the scene of one of the most heroic incidents of modern history. A short distance from the walls stands the Jumma Musjid, which, although somewhat lacking internally in the good taste and harmony of color and arrangement which characterize most buildings of the epoch, is unrivalled in grandeur of line and in external effect. At sunset, when seen from the eastern side, a violet silhouette against the glow of the sky, nothing could exceed its elegance of outline, and it has almost the illusion of a whole city, with its long array of domes, cupolas, spires, and finials, its level line of arcaded cloisters, through which the light pierces, giving to the vast pile an air of lightness and grace, and, dominating all, the two tall minars and great balloon-shaped marble domes.

Much of the merit of the Agra and Delhi mosaics was formerly attributed to Austin de Bordeaux and other Europeans in the service of Shah Jehan; but few patterns have been found, however, which can be referred directly to European inspiration, and it is everywhere apparent that the Moguls availed themselves of the mechanical skill and ingenuity of these Western artificers in working out their own designs, for instances are rare in Italy of workmanship so delicate in execution and at the same time so thoroughly subordinate to the general scheme of the architect.

V

One is usually more or less prepared for what awaits him at Delhi and Agra, but when we were advised to stop on the way north and see Ahmedabad for the first time, we did not expect to have the satisfaction of discovering for ourselves, as it were, a new type of city, and of becoming accustomed to a new phase of Indian art. The guide-books and other works which we had studied before leaving Europe made but little mention of this city, and we knew next to nothing of the marvels of wood-carving with which its streets are lined, and its ornate little mosques all built alike of orange-hued sandstone, differing only in their degree of elaboration; the most striking feature of these mosques is their curious blending of modern and Hindoo art, or, more explicitly speaking, the way in which the plans of Moslem builders have been wrought out and embellished by artisans of Hindoo or Jaina race. In this case the marriage of these two elements has been a happy one, for the architectural results are often remarkable for elegance of form and sculptured detail, and resemble nothing else in the world.

While driving about in the town with the vague hope of finding some fragments of this seductive wood-work, we came suddenly upon a signboard in front of an old house bearing the name in plain English of a New York association of decorative artists. Here we found many of the most skilful workers of the province engaged on American orders, such as chimney-pieces, sideboards, sculptured beams, and panels. This establishment had been recently inaugurated by Mr. Lockwood de Forrest, who has since accomplished so much in popularizing Indian art, and at that time Anglo-Indian art had scarcely awakened to the fact that these things were even worthy of consideration even from an artistic or a commercial point of view. Mention was made in a former article of the general arrangement of these Ahmedabad houses, also common in other cities of Guzerat and in Bombay. The leading features may be again noted as being the deeply recessed lower story forming a veranda, and the wooden pillars with elaborately wrought consols supporting the upper stories or balconies; the whole façade is often covered with a wealth of carving, painted with tints which are rather gaudy when new, but which are exquisitely beautiful when half effaced and weather-worn. The heads of elephants and spirited horses, figures of dancing girls, nymphs, and the gods of the Hindoo pantheon are mingled with floral scroll-work, or more conventional arabesques. The doors of these houses, although massive and heavy, both in appearance and in actual weight, are often exceedingly interesting and of great artistic beauty.

Archæologists and others who have written on Indian art have made little mention of the domestic and street architecture of the country, or have dismissed the subject with a few words, confining their field of observation to the public edifices. One of the very first to appreciate this phase of indigenous art was a well-known English architect, who caused a series of large photographs to be made of houses, windows, doors, and ornamented panels for the South Kensington Museum, and it is through his endeavors that a thoroughly illustrative collection has been made there. Although he has lived to see his labors appreciated, he had great difficulty at the outset in creating an interest, owing to the conservatism of certain directors or others in authority, who recognized only the art of Greece and Rome, stigmatizing everything in India as "Alhambra Rot." Far from discriminating intelligently between the different schools, or even between the good and the bad, they wished to know nothing about it, considering from their classical standpoint that it could have no interest for the world at large.

In contrast to this somewhat intolerant spirit, one meets now and then intelligent natives of India who appear to have discovered for themselves the intrinsic worth of these things at a time when most Europeans were still indifferent to them. There used to be a large "Europe Shop" in Ahmedabad, resembling in the character and variety of its merchandise an American country store, which was kept by an elderly Parsee, and I once had occasion to replace some missing article from his extensive stock. The old gentleman, with white mustache and the mutton-chop whiskers affected by Parsees of the old school, wearing the regulation tall black cap and white drills, was tilted back in his chair, giving orders to half-caste clerks and paying little attention to the rare customers. Some question of mine in regard to the antiquities of the neighborhood seemed to arouse his

TEAK-WOOD DOORWAY, AHMEDABAD

interest, and after diving and rummaging among a pile of old boxes he came out triumphantly with a neatly bound little volume, a monograph in English, describing the principal buildings of mark, and illustrated by photogravures. He had not only written the book, but had made the photographs, having first tried to draw the subjects and finding his skill insufficient; and he had also travelled over a large part of India for the sole purpose of enjoying and studying its architectural beauties. I do not cite this as being at all an exceptional case, since he belonged to a race remarkable for keen intelligence, and among which culture is often associated with wealth. No transition more abrupt and entire could be imagined than that from Ahmedabad to Ajmere. It is not that one city could be considered as exclusively Hindoo and the other as Mohammedan, for the former city was in its prime the capital of a flourishing sultanate and held an incredible number of mosques, while the other was at one time a favorite seat of the Mogul Emperors; but in Ahmedabad the decorative art of the Hindoos, a more cultivated race than their conquerors, was able to hold its own, and there is no trace in the carved house fronts of Arabic influence, and but little even in the mosques, which were profusely sculptured in the Jaina style; there are few if any of the dentilated arches which abound in Rajputana, and a white wall is a rarity among the richly colored but somewhat sombre-toned houses which line the streets. Should one go directly from this city to Ajmere the difference will seem as striking, for instance, as that which exists between Amsterdam and Capri, and would seem to be the work of a widely different race. Here everything is white, there is no carved wood, and the street architecture resembles that of the neighboring cities of Rajputana, of which Ajmere was once an important capital. Most of the town is more or less modern, and while its white aspect recalls in a measure the appearance of a Moorish city, nothing could offer more contrast to the blank walls of the Moors than the brightness and gayety of its bazaars,

WINDOW OF QUEEN'S MOSQUE, AHMEDABAD

made attractive by innumerable arched windows, balconies, and colored awnings. At Lahore and Amritsar we are confronted with another type, the outcome of a different art instinct. The tall wooden houses, as elaborately carved and decorated as those of Guzerat, display many of the geometrical patterns used by the western Arabs, and at Multan and in Scinde Persian influence begins to appear, and many other variations exist in which these leading elements are combined in different proportions.

VI

A lingering doubt still exists as to the possibility of completing or even beginning an art education outside of Europe, and a travelled American was recently heard to ask whether it were yet practicable in the United States. It might furnish such doubters with food for reflection, could they visit one or two of the art schools of India, and see with what success the experiment of initiating the native into the mysteries of the painter's craft, from a European stand-point, has been crowned thus far. In the life-class at the School of Arts in Bombay, we found the students working in various mediums, from a costumed model, one of the characteristic street types of the bazaar. Hindoo and Moslem, irrespective of class distinctions, met on neutral ground, and the class itself would have made an interesting subject for a painter. Some of the workers wore the conventional dress of their race or order, and others the semi-European garb now prevalent. There was a fair sprinkling of scarlet turbans and black velvet caps, and a young Parsee girl, clothed in the classical, clinging drapery of her race, was making what would be considered anywhere a very pretty

SCULPTURE AROUND THE DOORWAY OF A TEMPLE, MUTTRA (MODERN)

ébauche in black and white. The director of this institution, Mr. Griffiths, is an artist of rare ability, and to him is due the credit of inaugurating a school of industrial art, with the object of improving the quality and raising the standard of these various Indian handicrafts, and which is now one of the most interesting features of this institution. Like most innovators, he at first found difficulty in securing the co-operation of the government in developing his plan, and it was not until he had obtained the interest and practical assistance of Lord Reay that the matter was brought to a successful issue. This section of the School of Arts is now called the "Reay" art workshops, and it was opened in 1891 with a staff of eighty artisans. The long building where these ateliers are located, built in unpretending and economical fashion, resembles a weaving-shed, but is well lighted, and quite sufficient for the modest needs of the workers: the rooms have earthen floors, and only one, where finished products are exhibited, has any pretensions to decorative effect. Instruction is given in gold and silver chasing, enamelling on metals, engraving and repoussé work, wood-carving, ornamental copper and brass work, and iron work; also carpet-weaving. Each workshop is presided over by a master craftsman, assisted by a number of apprentices. The system of apprenticeship has

STONE BRACKETS AT MUTTRA

been found necessary in order that the students may not be enticed away by the prospect of higher wages, before their course of study is completed. If they are found, after a probationary period of several months, to have the requisite qualifications, they are formally apprenticed for three years, and receive five rupees a month for the first year, seven for the second, and ten for the third. Much attention is being given to ornamental metal-work, such as iron window gratings and balustrades, and the efforts thus directed will, it is hoped, result in domestic iron-work of a more artistic character than is found in the more modern native houses of Bombay, and more on a par with that which still survives in Ahmedabad and other older cities, which have not yet begun to substitute the cheaper machine-made work of Europe. The ornamental metal-work of the great Victoria Terminus* at Bombay was made at the School of Arts, and far more cheaply than it could have been imported from Europe. This station is one of the most imposing modern buildings in India, and although somewhat florid in its external ornamentation, is agreeable and harmonious in effect, as well as sumptuous in material and finish. In the department of wood-carving at the Reay workshops there are many examples of the application of elaborate decorative designs to art furniture, screens, punkah frames, and other household articles; and the workmen are encouraged to employ their own tools, rather than those imported from Europe, so that when they leave the school they may be better able to turn their hands to any work which may come in their way, without being dependent on foreign aids. In another room a few carpets were being woven on vertical frames, from fragments of ancient Persian carpets of great

* The station of the Great Indian Peninsula Railroad.

beauty, and these models were followed far more carefully, both in design and quality of color, than in the more extensive workshops of the north, whether located in government jails or in private factories, from which the great warehouses of London and Paris are supplied. The metal work produced here impressed me as being more artistic than that which is usually offered to the casual tourist in the shops, or by itinerant venders, particularly those partially enamelled or engraved. A most praiseworthy feature of this institution is the economical way in which such results are obtained, as if every rupee had been laid out to the best advantage. The Mayo School of Arts at Lahore is one of the most thriving and practically useful endowments of this kind to be found anywhere.

VISTA IN THE NEW ART MUSEUM, LAHORE

In the minds of the majority of people Lahore, like Thule, belongs to the fantastic realm of opera, and whenever the name comes up, the practical man at once mentally consigns it to the vague limbo of theatrical geography. Remote from the sea, and within a day's journey of the treacherous Afghan, travellers with round-the-world Cook's tickets seldom include it in their itineraries. In spite of this crushing indifference of the world in general, Lahore has gone bravely on, and built for itself an École des Beaux Arts and an Art Museum, in both of which it has dared to be original, and which deserve to be more widely known as models in their way. In place of the customary renaissance palace or Greek temple, we find an edifice which seems to embody in its internal architecture and adornment the principles which govern the conduct of the school—the encouragement and amelioration of native art. This institution was first proposed in 1873–74 as a memorial to Lord Mayo, the former viceroy, and it was then decided that it should have a distinctly Oriental character. Mr. J. Lockwood Kipling was induced to go to Lahore, in order to take charge of the new undertaking, in 1875. Mr. Kipling's fitness for the task, and his success in bringing it to completion, was owing as much to his previous training and professional experience in various directions as to his keen appreciation of the Indian art in generation, for it has usually been conceded that a good "all-round man" has the advantage of a specialist in such an undertaking. He had previously identified himself with what might be termed the new art movement in Bombay by his work on the stately series of municipal and government buildings—the Veneto-Gothic palaces in the new quarter, which offer such a grateful contrast to the stuccoed and yellow-washed classical temples of an earlier date, many of which, unfortunately, still survive. There were many obstacles in his way at the outset, as well as deeply rooted prejudice to counteract, and much study of the ground was necessary before he could carry out the very obvious and simple notion that, since India is heir to a distinctive and naturally descended style of art, some effort should be made to preserve it, and to collect and perpetuate its best traditions. To continue in his own words, he "was hampered by two or three influences: first, the excellent English administrators, who had never seriously thought about art at all, but who expected the latest kind of European improvements on the subject; and, secondly, the natives themselves, who were very reluctant to believe that it was worth while to study and draw buildings which they had been indifferent to all their lives: they also expected something brand-new from England." After some tentative experiments, he established a nucleus of students and craftsmen from which the school grew to its present importance. Since Mr. Kipling's retirement the school has been under the direction of Mr. F. H. Andrews, and the work is being carried on quite in accordance with the views of its founders. All the assistant masters with the exception of Mr. David are natives of the Punjaub, and the course of study comprises modelling and moulding in plaster, architecture and wood-carving.

CARVED WOOD BRACKET AND CAPITAL, BOMBAY

engineering, geometry, mensuration, drawing, and design. There are no fees for instruction, and the students are further encouraged by various stipends and scholarships. Some of the more advanced students have already been sent out to introduce the system into the schools of the northwest provinces. An annual art exhibition is held here, and artisans from remote parts of the province send in their contributions.

At the epoch of my visit to Lahore, in 1893, the last exhibition had just been closed, but many of the unsold articles still remained in the show-rooms, and I was particularly impressed by the beautiful reproductions and fac-similes of carved doorways and oriel windows in dark wood, or in fragrant "deodar" (a light-colored Himalayan cedar), which were offered at prices incredibly low. There were also marvellous screens with frames inlaid with ivory or brass, and deodar panels filled in with delicate geometrical lattice-work almost microscopic in minuteness of detail. Nothing of inferior quality seemed to have found a place here, and the examples of ivory inlaying, lacquer and metal work were all of excellent and thorough workmanship. It was one of the founder's chief objects to furnish provincial artisans, who have no shops or studios,

BALCONY OF THE PALACE OF THE SETHS, AJMEER

and no way of reaching the public, with a place to show their works, and thus to "link up the bazaar with the school." But in spite of his efforts and those of his successor, the greater part of the students look to government service rather than to handicrafts for a future. The best of them are generally sons of carpenters, goldsmiths, blacksmiths, and the like, who have an hereditary aptitude for design, which men of other castes do not possess. As an instance of the way in which the materials at hand were utilized, Mr. Kipling found that under the apparent hap-hazard method of working which Indian wood-carvers follow, there was a definite system of teaching, and the boys in the shops improved their spare moments by copying certain set patterns. These models were collected and carefully codified, and some of the fine old examples of wood-work of the best period, called "Akbari," being of the time of Akbar, were added to them, and all were found to be of great use in elementary teaching. In this way also the details of the fresco-painting in the mosque of Vazir Khan were utilized as a copy-book, but at the same time the students were made to exercise their inventive faculties in attempting original designs, and to develop their inborn instinct for harmony of color, in which, when left to themselves, they seldom go wrong. Instances of the application of this latent but hitherto untrained talent to practical uses have already begun to multiply, and the superb decoration of the Queen's new banqueting-hall at Osborne by Bhai Khan Singh (an assistant master) shows what can be accomplished under such favorable conditions. In the atelier of sculpture at the school were examples of unfinished but promising work, and among the studies from life, hung on the walls of the painting-class, are a few heads of Sikhs and other local types, notably those by Munshi Sher Muhammad, now an instructor, to whose ability and taste much of the decorative work in the new art museum is also due. These heads are painted in a straightforward and vigorous way which would have commanded respect in any Paris atelier ten years ago. If these clever exotics have not yet caught on to the most recent fashion of expressing the "soul of things" by a more emblematic mode of treatment—the theory of valuation, in short—and, ignorant of the joyous reaction which has taken place, are still struggling to render what their eyes see, it is only because the last art-wave set in motion by the pioneers of the new movement has turned its course westward, leaving them still groping for more light.

In the museum adjoining the school are several examples of early Hindoo sculpture showing unmistakable evidence of Greek influence, and it would be easy to believe that their authors had labored in the shadow of the Acropolis. The Jeypore School of Arts is up to the present moment the only one which flourishes in a native state, and although much of the work produced there seems to aim rather at achieving commercial excellence than at improving the character of industrial art, some of its pupils have distinguished themselves by good architectural and decorative work. The results of the growing interest in local art are everywhere apparent, not only in the larger cities which might be called relatively art centres, such as Calcutta, Bombay, Madras, or Lahore, but in many of the smaller cities as well. In the town of Muttra alone there are several noteworthy public buildings, like the "Hardinge Gate," giving access to one of the principal bazaars, of noble proportions, and built of the pale clay-colored stone of the country, which is admirable material for the delicate and sharply-cut work of Hindoo

sculptors. There is also a small museum on the outskirts of the city, which, although not imposing in size, is remarkable for its exquisite workmanship. Wherever a blank outer wall occurs, it has been made interesting down to the ground, by dividing the lower spaces into arched panels and by carving on these centres masses of fruit or flowers, vigorously treated, and with only a slight degree of conventionaliza-

IN THE COURT OF THE PALACE OF THE SETHS, AJMEER

tion. These examples, were others lacking in Muttra, would show conclusively that there is some vitality left in Hindoo art. At Jeypore there is a fine modern palace in the park, and one at Baroda recently built, with a large hall adorned with balconies of ancient carved woodwork. The Palace of the Seths at Ajmeer is one of the most attractive modern instances of elaborate decoration to be found anywhere, and Rousselet mentions it in terms of praise. The façade of this palace, fronting one of the principal streets, is completely covered by tiers of projecting windows of varying design in which white alternates with brown stone, all remarkable for breadth and at the same time delicacy of treatment, and the whole pile is wonderfully light and airy in effect, while the principal court-yard within has some admirable oriel windows, and the intervening wall spaces show much originality in their decoration. While many of the pupils of these Art Academies have shown incontestable evidence of ability, and in some cases a striking talent for portraiture, it is questionable whether they should be encouraged to engage in a career which does not at present offer any very alluring prospect of success, either artistic or commercial. There seem, on the other hand, to be far greater possibilities in store for them in those fields of decorative and ornamental art in which they are at present almost unrivalled: there may yet be a decade or two during which we may hope to see other palaces and public buildings erected of the fantastic and graceful architecture which admits of such varied combinations, before the growth of the utilitarian spirit and the exigencies of commerce shall have supplanted them all by blocks of stone and sheds of corrugated iron. It is even possible, as an Englishman has written, that some future municipal engineer may find it necessary to widen the streets of Lahore and set them straight with a plumb-line. Nothing can check the steady growth of these improvements; they have come to stay, and their triumphant excuse for being ugly is that they are cheap.

HINDOO AND MOSLEM

I

From the earliest period of which any historic record has survived, when the Vedic literature first took shape, through the following ages which saw the rise and fall of Buddhism, the final triumph of the Brahmanic faith and the successive Mahommedan invasions, down to the present day, India has been the battle-ground of antagonistic creeds. The first followers of the Prophet found a country which had long enjoyed an advanced stage of civilization and culture, but which, divided into many states and harassed by internecine dissensions, was unable to oppose an effectual barrier to their progress. When the flood of Mussulman conquest, stamping out on its way the worshippers of fire and pouring down through the passes on the north, had spread over the Punjaub, a dynasty of Mohammedan kings succeeded the Hindoo monarchs of Delhi, and prepared the ground in a manner for the formation of the great Mogul Empire. From the writings and memoirs of Bernier, Sir Thomas Roe, and other early travellers, and aided by the study and inspection of the numerous existing remains and monuments of that epoch, we may form some idea of its pomp and luxury, unparalleled in modern times, and recalling in many features the splendor of the ancient monarchies of the Euphrates valley. This last great period of Mussulman ascendency, beginning with the reign of the

Emperor Baber, the so-called founder of the Empire of the Moguls, the contemporary of Suleyman the Magnificent and François I., and extending into the following century when Shah Abbas reigned at Ispahan, and European travellers returning from Persia told marvellous tales of its sumptuous court, culminated in the reign of Shah Jehan at Delhi and Agra. Previous to the foundation of this empire, the occasional inroads of the Moguls are stated by Elphinstone to have been "the greatest calamity that had fallen on mankind since the deluge, as they had no religion to teach, no seeds of improvements to sow, nor did they offer an alternative of conversion or tribute." One invasion followed another from Genghis Khan to Tamerlane, until the advent of Baber, the first of the Tartar monarchs, who began his reign in 1526. He is now believed to have been "the most admirable, though not the most powerful, prince that ever reigned in Asia." With great administrative capacity, he was at the same time a soldier and an athlete, a scholar and a poet.

With Shah Jehan, the Mogul power may be said to have reached its climax; after Aurungzebe the decadence began, and the invasion of the Persian conqueror Nadir Shah gave it a blow from which it never recovered. Then followed the rise of the Sikh confederacy and the ascendency of the Mahrattas.

During all this time, nothing approaching a complete fusion of the two races, a blending of the Hindoo and Moslem elements, has taken place, but in many respects the ways and customs of each have been more or less modified by the intimacy and contact of daily life, so that it is not always easy to distinguish the one from the other by any outward sign. Even in the matter of religious observances, the lines of demarcation have been somewhat softened, and, to quote from Mr. Baines * and the illustrations which he gives, "in many instances where the two forms of faith exist more or less in numerical equality side by side, the Brahman officiates at all family ceremonial; and as it has been put by a local writer, the convert to Islam observes the feasts of both religions and the fasts of neither." This state of thought is very much like that described by Lady Mary Wortley Montagu as existing among the Macedonian Arnauts of her time, who, living between Christians and Mohammedans, and "not being skilled in controversy, declare that they are utterly unable to judge which religion is the best; but to be certain of not rejecting the truth, they very prudently follow both. They go to the mosque on Friday and to the church on Sunday, saying for their excuse that at the day of judgment they are sure of protection from the true Prophet, but which that is they are not able to determine in this world." Compare with this the following experience in the present generation as having occurred in the eastern plains of the Punjaub: "A traveller entering a rest-house in a Mussulman village found the headman refreshing the idol with a new coat of oil, whilst a Brahman read holy texts alongside. The pair seemed rather ashamed at being caught in the act; but on being pressed, explained that their mulla (priest) had lately visited them, and, being extremely angry on seeing the idol, had made them bury it in the sand. But now the mulla had gone, they were afraid of the possible consequences, and were endeavoring to console the god for his rough treatment." The scientific and ethnological side of the caste question has been exhaustively treated, but a stranger, even after he had digested the mass of erudition which has

* J. A. Baines, Census Commissioner for India, 1891.

HINDOOS AT A VILLAGE WELL

accumulated on this subject, would still find difficulty in distinguishing one subdivision from another, and even, in many instances, in discriminating between Hindoos and Mohammedans. On the other hand, there is such a marked difference between certain of the main divisions, whether religious or racial, as between a Baboo and a Rajput or a Sikh, a Bania from Ahmedabad and a Mahratta, that after having once noted their principal characteristics one is in no danger of forgetting them forevermore. Certainly no races of Europe can show such marked divergence of type as those of Hindostan. Then there is always the "caste mark," which is or should be daily painted on the forehead of every self-respecting Hindoo, and this may take the form of a dab of red paint, a circle or an ellipse, a slender crescent, or a round dot of gold, and the foreheads of certain holy men are decorated with white stripes. The "grande cordon" of the Brahman which elevates him above all lower castes is the white thread passing over his right shoulder, and which is as much a mark of distinction as the rosette of some European order in contrast with the rank and file wearing a simple knot of ribbon, or the lower orders who have no such distinguishing mark. And there is also another way of distinguishing the members of some of the more prominent castes, and that is by the form of their turbans, and in some cases by slight variations of costume, such as the coats or jackets fitted tightly around the chest with a curve flap, which in the case of Hindoos is fastened on the right side, and with Moslems on the left. The inexhaustible variety of shape and color among the turbans and caps is a striking element in the picturesqueness of Indian street life, and one which gives to the streets of Bombay the vivacity of an endless carnival. For in other eastern countries all headgear is fashioned more or less after one or two prescribed models. Among the Mahrattas alone there are several startling variations, and the turban, if one may call it so, worn by the nobles and grandees is shaped like a double-ended canoe, with some resemblance also to a cocked hat adorned with a gold-lace cockade, and the rakish Mahratta fashion of wearing it seems to embody something of the character of this once dashing race of freebooters who raided India for so many years. To attempt the most inadequate description of these varied fashions, or to portray them by a series of illustrations, would take the space of more than one article; and the stranger can hardly pass a day in any of the great centres without seeing at least one or two turbans of unfamiliar forms, and, as for their color, the tints in the most liberally assorted box of pastels would convey but a feeble notion of the infinitude of gradations which they display. These distinguishing marks of caste have invaded even the more democratic province of Islam, and certain fashions in which the Mussulman turban is worn are quite as distinctive as are the Hindoo head-coverings.

In Ahmedabad we first noticed a curiously plaited white turban built around a skullcap of delicate and subdued tints—a number of men wearing these turbans and long "kaftans" of white linen were coming out of a house where a great festival had been given, a dinner of a hundred covers. We found it impossible to procure one of these turbans in Ahmedabad, as they were worn only by a certain order of Mussulmans in or near Bombay, and upon arriving in that city we at once set out on a quest among the turban-makers shops. The special fabricant of this peculiar style of head-dress, when we found him, proved to be a little weazen-faced Moslem who sat perched in a window looking out into the bazaar, and from the "gharry" we watched the opening of negotiations by the servant who represented us. But he was unfortunately only a low-caste Hindoo, and his advances were received with disdain by the arrogant Moslem hatter, who refused to enter into any financial transaction with him whatever; but we finally obtained the coveted turban through the friendly offices of Hadj Mohammed, a Mussulman who kept an outfitter's shop under our hotel. Among the usages of the purely Mussulman community we recognize much which is already familiar to us in other Eastern countries, and quite as much which is strictly local, and there exists also the still more interesting borderland where the two great creeds seem to have reached the point of mutual tolerance, if not of ultimate fusion. Every shrine or place of pilgrimage held in honor by the disciples of the Prophet, and nearly every unfrequented or abandoned mosque, is usually confided to the guardianship of an ancient Mussulman, often a relic by descent of some heroic ancestor, who camps out with his family in a secluded corner of its cloisters. Here he leads a peaceful and ruminative existence, passing the long hot afternoon in a shady corner under the spreading branches of an ancient fig-tree or "peepul," droning aloud from the Koran to his pupils, with an occasional pull at his bubbling water-pipe by way of interlude, or a brief nap on his straw carpet. And while the venerable mulla slumbers, the monkeys or "langurs" let themselves cautiously down from the branches overhead and investigate the frugal contents of his larder, or gambol about the tank, while the swarms of green parrots keep up a riotous clamor among the leaves overhead. Ranking below the village menials in the graduated series of castes come the gypsies of India, who occupy pretty much the same position in the social scale that they do in other countries, while they follow similar

THE MULLA

callings. In point of numbers, and in relative prominence as compared with other castes, they are hardly important enough to be mentioned at all except for the vagueness and mystery surrounding their origin.* Many of them are tinkers, jugglers, and sorcerers, and although I have never seen it stated that snake-charming was among their vocations, a party of swarthy wizards who entertained us with a basketful of cobras at Ahmedabad had all the salient features of their confrères on the Albaicin at Granada. The village barber and his wife have a position above that of many other castes, owing to the variety and importance of their social functions. Hindoos alone have many different ways of wearing the hair, and we found amusement and edification at Saharunpoor in watching a row of these barbers seated on the ground, with their cases of tools beside them, as they operated on the heads of their constantly changing clientèle. Both Hindoos and Moslems are alike charitable to their poorer brethren, particularly to those who are bound by religious vows to lead a life of mendicity. The Mussulman khamsanah at a dâk bungalow treasures up what is left of wasteful Christian dinners, and distributes it to his needy co-religionists on Fridays when they assemble in force. Many and various were the races represented in these gatherings at Amritsar, notably those of northern descent, long-haired Beloochees, Afghans, and other waifs from over the border, all eager to profit by this semi-official bounty. One can hardly live a day in India without assimilating some new fact bearing upon the endless sub-divisions and

* Some years ago, at a dance given by a band of Andalusian gypsies, I noticed their marked resemblance to low-caste Hindoos not only in feature but in the quality of their skin and hair, and a Spanish acquaintance seemed firmly convinced of their Indian origin. This is also the theory of Mr. Baines, who finds many arguments to support it.

HINDOO AND MOSLEM BARBERS

infinitesimal gradations of caste, and as in the literary, artistic, and social worlds of other hemispheres, the principal divisions which would seem at first sight to the uninitiated outsider to consist of pretty much the same sort of people, are found, when attentively examined, to exhibit unexpected divergences, and to be composed of hostile units all animated by a common tendency to cluster together, to form nuclei, and then to subdivide again.

II

The Hindoo globe-trotter takes delight, not altogether free from a spark of malice, in pointing out the beam in the eyes of other Aryan brothers which has been thought to exist only in his own. "You too have caste," said one of the Hindoos at the Chicago Fair, "but your caste is founded on money alone." In a recent book about England and the English, written by a Hindoo, the author who had heard Englishmen talk about the baneful effects of caste in India as if they had none in England, says, "A poor man there is a Sudra;* and a rich man, a lord, a peer, a Brahman, a born legislator, statesman, and everything else." And yet upon the whole he is a "friendly critic," as the *Times of India* reviewer assures us, who found much to admire in British institutions. With the spread of education among subordinate castes, the supremacy of the Brahman, and the exclusive monopoly in matters intellectual which he formerly enjoyed, are rapidly waning. The class which seems to have made the most capital out of the new order of things is the somewhat loosely defined but widely distributed portion of the Hindoo population known as Bengalis or Baboos. When

* The lowest and most degraded caste.

they are conservative enough to cling to the primitive costume of their forefathers, which was evidently not designed to foster the vice of vanity among its wearers, there is little difficulty in distinguishing them from other subjects of the Queen-Empress. These orthodox Baboos wear nothing on their heads to cover their close-cropped shocks of black hair, although they usually carry a white cotton umbrella; their principal garment is a long piece

HINDOO WOMEN, SUBURBS OF BOMBAY

of white drapery called a "dhotee," leaving their arms and legs bare, and worn something after the fashion of a Roman toga. Other characteristic features of their costume are the low patent-leather shoes, and white socks, which have a tendency to hang down, leaving visible large surfaces of fat, brown shanks, as these people are inclined to be of full and portly habit. Gold-rimmed spectacles often add a touch of modern "actuality" to this somewhat archaic costume.

There is a prevalent belief among the more progressive members of this class that a European costume, or, what is more common, a sort of compromise between the dress of the undisguised Baboo and the Englishman, is the first step in the direction of worldly success. As a recent critic remarks, "In as small a matter as getting off a tram-car, I have repeatedly observed that Baboos in coats and trousers risk their lives in a flying leap, while others in dhotee and bare feet insist on the car stopping before they trust their precious persons to the ground." Whatever may be his dress he runs no risk of being mistaken for a member of any of the military castes, and in case of war it would probably never occur to the ruling powers to raise an army from among this industrious and prolific section of the community. But in a country where everything has been specialized from the very beginning, no one seems to respect this class the less, on account of its pacific disposition. And yet some of their severest critics may be found among their own order. One of their pundits with an historic name lately remarked, "You can no more make a gentleman out of a Bengali than carve a fine image out of rotten wood." He and others believe that the Bengali has little stability or force of character, and that new institutions or movements which originate among them fail to inspire any marked degree of public confidence unless propped up by the support of some European element, however slight. And as a general thing the Bengali will rely more on the word of an Englishman than on that of his fellow-countrymen. But on the other hand it cannot be denied that these people represent much of the brain and intelligence of native India. They edit papers and are born agitators, criticising the policy of the government, and saying whatever it pleases them to think upon political matters in their societies, as well as in their journals, for they are usually endowed with the gift of volubility and rapid utterance, and freely express their minds in "high-falutin'" and more or less Shakespearian English. With the steady progress of modern ideas and education the examples of Baboo English, which once delighted Anglo-Indian readers, are becoming rarer, and we may never have another book equal to the well-known biography of Onoocool Chunder Mookerjèe.* A gentleman

* The writer cannot do better than quote the opening lines of this remarkable work for the instruction of those not familiar with the author's style: "The Memoir of the late Hon'ble Justice Onoocool Chunder Mookerjèe. Let me hold my *Penna* after a few months, to write the memoir of the individual above-named: but quid agis? if any one put me such a query, I will be utterly thrown into a great jeopardy and hurley-burley, and say—a fool of myself! As a spider spins web for its own destruction, or as when the clown who was busy in digging a grave for 'Ophelia,' was asked by Hamlet, 'Whos grave's this Sirrah?' said. 'Mine Sir,' so in writing one's memoir I am as if to dig my own grave in it. To write one's memoir, or to write in such a way as the literary public may fall in love with, is a task difficult in the extreme, especially of such a man as the late Hon'ble Justice Mookerjèe. He was no poet that I may put some such writing in print, full of poetical thoughts, which the public did not see, or recite some such stirring events, as induced him to write into measured lines some such subjects, which the public are already in possession of and thereby please them."

An official while in town left a pony in charge of a native subordinate, from whom it escaped. The native explained the matter in a who has been for many years connected with the management of one of the northern railways does not think that they are actually supplanting Europeans, but that on the contrary they are often elbowed out by "poor whites," a class which formerly did not exist, the sons of Europeans, or "Eurasians," for the most part laborers and mechanics, when they can find employment. On the other hand, fewer Europeans now fill the posts of station-masters, engine-drivers, or guards, and natives trained for the work are rapidly replacing them. Natives, particularly of the Baboo class, now hold a larger number of official appointments than was formerly the case in accordance with recent official decisions. My informant thinks that they are excellently organized for office and routine work, though not reliable in case of emergencies, and personally he would rather employ a native for any post worth under 100 rupees a month than a European, as he can procure a better stamp of man in a native at that price. But these adaptive and versatile Hindoos are rapidly crowding out Europeans from minor clerkly employments, since they can make a better appearance on less money. Among their ranks may be found journalists, politicians, and scribes of every description, advocates, attorneys, and judges. Many have achieved distinction at the bar, in politics, and in literature. The poetess Toru Dutt, whom Edmund Gosse calls a "fragile, exotic blossom of song," was the daughter of the Baboo Govin Chunder Dutt, and before the age of twenty she had attained such a mastery of French that her romance *Le Journal de Mlle. d'Arvers*

letter to his "sahib": "I have the honour to report that the little horse, since your honour's departure, has assumed a devil-may-care attitude and has become violently obstreperous. This morning at 6 A.M. the said little horse eloped from my custody, but, with the favour of Heaven, he may return."

SNAKE-CHARMER

received much commendation in Paris, and her ancient ballads and legends of Hindostan are full of passages which few would wish to see changed, and which show a wonderful mastery of English verse. Without falling into the error of judging a race by rare exceptions and of "booming the Baboo" prematurely, it is evident that he is having a chance for the first time in history, and that he is not backward in making the most of it.

III

One of the vital problems of government in India to-day is the maintenance of harmony between the two principal religious factions. This is by no means a new question, but one which has taken many different forms since the days of the tolerant Akbar, who, although surrounded by fanatical priests and followers, showed himself to be far freer from race prejudice than some monarchs of the present day; and the latest development of this problem, reduced to its lowest terms by the press of India, is the "Cow Question," or "cow *vs.* pig." These two peaceable animals have been dragged into the controversies between the disciples of Mohammed and of Brahma, where they have been made to play not merely the part of animate symbols, but that of active participants in the frequent local outbursts of religious frenzy. Some years ago one of the first of many similar *emeutes* was caused by the discovery of a live pig in the sacred precincts of the great mosque at Delhi. To the stranger forced to be content with general impressions, and lacking the time, or perhaps the disposition, to look beneath the surface, the chief cause of contention between the partisans of the two great creeds might appear a trivial matter; but the real question lies deeper, and is not to be treated in either a facetious or a zoological vein. Far from seeing anything laughable in the aspect which these dissensions have taken of late, the local press inclines to treat the matter with great seriousness: and with good reason, since the immediate cause of the mutiny has again been admitted, after all, to have been the greased cartridges smeared with animal fat, objectionable alike to Hindoo and Moslem. While the cow is the more serious cause of these lamentable differences of opinion, and will always remain a *casus belli*, the pig is dragged into the conflict, and most unwillingly, by the Hindoos, to be used with never-failing success as a weapon of offence against their adversaries, and ofttimes as a missile. The Mussulman sees no reason why he should be debarred from eating beef by the prejudice of the Hindoo, but wherever the Hindoo is numerically strong enough he will prevent him. On the other hand, a Hindoo writer in the *Tohfa-i-Hind*, in descanting on the evils of cow-killing, says: "To kill such a highly useful animal to supply one day's food (for a few men) is downright folly, and those who destroy such an animal for the purpose of food deserve to be regarded with abhorrence. Besides, cows' flesh is most injurious to health. The writer has got a large number of ancient books on medicine in his possession, written by Mohammedans, in which cows' flesh is distinctly condemned as deleterious and productive of leprosy. Her blood, too, is described as a deadly poison in its effect. Again, in the old books on cookery, of which, too, the writer possesses a goodly lot, modes of preparing food of the flesh of other animals are given, but nowhere cows' flesh is mentioned. All this clearly shows that cows' flesh cannot be used by man without doing great injury to his body." This thorough-paced vegetarian is firmly convinced that cow-killing was introduced into India un-

BELOOCHEE

der British rule, in proof of which he points to the spread of leprosy, and what he calls "the increasing spread of famines."* The feeling among the Hindoos against the wanton destruction of these sacred animals by their gluttonous adversaries and former tyrants has reached such a height that an "anti-cow-killing league" has been formed and is rapidly growing in strength. A riot caused by this sentiment occurred last year at Gazipur, but serious consequences were averted by the prompt action of the authorities. A number of Hindoos convicted of having caused the disturbance appealed from the judgment of the chief magistrate of Benares, sentencing them to a term of imprisonment, and the main facts were again stated in court. One Wazir Ali, the "zemindar," or headman of a village, and a Mussulman, as his name implies, was about to give a feast to celebrate the marriage of his daughter. But the local butcher would not sell him any beef, on account of the feeling among the Hindoos, who are in the majority in that province. Then Wazir Ali bethought himself of his own cow, but not being discreet enough to keep his nefarious design to himself, the Hindoos got wind of it and spread the news throughout the neighborhood. Some of them ran to the next village, shouting, "Cows are going to be killed in Mau†

* *Times of India*, March 12, 1894.

† Mau, name of town.

to-day at Wazir's house! All go to the temple of Mahabir. Whoever does not go, let him be held guilty of eating cow!" When an armed crowd had collected, numbering between two and three thousand Hindoos, Ram Gulam Lal and a Brahman were deputed to go to Wazir Ali, and tell him that if he killed his cow, "his house would be looted and he himself probably killed."

Wazir Ali, at a loss for some way of feeding his guests, proposed to kill a buffalo calf, if he could find one, and appealed to the local authorities to protect him in this exercise of his civil rights. But the mob had determined to prevent him from killing either cow or buffalo, and threatened to loot the village; some one was heard to say that British rule would not last three years; but upon the arrival of the representatives of the law and the display of force the ringleaders were arrested, and the mob finally broken up and dispersed.

Opinions differ as to the extent to which the "cow-protection" movement is responsible for the late disturbance in Bombay. That it was one of the causes seems to be generally admitted. In this instance the agitation had been fermenting for several weeks previous to the outbreak, and the police were ready. In the list of resolutions issued by the local government of Bombay a few months after the riot some of these causes are alluded

AFGHAN

to, and there are many curious facts which give an idea of the prevailing character of these religious or semi-religious disturbances and the course which they usually take. There had been a growing ill-feeling between the two factions which had manifested itself in various ways, and, as the Commissioner of Police reports, the causes of the final outbreak "were both predisposing and immediate." He had with much difficulty prevented the leaders of the "Cow Protection Society" from parading thousands of these domestic animals through the streets on the occasion of their anniversary in April. A rival society was formed for the purpose of preaching the same views with greater energy; and their agents obtained a large plot of land, where they intended to sequestrate all the cattle which they had intercepted and purchased on the road to Bombay. "Pictures and pamphlets illustrating the sanctity of the cow, and the sin of slaughtering it, were also sold and distributed all over the Presidency, but chiefly in Bombay." The secretary of one of these societies went to the commissioner and urged him to prohibit the practice of slaughtering cattle, which had existed for centuries in Bombay, but he naturally refused to interfere. In spite of all the precautions taken, and the vigilance of the authorities, hostilities broke out, as had been anticipated, on a Friday,* and in the vicinity of the Jumma Mujid. When the crowd of Mussulman worshippers—which was unusually large, numbering over a thousand—began to leave the mosque at one o'clock, after the noonday prayers, it was evident that there was a concerted movement among them, which presently developed into a tumultuous rush towards the Masuti temple. Notwithstanding the efforts of a large number of law-abiding

* August 11, 1893.

Mussulmans, aided by the police, to quell the excitement, sticks were brandished, stones thrown, and with loud shouts of "Din! Din!" the mob attacked the Hindoo shop-keepers, rushing down the neighboring streets, and assailing the police and mounted "Sowars" with their clubs and with volleys of stones and tiles. In the meantime other riots had broken out in various quarters; and as the bands of infuriated Mussulmans were driven from one street to another, or dispersed by the police and the troops which had now been called out to aid them, they would again unite and attack the hated cow protectors and all who stood in their way. Detachments from the Bombay Volunteer Light Horse Artillery and Rifles, and also from the Marine Battalion, as well as several other strong bodies of native troops, now came to the rescue, and guns were posted at the intersections of streets. For several days the tumult raged—not, it would seem, in one continuous battle, but in a series of riots, followed by intervals of quiet, and again breaking out afresh. Hindoo temples and Mussulman mosques were desecrated, idols were broken, stables where cattle were kept set on fire, and even the poor buffaloes, which partake of the sanctity of the cow only in a remote degree, did not escape: shops were looted, and crowds of Mussulmans escorting the biers containing their dead were assaulted in their turn by the Hindoos. And so the struggle went on, until the arrival of fresh troops from Poona finally put an end to it. Among the most desperate combatants were bands of "Seedy boys" and Pathans, and even Mahrattas were dragged into the fray, but in no instance known was any European attacked unless a member of the police force or a soldier. Over fifteen hundred rioters were arrested, of which number the Mohammedans were largely in excess, and in some instances heavy sentences of imprisonment were imposed. In summing up the causes of this disturbance some months later, the Governor considered that one of the main causes of the outbreak was the infections spread by the riots which had broken out in other parts of India, and especially those at Prabas Pathan.*

Mussulmans are quite well aware that the tender sentiments of the Hindoos in regard to cows are of old standing, and also, on the other hand, that in all stations where Englishmen reside the supply of beef is regularly forthcoming, although precautions are always taken to avoid wounding the susceptibilities of the Hindoos. It appears also from the reports that no amount of foresight could have averted the uprising, but at the same time a stronger display of military force at the outset might have prevented much violence. And here we touch upon a tender point, for it seems that in England there is a party which is always ready to decry any resort to arms, or any unnecessary manifestation of force in India.

Now we come to another class of disturbances, of a more purely religious or rather sectarian character, in which the cow is relegated to the background, and the pig plays the part of the spark which explodes the magazine. Yeola, the scene of the latest riot, is a town where the Hindoo part of the population far outnumbers the Mohammedan section. According to the Hindoo version

* The beginnings of the disturbance were seen at Prabas Pathan, a village in the Junagadh territory, in the vicinity of the famous shrine of Somnath, where during the "taboot procession" an onslaught upon the Hindoos was made by the Mussulmans, in which eleven were killed and many injured. The incident naturally created much excitement in Bombay among both Hindoos and Mohammedans, and meetings were held by the respective communities, at which subscriptions were raised for defraying the cost of prosecution and defence in the judicial proceedings that were to follow the riots, and to relieve the feelings of the victims.—*Times of India*, January 1, 1894.

of this affair, the misunderstanding first began on September 15, 1893, when, as has been the custom from time immemorial, the Hindoos are wont to take their idol in procession accompanied by bands of musicians

PUBLIC LETTER-WRITER, LAHORE

playing the deafening music which is thought to appease his wrath, but which is peculiarly irritating to Mussulman ears, and after promenading him through the town with much pomp and ceremony, sitting in state in a towering car, gorgeous with red and gold, they conduct him to the temple. Unfortunately for the idol and his faithful followers, the procession was made to pass the Patel's mosque, where a strong body of fierce descendants of the Prophet was lying in ambush, eager to swoop down on the noisy infidels.* The Hindoos say that the

* In these religious processions each sect delights to parade through the enemy's part of the town, and it is only by the exercise of much diplomacy on the part of the local authorities that collisions are prevented.

principal magistrate, who happened to be a Mohammedan, the only other magistrate in authority having left the village, then showed himself, and obliged the procession to take another route, which allayed the excitement for the moment, but gave great cause of offence to the Hindoos. As succeeding events proved, the outbreak was only postponed, and the measures taken at the time were injudicious and satisfactory to neither party. The Dussera festival was to take place shortly, and as more trouble was apprehended by the local authorities, a number of orders and proclamations were issued, some of which appear to have conflicted with each other, and did not produce the anticipated effect. The procession was ordered not to pass any mosque between the 10th and the 17th of October, but was allowed to pass certain specified mosques at given dates and hours. Furthermore, no musical instrument except a gong should be played within fifteen paces on each side of a mosque. The Mohammedans, on the other hand, were not to assemble in their mosques "for any unlawful purpose" at these times, or their mosques would be locked up. This measure, as might have been expected, gave umbrage to the Mohammedans.

These various attempts on the part of the local powers to smooth matters over seem also to have grievously annoyed the Hindoos as well; for their most important ceremony on the day of Dussera, which fell this year on October 15th, did not take place at all. On this occasion they assemble in Balajee's temple, and take the idol out for an airing in the suburbs of the town. Although the temple was protected by a detachment of soldiers, the managers of the procession complained that their god Balajee had been insulted and deeply injured by the derisive yells and cries of the Mussulman roughs and irreverent small boys, that the ceremony was useless without the customary music of horns and tom-toms, and, furthermore, that if they could not start when they were ready, they would not go at all. Their state of mind was further aggravated when it was found that the stone bull had been removed from his accustomed place of honor in the Temple of Shree Trimbakeshwar, and, to crown all, the Mohammedans had forcibly entered by night the most sacred shrine and place of pilgrimage in Yeola, the tomb of the founder of the city, removed the god, and thrown him in the ditch. It was not until some months after these incidents that the actual uprising occurred.

Without attempting to further unravel the conflicting statements of either side, or trying to make them correspond, which is the business of the local chronicler, this, briefly, is what happened. While the excitement was spreading, and the agitators on both sides were diligently laboring, the accursed pig was discovered in the Patel's mosque, and under peculiarly aggravating circumstances. The pig had been cut in two, in order to defile the mosque in the most thorough manner, and, wild with excitement, the Mussulmans were rushing about and crying out for vengeance, when it was found that the mosque was on fire! Now their frenzy became uncontrollable, and they hurried in a body to the Mulhidar temple, where they massacred a cow within the holy enclosure, and in a manner exasperating to Hindoo feelings. While this was going on, the fire in the mosque, which had been kindled with cans of kerosene, was gaining ground, and the men who were working to extinguish it were pelted with volleys of stones from natives posted on the opposite housetops. They were ordered to refrain by those in authority, but upon their refusing to do so they were fired on by the police with blank-cartridges, and then dosed with buckshot. Other mosques and houses of Mohammedans were now on fire, the local magistrates began to arrive, and then fresh bodies of police and the volunteers. The tumult was finally quelled, but after it had lasted for seven hours, during which time much destruction of property had taken place, and considerable loss of life. The pig story is now discredited by some of the Hindoo journalists who are anxious to prove that their enemies were the aggressors in every instance.

The "Gaurakshina Sabha," as the cow-protection so-

FAKIR, TWILIGHT

ciety calls itself,* was established ostensibly for the protection and improvement of cattle, and so long as it occupies itself with its original object it cannot fail to be of great utility in a country where animals are often overworked and ill-used, in spite of the belief that human souls may be incarnate in their bodies. But while men of position on both sides and social leaders are alike interested in the maintenance of peace and order, there is evidence which strengthens the belief that professional agitators have been travelling from place to place using the name of this or of other societies to further their designs, and devising new schemes by which they expect to profit at the expense of their dupes.

A Bengal rajah who was recently interviewed, and invited to address a meeting on the subject of the cow-protection movement, declined to do so, but stated in the course of conversation his belief that "the cow question was the political question of the day;" and also that "cow protection and the protection of all our temples and religious institutions, religious rites and interests, depend on the peace of the country, and those who foolishly try to play with the foundation-stone in the shape of the peace of our society are self-destroyers, and in my opinion worse than persons who commit suicide." Another opinion on this subject, delivered by a Parsee while on a recent visit to America is worth recording.† He says that "the riots in India were not directed against British domination at all—all the leading business men, the educated classes, and even the great middle classes of Indians are warm adherents of British rule and policies of government. It is difficult to make people understand the true cause and exact scope of those riots who know little

* In Behar. † *Baltimore American.*

of the intricate lines of religious and secular thought and life in that country. The question which agitates India to-day is not some great problem of internal government, but the cow question."

Above all this tumult of misguided and over-zealous religionists, and calmly superior, the government of India sits, majestically enthroned, and armed like Jove with an ample supply of thunderbolts with which to strike the erring of either creed. In the address of the late Viceroy at Agra, he affirms the strict neutrality of the government, "a neutrality not based on indifference," but upon an equal respect for both the great historic religions of India and he also declares that "the government of India is under a twofold obligation. We owe it to the whole community, British and Indian, to secure the public safety, and to protect the persons and property of the Queen's subjects from injury and interference; we are also bound to secure to both the great religious denominations freedom from molestation or persecution in the exercise of their religious observances. The law secures to the Mohammedans the right of following the ritual which has been customary for them and for their forefathers, while it secures to the Hindoos protection from outrage and insult, and for this reason forbids the slaughter of cattle with unnecessary publicity, or in such a manner as will occasion wanton or malicious annoyances to their feelings. Let both sides understand clearly that no lawless or aggressive conduct on their part will induce us to depart by an inch from this just and honorable policy. Do not let it be supposed that the slaughter of kine for the purpose of sacrifice, or for food, will ever be put a stop to: we shall protect the religions of both sides alike, and we shall punish according to the law any act which wantonly outrages the religious feelings of any section of the

A FAKIR, BENARES

community. Let it also be clearly understood that we shall not permit any disturbance of the peace, and that wherever violence is exhibited we shall not be afraid to put it down by force."

The accounts of affairs in India, published by the Continental journals, and particularly those in which sectarian riots or other local disturbances are referred to,* are seldom trustworthy, since the prevailing jealousy of England, and the fact that she has so far succeeded in maintaining a stable government for the heterogeneous millions of India, which in itself is a grievance, leads them at times to misrepresent facts, and often to exaggerate local disturbances of comparatively little importance. When the enormous aggregate of the population is considered, it is easy to understand that far greater causes would be necessary in order to pervade all classes with discontent, to interfere with the regular working of the judicial machinery, and to imperil the peace of the whole empire.

IV

A figure which adds much to the joyous aspect of life in India, and, like the hump-backed cow, the crow, and the vulture, is part of its strictly local color, is the itinerant fakir. The fact that he seems to take himself very seriously does not prevent him at times from being indescribably grotesque. Of all the children of Aryan stock he is the most conservative, unchanged and unchanging; and even in India, where in these days one is seldom out of hearing of the locomotive whistle, he is an anachro-

* It is shrewdly imagined by government that the anti-cow-killing society is only a cloak for a lot of disaffected Hindoos to work under. —*Note by a member of the jury during the trial of the rioters.*

nism. Buddha, after the great renunciation, was the first to wear the yellow of whom we have any authentic tradition, and whenever the fakir appears in history, no matter at what date, he is always exactly the same figure that we meet to-day, plodding along the road on his way to a shrine. The fakir who conversed with the Emperor Jehanghir,* treating him as an equal, to the great scandal of the English ambassador, wore a crown of peacock's feathers, like one who used to hang about the palace of the Seths in Ajmere. The famous interview between the Emperor and the fakir is depicted in ancient Hindoo miniature, where they are both seated facing each other, on the roof of a little pavilion rising from the water; a boat is fastened at the door below.

* "I found him sitting on his throne, and a Beggar at his feet, a poore silly old man, all asht, ragd, and patcht, with a young roague attending on him. With these kind of professed poore holy men, the countrey abounds, and are held in great reverence, but for workes of chastisement of their bodies and voluntary sufferings, they exceed the brags of all heretiques or Idolaters. This miserable wretch, cloathed in rags, crowned with feathers, covered with ashes, his Majestie talked with about an hour, with such familiaritie, and shew of kindnesse, that it must needs argue an humilitie not found easily among kings. The Beggar sate, which his sonne dares not doe; he gave the King a Present, a Cake, asht, burnt on the Coales, made by himselfe of coarse graine, which the King accepted most willingly, and brake one bit and eate it, which a daintie mouth could scarce have done. After he tooke the clout, and wrapt it up, and put in the poore mans bosome, and sent for one hundred Rupias, and with his owne hands powred them into the poore mans lap, and what fell besides gathered up for him: when his collation of banqueeting and drinke came, whatsoever he tooke to eate, he brake and gave the Begger halfe, and after many strange humiliations, and charitirising, the old Wretch not being nimble, he tooke him up in his armes, which no cleanly body durst have touched, imbracing him, and three times laying his hand on his heart calling him father, he left him, and all us and me in admiration of such a vertue in a heathen Prince."—Sir Thomas Roe.

YOUNG NAUTCH GIRL

His usual and unique garment is a long strip of flimsy cotton of a faded orange hue, which is wound about him, leaving his legs and arms bare, and they, as well as his face, are gray with dust and ashes. Long strings of beads and rosaries, amulets, charms, feathers, brass chains and gewgaws give him the appearance of an ambulating junk-shop. Stripes of white paint diversify his solemn countenance, and he is often burdened with a heavy volume of Holy Writ, which is sometimes in very good condition with a new and "puckah" binding. A thick and shaggy shock of hair is part of the fakir's stock in trade, and when he has not enough to start business with, he ingeniously pieces it out with some brown substance having the nature or appearance of a "jute switch." It is usually gathered up on the nape of the neck after the present mode among European ladies, and it is then twisted into a series of knots on the top of the head. Lengthened out artificially, it is frequently wound about the fakir's head like a turban, tinted with henna, and its bulk is further augmented with strings of wooden beads, cowries, brass chains, or whatever he happens to have on hand. A few wear their hair closely cropped, and when it descends to the shoulders only it is anointed with oil or grease, and then powdered with dust, in order to give it that peculiar matted appearance so highly prized. There are others of exalted pretensions who cover their heads with a tall-pointed cap or helmet of some sort, hung around with bells and other metallic articles which jingle, and now and then we meet one wearing, like Jehangir's friend, a tall nodding crown of peacock feathers, which is remarkably effective in frightening horses.

But the fakir, sitting alone by the roadside, in the solemn twilight, ceases to be merely grotesque; hardly distinguishable from the dust but for the faded color of his drapery, motionless, and seeming to gaze fixedly at something invisible to profane eyes, he is a startling and unearthly figure, and any right-minded horse would refuse to pass him in the dusk. The fakir is always a seductive object to paint, for what could be more discreetly decorative than his scheme of color, the quiet opposition of his blue-gray skin like an elephant's hide, and the washed-out orange of his garment; but however lovingly he may be studied he will always look like an unfinished sketch, slightly "out" in its values, or, to be more precise, like a sculptor's "maquette" of clay, and will never be likely to find much favor as a subject in the world of commercial art. It is not an easy matter to show on canvas that the reason why his face has no modelling, scarcely any reflected lights, is because of the opaque coating of clay, to which cause is also due the remarkable texture of his dyed hair, and that the reason why he appears, at first sight, to wear tan-colored kid gloves, is because the gray dust has been washed off in some sacred tank.

Fakirs almost invariably pose well, and are singularly docile and accommodating as models, the inexhaustible stock of patience required in their vocation making it easy for them to keep the same position. Every one knows the oft-told tale of the saint who sat for sixteen years with one arm upraised until it stiffened in that position like the dead limb of a tree, and the nails grew into the palm of his hand; and of the other who placed a pinch of earth on the end of his outstretched tongue, planted a seed therein, and sat until the seed sprouted and the leaves appeared. In spite of the fact that their vows forbid them to touch the coin of the realm, they are not averse to receiving it in the gourds or little buckets which they usually carry. One who belonged to a sect distinguished above all others for saintliness was draped and turbaned with yellow and carried a slender wand which he never laid down. Having consented to pose, he took up a position in the sunlight, and was carefully instructed not to move. While he sat, his lips moved incessantly, and he never ceased to repeat prayers or charms; but one of his hands, having got out of position at the critical moment, I rose to replace it. At my approach he shrank backward with an expression of horror, but fortunately before I had touched him it was explained to me that the contact of an unsanctified hand would put ages of penance between him and the happy goal which was now so near.

An ascetic, with whom we had the honor of a personal interview, had invented an original method of attaining that elevation of spirit, through maceration of the flesh, which all must compass before they may hope for endless rest. We saw him on the road from Ajmere to the Sacred Lake of Poscha, dwelling alone in the wilderness. The fine road by which we descended a steep declivity among the hills made an abrupt turn at the bottom of the slope, and the driver had to rein in his horses, which were rearing and plunging at the sudden apparition of a small white tent and a silent figure squatting at the entrance. With three broad white stripes chalked across his forehead, and hair toned to the deep and streaky bronze hue so prevalent at the Concours Hippique, he was like a Japanese monster carved from a knot of wood.

FAKIRS AT BENARES

Just inside the tent stood an elaborate iron bedstead, and there was neither mattress nor sheet to conceal the framework of the structure, with transverse bars thickly planted with long iron spikes, on which, for eight hours of the twenty-four, the fakir was accustomed to stretch his emaciated body. At that moment he was taking a rest, and his eyes, the only signs of life in his wooden countenance, were fixed on us. The bedstead had been constructed in Ajmere at the expense of one of his disciples, a wealthy Hindoo merchant. This valley was the playground of divers striped and spotted brutes of the cat family—to such an extent that iron-barred refuges for goats and goatherds had been built at intervals along the road—and we have often since thought, with a certain uneasiness, of the lonely fakir whose only defence was his sanctity, and wondered whether he had been rewarded with the martyr's crown.

When the hot wind of April was at its height in Benares, a few weeks later, and the mercury daily stood at 100° or 110° Fahr. with an upward tendency, while it marked 159° in the sun (according to the *Pioneer*), we could not but admire the fortitude of another devotee whom we daily saw at the boat-landing on the Ganges. His idea of self-abasement was imaginative and Dantesque. From a sort of gallows on the bank of the river, in a spot at once exposed to the full power of the sun, the reflected heat from the calcined bank, and the burning wind which swept the dust and parched leaves into whirling eddies, he hung suspended by his heels, with his face covered by a figured prayer-cloth. With each oscillation of the dangling figure, as it slowly swayed to and fro, its head passed within a foot of a hot fire, made of the pungent flap-jacks with which the Hindoo cooks his rice. Another, whose aspect denoted the highest degree of self-immolation, galloped down the road mounted on a frightened cow, past the verandas of Clark's Hotel. A shred of yellow cloth concealed but little of his dusty anatomy, wasted by vigils and long fasting, and he waved a tattered umbrella as he tore past, yelling at the top of his voice. For the daring simplicity and originality of his "make-up" he deserved the academic palms of his order.

Benares is the principal gathering-place of this motley tribe of zealots and ascetics, and here they troop during the spring festivals from all quarters of India. Many are the strange varieties and idiosyncrasies of costume or manner which prove that charlatanism, whether religious, social, or æsthetic, is not monopolized by Western races alone. Along the roads leading to the Holy City they march in groups, singly, or in couples, incrusted with clay and dust, and many of them carry a primitive sort of umbrella, made of fan-palm leaves, which seems to cause them much embarrassment when not actually in use, since they cannot shut it up, and it is always in the way.

When one drifts down the Ganges in the morning, along the crowded stone steps of the "ghauts," rising in graded terraces like the seats of the Coliseum to the great palaces and temples above, the boat passes close to the little platforms of plank built out from the steps over the swirling current; and here, on these platforms, sheltered under huge tent-like umbrellas of straw matting, sit rows of "holy men" and saintly Brahmans in rapt meditation and silent ecstasy, occasionally unbending for a little friendly gossip. Here they glory in the happy ending of their pilgrimage, and enjoy what must be the nearest approach to perfect beatitude vouchsafed to man, for they have arrived at their goal, and they have no baggage to distract their thoughts from pious meditation, no

FEAST OF GANESHA, BENARES

huge overland trunks nor bundles of wraps to worry them, no hotel bills to pay, no care for the morrow, for what they shall eat or where they shall sleep, and the more ragged and unkempt they are, the more shall they find admiring disciples and worshippers among the fair, who shall pay a worthy tribute of "pice" for their wisdom. The brave apostles of other creeds may well feel disheartened at the utter hopelessness of making proselytes among them, for what greater bliss could they offer in exchange for this? If it be so ordained that they are to die on these steps, among hurrying feet, in the full glare of the sun and exposed to the burning wind, they shall pass away in perfect content, sure that their souls will attain the long-coveted rest without first undergoing probation in any inferior form of animal life. "Die at Benares, or die on hereditary land," is a saying held in repute among orthodox Hindoos, for this is their Mecca.

V

Festivals religious and profane, some of which might be qualified by both adjectives, fairs, pilgrimages, and religious gatherings follow each other in endless succession. Always rich in pictorial interest and incident, they are nowhere seen to better advantage than at Benares, and in the spring-time, when the religious exaltation of Holy Week and the seductions of the Carnival are happily blended, when the pious Rajah comes to spend a week or two in his palace looking down on the sacred stream, when he is carried in a gilded palanquin to the sound of music, and placed in a peacock-hued barge under awnings of gold brocade—for this period of purification is often followed by a pilgrimage in alien and Philistine garb to Vichy or other distant shrines held in repute among

Hindoo princes. This season of spring-time at Benares has nothing in common with that of other climes, and it might rather be likened to the end of the year, for the last green leaf is scorched and shrivelled by a wind like the breath of a blast-furnace. On the occasion of the "Holi," when white-robed crowds sprinkle each other and everything else—their doorways, their sacred cattle, and the very ground—with magenta-colored powder, and when, in the red after-glow, torches and lanterns are just lighted, all reflected in the broad reaches of the Ganges, and with the high palace walls and temple spires rising above, the scene becomes the wildest, most crimson-tinted saturnalia imaginable, phantasmagoric and unreal. At this season also the festival of Ganesha takes place, lasting for several days, when it is almost impossible for love or money to hire a boat, for everything that floats is engaged to take part in the procession of boats, and each one, newly swept and garnished, the hurricane deck provided with an awning, carpeted, furnished with chairs, tables, and even the household god in an illuminated shrine, is engaged for the duration of the fête by some wealthy Hindoo and filled with his friends. Even our own boatman, whom we had hired by the week, stipulated to be let off at this season, as there was always a chance of making a fabulous sum out of some native capitalist arriving at the last moment. It was our good-fortune to see a Nautch dance under the most favorable conditions, given by the Maharajah of Benares for the benefit of some friends, who had stayed on, in spite of the heat, for this occasion. We were driven down to the landing-place in the cool of the evening, for the mercury had fallen gradually with the cessation of the wind to somewhere in the nineties. Here on the steps the secretary of the prince was waiting, accompanied by his two sleepy

NAUTCH DANCER

little boys, some men with torches, and a bearer with a silver staff, who made way for us through the closely packed throng; the boat resembled a small river steamer, with an upper deck sufficiently furnished, lighted by lanterns, and propelled by two paddle-wheels, which from motives of economy were turned by coolies with hand-spikes instead of by steam-power. Up the stream the whole length of the city front we moved slowly among the swarm of illuminated boats, an integral part of the long defile, and yet not of it. By the light which shone from the tiers of palace windows, from the doors of temples and shrines, from the flashing of fireworks and the gleam of hurrying torches along the steps, it was evident that all Benares, with the exception of the favored few in the boats, had poured out upon the ghauts. From the nearest boats floated strange music and the voices of the Nautch girls; most of these boats are constructed something after the fashion of a Nile boat, but without masts and sails: the greater part of the hull is taken up by the cabin, with a row of windows on each side, provided with wooden blinds, and the roof of this cabin serves as a promenade deck, shaded by an awning. These upper decks were brilliantly hung with lanterns, crowded with revellers, musicians, and dancers. From a passing boat with closely shuttered windows, through which the light streamed out, came the concert of sound which usually accompanies the last stages of revelry; the boat was manned by a party of the Rajah's retainers, and in response to a hail from the secretary some bottles of champagne, cakes, and ices were passed out from the closed cabin. The curiosity of the ladies as to what was going on inside of the cabin elicited only a polite but evasive response from the secretary.

The heated, lifeless air of the night, and the strange

odors wafted from the steaming water, the monotonous throbbing of the paddles, and the flickering of myriad lights on the crowded shore, all tended to produce a hypnotic, semi-somnolent condition of mind and body, and we should have been well content to drift on thus forever—but a turn of the river brought in sight the gleaming pavilion of canvas built out on floating barges, where the spectacle was to take place. The tent was already densely packed with Hindoo spectators, a line of statuesque torch-bearers stood around a long carpet, and at the end of the carpet lay a pile of cushions under a canopy, all of gold-worked crimson velvet. This was the Rajah's place; but as he had sent word that he could not be present, the music struck up when our party had seated themselves in a row of chairs on a raised platform at the right. Then the dancing began—dances by several bayaderes, and single dances accompanied with song or recitative, ending with a performance by the court actors. After a preliminary ballet, in which two or three took part, a dainty little personage came forward; graceful, gazelle-eyed, enveloped in a filmy cloud of black-and-gold gauze, which floated airily about her, she was the living incarnation of the Nautch as interpreted by the sculptors of Chitor; from the air of laughing assurance with which she surveyed her assembled subjects, it was evident that she was accustomed to homage and sure of conquest. She held her audience absorbed and expectant by the monotonous and plaintive cadence of her song, by long glances full of intense meaning from half-closed eyes, and by swift changes of expression and mood, as well as by the spell of "woven paces and of waving arms." This paragon of Nautch girls, like most of her sisterhood, wore nose jewels, but to our eyes they did not detract from her beauty, nor did they appear more unchristian than the bulky pendants which women in other countries suspend from the cartilages of their ears; the diminutive cluster of pearls or brilliants seemed rather to play the part of the black patch on the powdered face. As we were afterwards to learn, one may see many a Nautch without retaining such a vivid impression; much of its force was owing, no doubt, to the fitness of the place and the charm of strange accessories, the uncertain glare of the smoking torches, the mingling of musky odors with the overpowering scent of attar of roses, and of wilting jasmine flowers; these perfumes were intensified in the close air of the tent by the heat of the night—the prelude to the fiercer heat which comes with the morning and the rising of the hot wind.

RECENT IMPRESSIONS OF ANGLO-INDIAN LIFE

I

Bearing in mind the time-honored predilection in favor of first impressions, and knowing by experience how rarely it happens that subsequent visits to a spot which one has left with regret do not dispel some illusions, it was not without doubt and misgiving that the writer approached Bombay for the third time, on this occasion by rail. After mentally fortifying one's self against possible disappointment, it is always an added, often a half-unexpected pleasure, to find that the charm still remains. In this instance, if the charm should be analyzed, it might be found to lie partly in the strange and exotic character of the surroundings. Having determined then beforehand to take every precaution that the first impression might be renewed as far as possible, and knowing that one's environment at the hotel has much to do with it, we did not take the advice of well-meaning friends who pointed out the superior advantages in the way of comforts of the hotels in the "Fort," but went straight to a more suburban quarter in the vicinity of Malabar Hill. The chosen hostelry was the type of the old-time colonial hotel, a three-storied barrack, surrounded by tiers of trellised wooden galleries. One entrance was through a triangular garden-patch, overarched by rustling banana leaves, and by a pathway littered with their brown, filmy skins. The lower floor of the hotel was a vast apart-

THE FORT, BOMBAY, FROM MALABAR HILL

ment, with pillars supporting the story above. A large part of this space was occupied by the dining-tables, one or two private dining-rooms, and a species of hotel parlor at one end, furnished with the dusty black-wood furniture peculiar to Bombay and a few bound volumes of *Illustrated London News.* These little rooms, occurring at intervals, were fenced in by board partitions reaching half-way up to the ceiling. Our quarters on the third floor opened, like all the others, on the wooden gallery surrounding the building, where the lodgers were accustomed to keep their lounging-chairs, designed for the encouragement of laziness and the convenient consumption of "pegs" and cheroots. Some of these chairs were of the familiar bamboo kind, and others, which are seldom seen out of India, being too heavy to do duty as deck-chairs, had massive wooden frames, and a long rail on each side, across which the patient may hang his inert legs. There was a view from this elevation of a back-yard, and of more or less dilapidated out-buildings, where a great deal of slipshod half-caste house-keeping was going on, in the shadow of the unfamiliar trees of the country; beyond this, the distant church spires and buildings of the city, tall factory chimneys, innumerable waving cocoanut tops, a hill capped with straight-stemmed fan-palms, all dim of outline and undecided in the smoke and yellow haze: at whatever time of day one looked forth in this hot October weather it was always an afternoon sky that one saw. In the freshness of the early morning, before sunrise, when it was our custom to enjoy the chota hazri, or "little breakfast," which was placed on a table outside the door, there was still the same vaporous horizon with just a faint flush of rose: but one might know that it was morning from the clamorous activity of the crows, kites, and broad-winged buzzards which wheeled past, keeping watchful eyes on our breakfast-table. The writer cannot but regret the time squandered in fishing for crows, with indifferent success, by means of something edible attached to the end of a hanging string; but the temptation was sometimes irresistible, for while we sat at the table one or more of them, perched on the rickety shutters, or swinging on a neighboring tree-top, watched us with glittering eyes and heads pertly cocked, and if we stepped into the room for a moment, there was a sudden swoop, a rustle of sable wings, and the swift flight of the glossy pirate with a dripping egg or banana, closely pursued by his less daring brethren. It is not of much use to play tricks on the Indian crows, and the earlier one accepts (temporarily at least) the prevalent belief that they contain the souls of those who were up to sharp practice during their human incarnation, the easier it becomes to understand their ways. Witness the case of the young torpedo engineer who, being plagued by them beyond endurance, carefully concocted a torpedo in a flower-pot seductively baited, to which he attached the wires of an electric battery. Needless to say that he was hoist with his own petard, while the "sandhedrin of gray-headed crows" gravely chuckled from the neighboring tree-tops. The writer once offered a liberal reward to the house-servants at the hotel to induce them to catch one alive for artistic purposes, but no crow was forthcoming.

CHOTA HAZRI

This early breakfast in the open air had a savor which the more elaborate functions at the table d'hôte did not possess. It is true that the menu was limited and unvarying, confined to tea, toast, and eggs, with whatever fruit happened to be in season; that the salt was of doubtful whiteness, and the pepper-box an ex-receptacle for Keating's insect powder; but none of these things had power to detract from the enjoyment of the situation.

This rickety balcony overlooking the swaying, lustrous cocoanut fronds had attractions unequalled by the most inviting of the damask-lined retreats sacred to good cheer which look down on the tumult of the boulevards; and the mere fact that one was obliged to be always on guard against the sudden raids of the feathered buccaneers added an additional zest to the "little breakfast." When mangoes were ripe, and were served to us delectably iced and wrapped in a napkin, one could only look forward to the sailing of the steamer with sincere regret. A brief gastronomic flirtation with another fruit did not leave as pleasant an after-taste as the brief acquaintance with the sumptuous mango, for this much lauded and abused delicacy, commended as much by its admirers as it is execrated by its foes, is of gigantic size, and endowed with a correspondingly aggressive odor, so that one cannot indulge in it surreptitiously, but must take the whole neighborhood into his confidence. In the early afternoon before the landward breeze began to stir among the tree-tops one desired nothing better than to lie at full length in the long chair, with an iced peg and a cigarette, watching for the first streak of wind-ruffled blue sea to appear on the horizon; and if for a moment one went inside, to dive into a trunk and lift out trays, the atmosphere felt like the sudorium of a Roman bath, and an entire change of raiment became expedient, and yet the soft breeze, as it gained in strength, lifted one's papers off the table and scattered them over the room. This apartment, arranged to open on a veranda at each end, so that the wind might draw through the open work of the partition which divided the sitting-room from the bedroom, and with blinds at each end, which could be so slanted as to leave full play to the lightest breeze, had its drawbacks, for the bath-room was somewhat dark and gruesome, and it took time to become accustomed to the formidable size of the cockroaches, two of which had their lair under the washbowl in a recess of the wood, whence their exaggerated antennæ protruded, while the owners clung, back downwards, to the rim.

In these early October days one was only cool while fanned by the punkah at dinner-time, or under its rhythmic sway at night, or while driving in the breeze along the Back Bay, far more decorative in its southern fashion than the Rotten Row or the Bois, and which adds so much to the attractions of Bombay. At the table d'hôte, notwithstanding the punkahs, one was always conscious of a beaded brow while slowly absorbing iced fluids; as in other hotels of the same period, the crockery had evidently been in use since the days of Warren Hastings, and must have done faithful service for many different social castes, for some pieces might have graced the table of a former governor-general, while the majority, notched, chipped, and discolored, represented more democratic levels; and the knives were, one and all, thin and pointed with long usage and daily scouring in the sand by native servants. The manager was an anæmic Irishman, whose daily routine included the absorption of an unlimited number of pegs, varied by an occasional drive to the "Fort" in an antiquated two-wheeled buggy, by the way of exercise. On the morning after our arrival I came down at 6.30 with a color-box, intending to begin a sketch among the carved and painted houses of the quarter, and found him sitting outside at a little table, on which stood a tall glass of whiskey and potash water. His face was red and plentifully perforated with open pores, suffused with moisture, but he looked comparatively cool, clad in white drills. Glancing at my painting-traps, and realizing with amazement, in which I detected a shade of compassion, that I actually intended to walk, he assured me that such excessive exertion was usually followed in this climate by sudden death. In turn I assured him of my entire resignation, founded on a hopeful belief in the perfect beatitude of nirvana, etc., and he allowed me to proceed, having washed his hands, as it were, of all responsibility. When we started on an indefinite cruise through the Mofussil regions he gave us much kindly advice, but said that travelling by railway at night exposed one to fevers, and was extremely dangerous, in which he was partly right. I think he never expected to see us again, but when we returned some six months later, in the stewing month of April, we found him in bed, emaciated by a malady brought on by excessive consumption of pegs and want of other exercise, but he recovered sufficiently to be shipped northward on an Anchor liner. At this hotel we had our first experience of the bedroom punkah, and it was not altogether satisfactory. In order that the punkah frill might sweep within a few inches of our faces the mosquito nettings were removed, as we vainly believed, what we had been told, that mosquitoes were unable to perform their alimentary functions in a strong current of air. At first the soft fanning, the reg-

THE CHUPRASSI

ular dip, and the long wave of cool air which passed over us were delightfully soporific, but we had not calculated on the punkah-wallah habit of dropping off to sleep; and although the cries and objurgations addressed to these drowsy menials from neighboring rooms failed to arouse us, we were soon awakened by the sensation of heat, and by the feeling that we were helplessly in the power of the singing miscreants. Our landlord had expressed astonishment at my demand for a punkah, since the anticipation of coming "cool weather" had lowered his anæmic temperature, and he had slept under a blanket for the two previous nights. A notable feature of the hotel were the long corridors like dark tunnels, the blaze of blinding yellow light at each end, with green leaves framing vignettes of golden haze and smoke and stiff fan-palms, or a distant blue line of water dotted with white lateen-sails, and the pair of punkah coolies at each open door, one asleep, with his mahogany shins stretched half-way across the passage, and the other languidly pulling at the cord which hangs from the fanlight over the door. Glimpses of the interiors were not easily had, although the doors were all ajar, as tall screens of carved black wood, panelled with turkey red, stood just beyond the thresholds. The company at this hotel was cosmopolitan to a degree, made up of people representing the different Anglo-Indian castes, and travellers who were arriving or departing by the weekly liners. A veteran colonel, just back from a campaign in Beloochistan, consoled us, when we complained of the heat, unjustly, perhaps, for the mercury never rose to the height which people take as a matter of course during the progress of a New York summer. He said that in Beloochistan they were accustomed to emerge from their tents, when an interval between dust-storms permitted, at 4 A.M., and sit

PUNKAH WALLAH

outside to drink in the freshness of the morning, when the mercury fell to 104° Fahr. My vis-à-vis at the table was an energetic young American, absorbed in the pursuit and capture of wild animals for a transatlantic menagerie. We were taken by our plausible friend to see a couple of unhappy tiger cubs, and were nearly induced to purchase one of them, but, remembering in time the restricted accommodations of our apartment on the Avenue Wagram, and the unsympathetic character of the concierge, we wisely backed out at the last moment. But of the several hotels in Bombay which we occupied at intervals, the one which I remember with keenest satisfaction stood at the end of an alley of slender-stemmed and stately fan-palms, and on our right, as we approached it, a sunburnt hill-side, from which red rocks protruded, rose into a high ridge crowned with still taller fan-palms. Curving across and above the gate-posts was the quaintly alliterative name of the Parsee landlord, Rustomjee Ruttonjee; but as this hotel differed but slightly from the others in service and cuisine, its chiefest attraction was the entire loveliness of the view from the windows. When one reluctantly awakens at 5 A.M. and looks down on the dull gray twilight of a European city street, usually saddened at that hour by a leaden sky, it is not always with a feeling of joy that he thinks of the coming day; but here, in the stillness of the early morning, when the waning moon hung in the mellow western sky over the purple sea, dotted with white sails, which showed here and there beyond the solid floor of matted tree-tops, so thickly interlaced that the dark ground was only visible in places, stretching away from under the windows, and hiding the Mahaluxmee Battery and the sea-road, it seemed a waste of time and of life to lie abed.

In the near foreground below a round green pool,

fringed about with drooping banana leaves, reflected the light of the sky, and on the topmost branches of a tree which almost touched the windows sleek emerald-green parrots sat and plumed themselves. At sundown, a strong sea breeze blew the cocoanut tops about, and they waved and tossed like sable plumes, sharply cut against the vapory red horizon. There is a delightful spot near the shore, and close to the Mahaluxmee Battery, conducive to meditation and vague speculation as to what is

SUNSET FROM MY WINDOW

going on in the far-off west beyond the sunset—and here the Parsees, especially those of the wealthier class, are accustomed to station themselves when the red sun sinks behind the purple rim of the sea, shot through with iridescent crimson and violet tones. This brief halt does not have the appearance of a religious function, although most of them gaze fixedly at the great luminary as it disappears, but all seem to be enjoying the coolness of the air, and relaxing at the same time into a little friendly gossip with their neighbors. Their horses and coachmen look sleek and well-fed, and, like their masters, have a comfortable and prosperous air. But few of the men, and those usually of the older generation, stick to their hereditary costume, although many still wear the shiny mitre-like hat, and most of them are adorned by English tailors; some of the young men still keep up the narrow turban closely built around a skull-cap. Nearly all the ladies wear the pale, delicately tinted shawls which harmonize so well with their melancholy black eyes and clear complexions.

Of the more correct and orthodox hotels of the "Fort" the writer has nothing whatever to say in disparagement, and the American or English tourist who chooses to sojourn there may, with but a slight stretch of fancy, imagine that he is still at Charing Cross or the Grand Midland, and enjoying the superior comforts of those famous hostelries. To the hotels in more remote Mofussil capitals the transition from those referred to is by no means abrupt, and in spite of the changes which are being rapidly effected, most of them still retain features which, to say the least, are unmistakably local, and which cause the experienced traveller to prefer the dâk bungalow where it still exists. In one of these northern centres it was only with great difficulty and by the display of persistent energy that we succeeded in reaching the dâk bungalow at all, in consequence of the aggressive enterprise of the hotel "touts" at the railway station, and their influence over both servants and drivers. The hotel which was most difficult to escape from, and which had a rather undesirable reputation, was the Lord Donneybrook. Its rules and regulations, printed with the old-fashioned, worn-out type which has probably done unremitting service since the days of Clive, were surrounded by an ornamental border such as one still finds on bottles of "Bengal chutney"; among other items we read that "A single person occupying a double beaded room, will have to vocate it for a single beaded one, if required for a married couple or 2 persons." Also that "Visitors will be good enough not to strike the Hotel servants, any complaints made against them will be attended to." Notwithstanding our directions to the driver, we were taken to this hotel, but fearing that we might fail in complying with its somewhat lengthy schedule of rules, we persisted in our original design of going to the bungalow, and probably missed one of the choicest experiences of a lifetime. We had no reason to regret having chosen the bungalow. It was a long, narrow, one-storied structure, with a veranda extending the whole length of its front; the apartments were all exactly alike, consisting of a living-room or parlor, bedroom and bath-room, each with a door on the other side giving access to a little private piazza. As we arrived just before Christmas, which is the great season for Mofussil travel, the place was crowded, but the khansamah and his twin brother, grave and portly Mussulmans, became unusually sympathetic and attentive when they realized that we appreciated their efforts. Never in India did we find such cookery at a hotel, for there was no table d'hôte, and each guest was served in the privacy of his apartment. Every dish was brought in hot, chops and steaks were placed on the table, still sizzling on the grill, according to the local fashion; there were juicy teal and partridges, and the curry was generously spiced. For all this we were only required to pay the sum of five rupees a day (for two persons occupying the same quarters) in addition to one rupee each for room rent. The expectations of the khansamah and his brother did not end here, and they were not disappointed;

but one day they reluctantly called our attention to an item in the printed list of rules allowing each person twenty-four hours occupancy only in case the room was wanted by a new-comer, and at the same time showed us a written complaint in the bungalow book, where we had been obliged to inscribe the date of our arrival, and alas! we were now the oldest inhabitants, having sadly overstayed our time. The khansamah insinuated that we should make a little trip which we had projected to a neighboring point of interest, and after two or three days' absence he would send a carriage for us and reserve our rooms. "Chota hazri" was usually laid on the table in the outer room at an early hour, and we were invariably awakened by the chirping and twittering of the sparrows, which, far from waiting for any invitation to help themselves to butter and jam, resented our appearance on the scene with indignation and vehement scolding. The diminished pat of butter which remained for us was usually pitted with the marks of their beaks. It was quite impossible to keep out these impudent marauders, but it was amusing to watch the manner of their entrance and exit. The door opening on the veranda was closed by a transparent mat of cane or grass, which touched the floor, and they had an ingenious manner of crawling under it in spite of its weight.

The only incongruous note in the bungalow * was the punkah, whitewashed like the high, bare walls of the sleeping-room, and tied up against the ceiling. It was then the height of the short winter, following the nine months of furnace heat, and the sight of this unseasonable implement sent a chill through one's marrow.

* This famous bungalow has been suppressed, the hotel-keepers of the city having represented to the local powers that it ruined their business and was quite unnecessary.

It is only of late years that travellers have begun to invade India in any considerable numbers, and consequently hotel accommodations are often insufficient, except in the show places and in the most populous business centres, so that in many cities of over 100,000 inhabitants the public bungalow is the only accommodation to be found. This is now often supplemented by the "waiting-rooms" at the railway station, provided with restaurant and two or three bedrooms. But during the "cold weather," the popular travelling season in this country, both bungalow and waiting-rooms are often full, and the traveller has difficulty in finding a place to lay his head. We were once obliged to throw ourselves on the mercy of the station-master, who finally made us comfortable in an unoccupied saloon-carriage belonging to the executive engineer of the district.

THE KHANSAMAH

For any one who has work to do, the privacy and seclusion of the dák bungalow offers material advantages. As each meal is cooked separately and served in the traveller's apartment, he escapes the stiff and fussy table d'hôte at the hotel, an institution which never seems to be quite at home in India.

But the cookery is usually rather heavy, as the khansamah's favorite utensil is the frying-pan, and one need not expect to find superfluous luxury in the way of furniture. The rooms being unprovided with windows for the most part, and as the little light which there is enters through the curtained half-glass doors, they are dark and chilly in the winter-time, and have a ghostly and uncanny feeling about them, even by daylight, so that the occupant often prefers to take his meals on the sunny veranda during the daytime. There are seldom any fastenings to the doors, and it is sometimes impossible even to close them. When the khansamah brings in a smoky kerosene lamp at nightfall he pulls down the transparent curtains or "dhurries" of split cane over the glass part of the doors, thus enabling any one outside who wishes to study the habits of the occupant to look in, while remaining invisible himself. But when the crackling fire of brushwood is lighted in the chimney, the room loses something of its gloom and loneliness. Fireplaces are found wherever the winter is felt, but seldom south of the tropic, and during the long periods when the rooms are locked up and deserted they serve as refuges for bats, lizards, and the ubiquitous mongoose. It is not customary at these caravansaries to make out a bill for the departing guest, as the khansamah is usually more skilled in mental arithmetic than in writing, but we found that such documents, when we could get them, had a certain literary value. The presiding genius of the Ahmedabad bungalow, known as Shaikh Boodhoo, was a hairy, shaggy-browed Mussulman, somewhat advanced in years, as the major part of bristling blue-black beard was quite white at the roots—and, by-the-way, it is not always easy to determine the age of a Mussulman, since he cultivates baldness from infancy, when conscientious enough to follow the dictates of the Prophet, and he usually begins to dye his beard at an early period. A constantly recurring item in his weekly account was "Lamp oil burn," and he sometimes began his bill with the lines "For feeding 1 gentleman and a Lady. Rs. annas." At another place of entertainment the khansamah, who did not even pretend to speak English, much less to write it, when the bill was called for summoned his little boy from school to perform this literary task. The result was a very creditable piece of penmanship on pink paper, with fourteen repetitions of the line "Food for 2 men Little Big Breakfast Dinner Rs 6–8—"; and the document ended with. "For Writing of this Bill 8 annas." He got it, for the laborer was worthy of his hire. A feature of the Ahmedabad "rest-house," and a rather depressing one should the visitor have an ill turn, was a small band of frowsy, ill-kempt white vultures, which were accustomed to strut and amble about the compound, and to look in at the door in the early morning to see if perchance there was any streak of luck for them. But if the stranger appeared in his normal state of health they would rise clumsily from the ground, and flop heavily and sadly away to some more promising neighborhood.

II

Travellers who visit India for no other purpose than the indulgence of globe-trotting proclivities, and those as well who have a special object of study, will often find their circles of interest gradually widening: few can escape being attracted by the strange and piquant contrasts of modern Anglo-Indian life, thrown into such strong relief by the mediæval background of unchanging native custom. While the Ameer of Afghanistan has recently concluded the alliance with England, has strengthened his defences, and according to a French journalist has sent to a London firm an order for a million uniforms and a tailor to fit them on his men, the account of the pageants and ceremonies at Cabul on the occasion of his son's betrothal reads like a chapter from Froissart's Chronicles.

At official functions, such as durbars, or at fêtes given by native princes, and at semi-official gatherings, characterized by an intermingling, if not a momentary blending, of races, one has the best opportunities of observing these curious oppositions, to borrow a term from the painter's vocabulary. One of the most interesting affairs of this kind at which the writer had the good-fortune to be present was a garden-party given by the lieutenant-governor of one of the northern presidencies, and the ostensible reason for this function was the reception of certain native dignitaries and the delegates of neighboring chieftains. The park-like grounds surrounding Government House, with long vistas of greensward, winding among tall trees, shrubbery, and parterres, gorgeous with the winter flora of India, were decorated with tents and marquees where refreshments were served, chairs and benches were scattered about, and there were tennis-courts of seductive smoothness. It was late in December, clear and calm, but the chill in the air as the sun went down seemed hardly in accord with all this summer luxuriance and the costumes and parasols of the ladies, although some of them compromised by wearing fur capes. At similar entertainments in Europe, the smart gowns and hats of the ladies give the keynote of color, but here they were quite outshone by the groups of native grandees, all attired with more or less splendor, and presenting much the effect, wherever a few of them

THE GARDEN PARTY—SUNSET

were gathered together, of bouquets of multi-colored orchids. In the suffused red light of sunset, all these marvellous combinations of changeable silks, scarlet cashmere, and embroidered velvet, with gold lace galore, glowed with additional lustre.

Against the sober green of the foliage all the strangely shaped turbans of silk and satin, pale lavender, and white and gold, or with changing tints of palest blue or cream color, seemed to compete in brilliancy with the masses of flowers around them. There is often a subtle something, either in the bearing or in the fashion of dress of these worthies, particularly those of portly presence and prestige, which reminds one of old portraits of Henry VIII. or François I. in all their purple and fine linen. The more barbaric red-and-gold liveries of the "bearers" and other servants added a more positive if less delicate note of color. Strolling about among the groups of Europeans were two brothers, one the type of the ideal Sikh, with handsome aquiline features, pale brown skin, and black beard, set off by a loosely wound turban of pale lemon color, and a long, tightly-fitting kaftan of black velvet. For the most part these native personages showed a tendency to group themselves together, and to sit silently apart from the Europeans, not, it would seem, from any consciousness of being out of place, for they performed their social duties with much seriousness and dignity, but perhaps they dreaded the effort and difficulty of carrying on, in an unfamiliar tongue, conversation suitable to the occasion. It may be that some of this aloofness is the result of hereditary habit, not unpardonable in a race where one family, at least, has always lived up to its standard as an example for the others. Where they show a disposition to cultivate the society of Europeans, they are not always the gainers to any large extent. Naturally they are at once sized up by their shrewd, if not always unfriendly, critics, and measured according to Western standards, and even a Serene Highness is at once set down as a good fellow, a dunce, or a cad. The fact that but few of the reigning dynasties have been long established, or date back to the early days of English rule (a fact which has nothing to do with their "claims of long descent," in many cases of undoubted authenticity), and that all of them owe their present position and continuance of power to the supreme government, has doubtless something to do with the rather patronizing tone often taken by Europeans when speaking of native potentates. At a polo-match, which took place near the cantonment in the same district, the great mass of the spectators were Indian, although few of the higher castes were represented among the invited guests. The Rajah of a neighboring state, who was himself a polo-player of renown, had sent his team which had already made a record of many victories. A line of regimental mess-tents afforded the best positions for viewing the contest. These tents, or rather marquees, were in most cases lined with the decorative cotton prints now so well known in Europe, carpeted with rugs, and furnished with lounging-chairs; the silver of each regiment, often including monumental trophies won by their teams on other fields, was displayed on the refreshment-tables. There was a fair showing of ladies, and among the younger men, mainly of the military caste, but never by any chance in uniform, were many faces recalling the ruddy, sunburnt types so familiar at Zermatt in the season. There is usually a striking uniformity among modern Britons of this type, whether one meets them tranquilly lunching on the apex of the Matterhorn, or tearing about on polo ponies at Benares in the season of the hot winds and in the heat of the day, when the prudent coolie, with more respect for his complexion, has gone to bed under his sheltering eaves.

On this occasion I was the guest for the day of Sigismond Justh, the Hungarian novelist, who was studying life from the officers' quarters of a native regiment, and as we both became interested in reminiscences of Paris, and in the adventures of a young officer of engineers, who had just crossed the Pamir from Siberia by a new route, we failed to see the end of the match which was fought out in a distant part of the field. The mess dinner which followed appeared to verify my friend's conviction that these gentlemen had mastered the art of being comfortable, and of living together in harmony, quite after the manner of a large family. There was an air of homely comfort with a spice of luxury at the mess bungalow, as well as at the private quarters of each officer; screens were placed wherever an insidious draught could penetrate, and there were wood fires in every room.

My Hungarian friend had visited, during the previous winter, a military station in Algeria, where the officers, with all the amiable characteristics of their race and all the *bon volonté* possible, had somehow failed to surround themselves with that atmosphere of home comfort which the Briton in exile knows so well how to create. During the interval before dinner we made the round of the camp and visited the hospital barracks with the captain, most genial of hosts, as it was his day for inspection. We met on the road a group of regimental musicians, practising on strange instruments, one of which resembled a bagpipe, and their leader, a young Afghan of formidable physique, who had rather the air of a brigand than a refined musician and an improvisateur, in obedience to a word from the captain promised to bring his men to the bungalow after dinner. When we returned we found them installed in the drawing-room and tuning up their instruments. The captain, provided with a ponderous volume of Afghan songs and ballads, was assisted by the towering young brigand, who led the orchestra, in drawing up the programme, while the other musicians, nearly all members of a tribe of gypsies from the hills of the border-land, and having the appearance of Pathens as well, swarthy and long-haired, seated themselves along the base of the white wall, holding their peculiarly shaped instruments. Never have I seen a stranger and more picturesque contrast of races than was presented by this group of half-savage minstrels on their good behavior, and the young officers in braided mess-jackets of scarlet or drab, and the two guests stretched out in bamboo chairs, wearing the conventional black and white which is always *de rigeur* on festal occasions. There was a quality in this weird Afghan music which suggested the prolonged and plaintive cadences of the Spanish gypsies, and it appealed the more forcibly to the poetic nature of my fellow-guest from its affinity with that of his own country.

At this cantonment we found the usual little club or neutral ground for informal social meetings, which, as in other small stations, had a domestic, homelike air, rather than that of a public rendezvous; ladies came in, and played on the piano or sang duets with men in tennis costume, who dropped it from time to time, and there appeared to be a conspicuous absence of that formality usually to be found in the larger clubs. Residents or visitors all seemed to be on the same terms of good-fellowship, and, as at the mess-table, quite as if they all made part of the same large family. This enforced intimacy, where people are thrown together of necessity, may have its disagreeable side, but the writer is free to admit that he was not made aware of it, or it may be presumed that those clubs at which he was presented were exceptionally fortunate as regards the personal and social qualities of their members. In the principal Mofussil capitals, where the European element is larger, these clubs naturally have a more metropolitan character. As at the smaller ones, there are always well-kept, cemented tennis-courts, a billiard-room, library, and reading-room, where the leading journals of every country, Harper's and other American magazines, are almost invariably found, as they are everywhere, except in some of the best-known Parisian *cercles*, where the *Police Gazette* is often the only representative of American illustrated literature. But in the great cities these institutions are planned on a more generous scale. At the "Byculla Club" the stranger cannot but be impressed with the faultless service and the air of luxury pervading the living quarters of resident members, and which might well have the effect of deterring many a bachelor from launching into the untried, from giving up the certainty of an easy existence for the perils and uncertainties of house-keeping in a country bungalow, or, worse still, of married life in an Indian hotel. Economy of space, always an important consideration in Western capitals, does not appear to have fettered the gradual growth and extension of the club premises in every direction. Ample stabling accommodation is provided for the horses and carriages of resident members, and in a climate like that of Bombay, where plenty of air and space are of primary importance, the height and spaciousness of most of the rooms are very satisfactory after the comparatively cramped quarters of most hotels in the Fort. The "Yacht Club," which is in a way the Jockey Club of Bombay, stands close to the sea and near the Apollo Bunder, the popular gathering-place when the band plays there at

UNDER THE PUNKAH AT THE YACHT CLUB

sundown, as well as a landing-place for passengers by sea, presents at first sight the appearance of a summer casino, with its framework of varnished wood, innumerable awnings and flags, and strengthens the illusion which the traveller sometimes has, on landing at the "Bunder," that he has reached an Oriental watering-place rather than a bustling commercial seaport; for there is an absence, in this quarter at least, of the unsightly surroundings which generally mar the approach to other great capitals. At the dinner hour, seldom earlier than half-past eight, the lofty dining-room, with a multitude of small tables, at which parties of four, six, or eight are seated, ladies in evening dress, and men who are usually types of the civil or military orders, gives one an impression in which much that is agreeably familiar is flavored with something more novel and exotic. There are no long punkahs suspended overhead, but the servants at each table, in blue liveries adorned with silver lace, wield great palm-leaf fans brilliantly draped and frilled, and the sight of all these slowly-moving masses of color shot through with the sparkle of gold or silver threads, the twinkling lights, and the intermittent fanning of the sultry sea-breeze which draws in through the open spaces over the wide tracts of polished floor, all stamp the scene with the unmistakable character of the South—not that which we know at Monte Carlo or on farther Mediterranean shores. but the true South which lies beyond the tropic.

III

. . . "And Yama said, For this question it was inquired of old even by the gods; for it is not easy to understand it; subtle is its nature. Choose another boon, oh, Nachiketas! Do not compel me to this!"

It was intimated to the writer a year ago, more or less, that some comments on the present financial situation in India, what is properly known as the Rupee Question, would be timely and acceptable. Since that time each successive mail has brought in reviews and solutions of the state of affairs, suggestions, statements and reports, complaints, amendments, and explanations, each offering the only practical solution of this financial equation. Hindoos, Parsees, and Mussulmans have all rushed into print, bankers, Japanese ministers, and retired army officers have all written letters expressing their conflicting opinions with more or less lucidity where technical experts, fearing to commit themselves, have shown a wise reticence, or have only added to the general perplexity.

To attempt the unravelling of this tangled skein is a task which few skilled financiers would care to undertake, but it is still possible to present a few of the causes which are thought to have led to the present depreciation of the currency, and some of the devices by which the home government had hoped to help India out of the difficulty, but which have so far proved inadequate. When the East India Loan Bill (£10,000,000) was brought up from the Commons and read for the first time in the House of Lords (December 19, 1893), Lord Kimberley then moved the second reading of the bill and explained at some length the circumstances which rendered necessary an application to Parliament for further power to raise a loan in England for the service of India. He then said in his speech in regard to the closing of the mints in that country, an experiment which it was imagined by the government might check the downward tendency of the rupee—"If it should so happen that this policy of closing the mints should entirely fail, we shall be thrown back into our original situation, which is a very grave one, because at the present price of silver the exchange, if measured as it is usually measured, stands at no more than one shilling and one-eighth; and speaking in round numbers, at that rate of exchange the government of India would be landed in a deficit of no less than 6,000,000 rupees. That would be a deficit of a most serious and alarming character." Turning to another point the Secretary of State remarked: "With regard to the trade in silver, of course before we closed the mints silver went to a large extent to India for the purpose of being coined into rupees. Any one might present silver at the mints, and that silver was coined and he received the rupees. Naturally at all times there was a good deal of silver that did not find its way to the mints, but now all the silver sent must be for other purposes. The question naturally arises: What are these other purposes—what is the reason for this very large, continuous demand? . . . Quite recently I have been able to ask the opinion of Sir David Barbour, who was financial member of the Council of the government of India, and who has just returned to this country. He tells me his opinion is that there exists in India always a very large demand for silver, and that demand has been stimulated in the ordinary way in which a demand is stimulated for a commodity by the large fall in the price of silver. The natives generally consider that this is a most favorable opportunity to purchase silver for the purpose of ornaments; and Sir David Barbour thinks that probably accounts for the larger part of the demand. When we remember that the population of India numbers 287,000,000, we see that any increased demand from so vast a population may easily produce a very considerable result. The other cause may be connected with speculation. At all events, there is the fact that this very large amount of silver is now going into India."

In the course of the same debate the Marquis of Salisbury expressed his opinion that there was no possible way of making the rupee rarer by artificial means, and deplored the measures which had been taken; also that the attempt to create a "rupee vacuum" by processes analogous to those of physical science would surely fail, for in spite of the most skilful manipulation rupees were still creeping in by channels both obvious and obscure. He also believed that the "private mints" of India were unusually active.

Ever since the close of the civil war in America there has been a disposition on the part of India to attribute its financial embarrassment to the United States, and the silver policy of our government has had beyond a doubt much to do with its recent misfortunes. Among other remedies proposed, the introduction of a gold standard has been taken into consideration, and an import duty on silver has been imposed, which it is expected will enable the government to derive a larger profit from its monopoly of coining rupees from cheap silver, and thus avoid the complications which would certainly arise from further taxation. A Hindoo banker who has written a memorandum on this matter (March, 1894) gives an additional reason for the step that the price of silver has been so much lowered in England and America, that 100 tolas* of

* A tola is worth approximately 180 grains troy.

silver, which cost 106 rupees before, can now be purchased in Bombay for from 85 to 86 rupees. It is the opinion of many that if bimetallism had been adopted long ago, the country would have been saved from the evils of its present monetary policy, but at present this could only be done by concert with the leading nations of the world.

Among the many criticisms called forth by the action of the government in closing the mints, that of the Japanese Minister of Finance is one of the most intelligent, and sums up the situation in a few words: "The stoppage of free silver coinage in India," he said, "has only increased the amount of current silver coin, and materially injured the popular confidence in that metal. The primary object of the stoppage was to limit the increase of silver coin and to prevent its depreciation; but that the contrary result was obtained can be attributed to nothing but the ignorance of the British authorities on Indian affairs. The reason of the unexpected result appears to be as follows: Indians have little confidence in each other, and only those are respected as men of wealth who possess most gold and silver money, and adorn their persons with most ornaments of the same metal. They bury their rupees in the earth, and do their best not to spend them. But with the stoppage of silver coinage silver coins no longer increased, and the Indians began to unearth their buried coins, which were brought into the money market. Thus, though silver was no longer coined, its circulation suddenly increased. This was a most unexpected result, and the English did not foresee it when they gave the injurious order." Forced by the cries and lamentations of the sufferers to continue its series of financial experiments, the "British Raj" has imagined an "automatic method" of keeping the rupee's head above water for a while longer, and has provided means to pay in gold for all the rupees offered at the fixed rate of 1*s.* 4*d.* each. Thus the rupee would be automatically kept from rising beyond that figure should it ever reach it. In the meantime the leading journals of the country continue to denounce the tardy and fruitless measures of the home government, to assert that it has lost the confidence of the people of India, and to lament over the miseries of a great empire sorely oppressed by such a grievous burden. In spite of all the measures proposed and carried out, the rupee has continued to dwindle until no one dares to prophesy what will finally be left of it; but at the same time the average revenues of the empire have been unchanged, there has been no occasion for extraordinary expenditures, such as war or famine, and, according to a reliable authority, there is surplus money to the value of 9,000,000 rupees locked up in the treasury—as useless an experiment, this observer thinks, as locking up silver dollars in the American Treasury. Among those who have suffered the most, and who, it would seem, have often just cause for complaint, are the officials, officers, and public servants, whose salaries are paid in rupees at rates fixed by the government when the rupee was worth its nominal value of two shillings. In many cases these salaries have not been increased, and while usually sufficient for current expenses in India, fall wofully short when officials thus paid have families in England, and are obliged to send home drafts payable in pounds sterling. To meet the necessities of this class the fixed rate of exchange was devised, and a "compensation allowance" granted.

Although it is doubtless a disreputable source of gain to profit by the misfortunes of our neighbors, it must be admitted that it is not always an ill wind which blows the traveller to the "coral strand" at this critical moment. However conscientious he may be, he can hardly help profiting by the situation if he carries a letter of credit, circular notes, and, moreover, a few "five-pun" notes in his pocket, which will bring him in, if I am not mistaken, an additional premium. While he will find the cost of living at hotels nearly or quite the same as it was ten years ago, he will also find that the prices of imported goods and native commodities of all sorts have remained nearly stationary, for competition has increased, and dealers have been afraid to raise their prices for fear of losing custom. Some keen observer has been looking about to find those who have profited by the fall of the rupee, but he has as yet discovered no one—not among the poor Ryots, who were supposed at one time to be making their fortunes and burying them in the ground, nor among "middle men;" and certainly not among the English merchants and importers, who buy in sovereigns and sell in rupees, and whose business, to use his own words, "is rapidly going to pot and to rot, and disappearing just as fast as the rupee has disappeared."

IV

It is quite possible to dislike reforms and to entertain a rooted aversion for the improvements proposed by philanthropists, which, when carried out, do so much towards destroying the local charm of a country like India. At the same time, one cannot but admit that there are dark and filthy corners in the social fabric which are sadly in need of wholesome purification, although the new elements introduced during this process are apt to be, like the restored patches on the Doge's palace, somewhat incongruous and out of harmony with the rest. In view of the extent to which this country has been made a field

THE POLO-MATCH, FROM THE MESS-TENT

for all manner of experiments—financial, moral, and educational—it would be an interesting theme for any student of social problems to make a thorough study of these various schemes for the amelioration of alien races from their very start, and to note how far they have proved successful. That many of them have been productive of good results thus far is sufficiently evident, and particularly those bearing on the physical well-being of the Indian. The Hindoo, the Mussulman, the Parsee has each his own "gymkana," or open-air club, for the encouragement of out-of-door exercise and athletic sports; each race now has its experts and semi-professionals in the cricket-field as well as in polo and tennis. Much interest was recently awakened by the address of a distinguished Hindoo scholar, the vice-chancellor of one of the principal universities, in which he deplored at length the premature decline of the Hindoo graduate, his feebleness and want of physical stamina, much of which he attributed to the prevalent custom of early marriage, as well as to the lack of regular physical training. He contrasted this lamentable state of the intellectual Hindoo with the greater vigor of the Parsee and Mussulman youth, and their longer tenure of life. Some of the learned gentleman's conclusions have been disputed, and the abnormal poverty of the Hindoo students, particularly the Mahrattas, is believed by many to be an important reason. The cause of physical culture, however, received an impetus, and within a few years there has been a large increase of bicycling, tennis, and cricket. Merely to enumerate these laudable efforts, many of which originated in the governing country, would necessitate an article by itself. The Hindoo peasant and laborer sees his oldest and most cherished institutions attacked and slowly undermined in the interests of progress, and one of them is the village well,* that most picturesque place of rendezvous in all primitive communities.

The mild Hindoo has not yet become reconciled to compulsory purification, and it may take time to induce him to abandon customs which his ancestors have followed for ages. But a very sensible innovation has been recently introduced, and one to which all classes have taken kindly.

* A writer in the *Pioneer* has given us a very forcible description of the old state of matters, while he finds the somewhat complicated remedies proposed not altogether satisfactory: "Take, for instance, a village on the banks of a river. Now this, one would think, has the advantage of pure water, and so it should; but then there is the trifling objection of a half-burnt corpse polluting the stream, and the nameless other causes which make the banks of a river to be avoided as a place for enjoying fresh air. But the real horrors of village life come into view when the village is away from the stream. To the outward eye most of the houses are very clean. It is part of the religion of the people to keep them so. The same people, however, who religiously wash the outside walls of their homes and keep the floor scrupulously clean pursue a different line of conduct with respect to themselves. They are scrupulous in washing, but their bodies, like their houses, are whited sepulchres, if one can use the adjective to the Bengali. They wash their bodies, their clothes, and even their cattle, but then they fill their water-vessels with the water in which these various washings have taken place, and take it home to cook their food, and also for drinking purposes. Then next to the carefully washed home one can see a heap of rotting, festering vegetable matter, just at the season when such matter attracts disease, when the hot-weather sun extracts every noxious gas that can be generated, and diffuses it throughout the village. In the rains the same rotting mass is washed about, and spreads malaria as it dries. The houses themselves are built in the midst of paddy-fields. A hole is scooped in the earth, out of which enough muck is scraped to make the flooring of the hut, and then is carefully left unfilled, in order that it may serve as an emporium for all kinds of filth and rubbish."

One of the remedies proposed was to build an iron dome over the well, and provide an iron pump and the necessary machinery (at the expense of the villages), while another suggested building up the well and laying a pipe down to the spring at the bottom.

in the shape of postal packets of quinine, sold at reduced rates by the local postal authorities. Nothing seems to have escaped the strong search-lights which have been thrown on the sore spots of India by medical, moral, and sanitary commissions; and even opium eating, that mainstay and sole dissipation of innumerable classes from Rajpoot to Ryot, has narrowly escaped being a matter for legislation. The "Opium Commission," which has recently been stirring up all India to its very depths, was instituted for the purpose of attacking the abuse of opium, and restricting its sale and consequent consumption. The Indian daily papers during the past winter have been nearly monopolized by reports of its proceedings, by the evidence on both sides, and by the letters and protestations, written by people of every race and caste; and it may be said without reservation that the results of these investigations have been an undoubted triumph for the opium eater, and that far from lessening the consumption of the drug they are likely to increase it beyond all precedent. Even the disinterested motives of those who originated the commission have been questioned by the uneducated classes in the Punjaub, who believe that it was sent out by English merchants with the object of stopping the opium trade in order to introduce their own whiskey as a substitute. In short, so different has been the effect of this investigation from that which was anticipated, that few can read the reports without feeling inclined to try the drug and see how it works on their own systems. The mass of accumulated evidence and statistics would fill several "Blue Books," but the report of each day's proceedings is more or less an abstract of the whole, each nearly complete in itself, and each strengthening the cause of the opium consumer. Wherever a medical officer reported on the condition of his men just returned from

MODERN FIRE WORSHIPPERS

active service in Burmah or elsewhere, it appeared that the best soldiers, morally and physically, those who were always exempt from such maladies as dysentery, fever, cholera, and rheumatism, were the opium eaters; they were able to go longer without food or stimulants, and to do more work. The testimony of physicians both European and native was almost invariably in favor of the drug when used moderately in the simple form known to native consumers. Surgeon-General Sir William Moore said "he had often smoked opium, and really did not see where the wickedness and immorality came in. As a matter of fact, one might see more immorality in a London gin-shop in half an hour even on a Sunday night than in an opium-shop during a whole year." It has been found that opium is cheaper than wine or spirits, less detrimental to the system, and just the right agent to stimulate the indolent Oriental nature, as well as to counteract the weakening effects of a vegetable diet and scarcity of food. Many a poor "Ryot" who can hardly pull himself together for want of proper nourishment is enabled by its aid to do a good day's work, while at the same time it serves him as a specific against the maladies resulting from unhealthy surroundings. The prospect of opium being unobtainable except as a medicine was viewed with alarm by all classes; witnesses from every part of the empire anticipated dire results and an appalling death-rate. (Report, Ajmere, January 30th.)

Great and wide-spread was the consternation when people were at last reluctantly compelled to believe that the commission had actually begun its work. Many a veteran Sikh who had fought with the best in the dark days of mutiny, and could look back on a long record of honest labor during the Roman peace which followed, all accomplished by the aid of his little "dabbi," or box of opium, must have been sorely shaken in his loyalty, or have believed that the British Raj had lost its head. While scientists, philosophers, and empirics in Europe have been experimenting for ages to find the Elixir of Life, these simple Orientals have contented themselves with producing by homœopathic doses of opium effects analogous to those hoped for from the discovery of Dr. Brown-Sequard; and if they have not succeeded in renewing their youth, have certainly managed to make it last longer. Many who understand the nature of the people fear that if they were unable to procure their daily dose of opium they would resort to cheap alcoholic stimulants far more disastrous in their effects. There are others who say that the "political barometer is unsteady," and that it is a bad time for officious or meddlesome interference with native customs.

The subject of "child widowhood" and the generally inferior condition of women in India has been attracting much attention of late, and now we are beginning to hear the other side of the question. We are told that all are not so badly off as some of these eager reformers would have us believe.

Intelligent and progressive Hindoos have begun to compare their own marriage customs with those which obtain in Christian countries; and while deploring the evil which often results from the system so long in use, according to which the bridegroom marries in the dark, as it were, and is seldom enlightened as to the qualities, intellectual and physical, of his bride until it is too late to retract, are beginning to make comparisons and to ask questions difficult to answer. While they are generally disposed to accept the superiority of things European on trust, like articles purchased in a "European shop," they find it hard to understand why divorce and legal separation, which are not sanctioned by Hindoo custom, are so prevalent in Europe. But if the existing abuses are to be remedied by the education of women rather than by legislative interference with long-established custom, there is abundant reason to suppose that every advantage enjoyed by their sex elsewhere will eventually be given them. On every hand new schools and colleges for girls are being opened, which often have classes for young married women; and they have long since begun to avail themselves of the opportunities offered for higher education, and are competing successfully with their brothers even for the degree of M.A.; but at present Eurasians and Parsees head the list of university honors. An English reviewer who does not altogether believe in "the disabilities of Indian women, and the hide-bound system which allows them no opportunities of shining," has lately written in the *Calcutta Review* some reminiscences of the Begum Sumroo, a lady who came to the front in the early part of this century, governed a native state, led armies, and altogether triumphantly established the ability of her sex in that country.

V

One cannot remain twenty-four hours in India without becoming aware that caste distinctions flourish among the English as well as among the disciples of Brahma; and if one has not given any previous thought to the matter, the conviction that such is the case may give him the degree of satisfaction which usually results from the discovery of the new and unexpected. The impression may have taken form and substance from the outward-bound P. & O. steamer, that microsm of Anglo-Indian society. Although the code is as yet unwritten, it is none the less

MARKETING, SAHARANPORE

potent, and the sagacious Hindoo contemplates its workings with inward amusement, for he has often been sermonized on the evils of his caste system. It is perhaps merely an accentuation, a slight exaggeration, of the leading divisions recognized in the mother-country, which, after all, have some *raison d'être*, for they resemble in no small measure those adopted by the parent race in the primitive days of India. But there is only a little friction here and there, a shadow of discontent among those who fancy that they have not been assigned the highest places at the table. Here, as elsewhere, it is among those whose claims to precedence rest upon visible foundations that one finds the most broadly democratic spirit, together with an easy-going disposition to ignore the whole business. The cultivated Eurasian of either sex, nevertheless, often finds it rather uphill work to reach the higher social levels, for the same race prejudice exists here as in America, and with less reason.

Strange as it may seem, one cannot get away from the impression that money is not the corner-stone of the social edifice in this military hierarchy, and that the possession of even a shred of power confers more distinction than the possession of unlimited bonds. Titles, being as familiar as the current coin of the realm, have not that prestige which attaches to them elsewhere, and a rising M.P., or a political "organ" of any sort, usually receives as much attention as the owner of an hereditary name. This state of matters is readily explained when one bears in mind that the men who govern India to-day are the civilized successors of the Vikings who wrested the empire from the misrule of the Moguls and Mahrattas, and founded a military despotism, which has gradually been replaced by a milder sway, with as much republican latitude as is consistent with that common-sense which seems to be the ruling principle of the Indian government. Those who hold the reins of power are not, as a rule, overburdened with money; and one may enjoy the strange spectacle of a vast empire, numbering over 287,000,000, having among them many who possess extraordinary wealth, not to speak of princes holding treasure and territory by inherited right, governed by men in many cases "actually living in straitened circumstances" in order that they may properly perform their duties. (*Vide* speech of the late Viceroy.) Obliged by the exigencies of their position to keep up a certain show of state and to entertain extensively on salaries which, with the ever-decreasing value of the rupee, are often barely adequate for necessary expenses, and would hardly give them the position of social units elsewhere, it is, after all, not to be wondered at that these men who hold sway over millions should make the most of this reversal of the usual state of things. When they return to the mother-country, after long years of honorable service, and are lost in the roar of London, too often with little to show for it in the way of gain, they may sometimes regret the importance and influence attached to their late position in India, if not its comparative pomp and luxury, as well as its harassing cares and responsibilities. Like the nations of Europe, India has its decorations, which are usually awarded for distinguished services, military or civic, or for exceptional merit, to judge from their brief and brilliant lists, and these distinctions are not to be had for the asking, or to be gained by what the French call *tripotage*. The "Star of India" is usually conferred upon those who have achieved greatness, and there is another order reserved for those who are born great or have greatness thrust upon them, as the rajahs and chiefs of state, or other members of reigning families.

It seems a fitting place to venture the observation that between the attitude of the government towards the native population of whatever race or caste, and the attitude of the individual Briton when he comes in contact with the humble Hindoo, there is a wide difference, which, however, is being gradually lessened. It has often been remarked by Anglo-Indians that wherever a difference occurs between an Englishman and a native, to be settled by law, the chances are that the latter will get the best of it; and while the government seems anxious that no shadow of suspicion should tarnish the reputation for fairness and equity which its officers are expected to maintain in their dealings with the native, and while it is ever too ready to make concessions, the manner of the European in his relations with the humbler classes often seems arrogant and overbearing. This attitude is sometimes, however, a mere affectation of brusqueness arising partly from the habit of command, and it is, moreover, invited by the servility and obsequious demeanor of the laboring classes and domestics. But these subordinate castes can hardly be held responsible for what might be termed an inherited manner, the result of long ages of oppression and serfdom, and even now, when they are gradually becoming accustomed to privileges which their predecessors never enjoyed, they still maintain their traditional attitude of conquered vassals. But, on the other hand, among the educated classes, and those who have reaped the most benefit from the established order of things, may be noted an ever-increasing and even aggressive consciousness of equality, often expressed by that studied insolence of manner which is the aim of a certain class of republicans, while among the European element there is certainly less of that bullying spirit which was formerly considered the correct thing; and it is a fact worthy

THE TEMPTERS

of note, also, that from this class, which has profited most by English rule, little or no assistance could be hoped for by the government in time of peril. Notwithstanding the financial difficulties in which the government of India is involved at this present moment, the discontent expressed by the native journalists, and the general poverty of the country,* which is by no means an evil of recent date, one cannot but carry away the impression that India is a well-governed country, and that much of the credit is due to the men chosen to fill the higher offices, and to the superior equipment of those whose positions are gained through competition. The mills that grind are not too much *en evidence;* and whenever one comes in contact with officials in their official capacity he feels that he is dealing not with automatons, but with men who do not find it necessary to assume that aggressive and autocratic demeanor which most republicans have learned to accept so meekly. There are few of the monopolies † existing in Europe, such as the exclusive right of government to manufacture incombustible matches and rank tobacco, as well as to exclude rival articles of better quality. It should not be imagined, however, that the condition of the people, particularly among the agricultural laborers, or Ryots, leaves nothing to be desired, and the "poverty of India" in general may be considered as a problem for which no permanent solution has yet been found. As a consequence of the increasing financial embarrassments the germs of the strife between labor and capital have at last reached India, and have given birth to strikes conducted with truly

* "It has been calculated that the average income per head of population in India is not more than twenty-seven rupees a year."—Lord Cromer, in 1883.

† The salt monopoly is a notable exception.

Western pertinacity. We hear of strikes among railway and freight-house employés, among factory hands, and, lastly, a rebellion among the punkah wallahs, who refused to continue their refreshing ministrations during the late heated term at the old rates. Many are the schemes which have been set on foot for the improvement of the lower castes, of the Ryots; and even the wretched Pariah, the outcast and scapegoat of his race, has not been forgotten, since it has been proposed as an experiment to found a colony of Pariahs somewhere near Madras, and then make them self-supporting agriculturists instead of a burden to the community. Some of the most sensible of these humanitarian projects relate to improved sanitation, as has been mentioned elsewhere, but they do not always meet with the enthusiastic reception which they merit either from the English press or from the people whom they were intended to benefit.

What is to become of India even in the near future, what social and political conditions of things will be finally evolved from the various elements now in fusion, are questions of absorbing interest, and of which it is difficult to foretell the final issue.

THE END